ALSO BY JOHN N. MACLEAN

Fire on the Mountain

FIRE
AND
ASHES

FIRE

AND

ASHES

*On the Front Lines of
American Wildfire*

John N. Maclean

A JOHN MACRAE BOOK
Henry Holt and Company | New York

Henry Holt and Company, LLC
Publishers since 1866
115 West 18th Street
New York, New York 10011

Henry Holt® is a registered trademark of
Henry Holt and Company, LLC.

Library of Congress Cataloging-in-Publication Data

Maclean, John N.
    Fire and ashes: on the front lines of American wildfire /
John N. Maclean.—1st ed.
        p. cm.
    "A John Macrae book."
    ISBN 0-8050-7212-8
        1. Wildfires—United States—Prevention and control.
    2. Fire ecology—United States.   I. Title.
    SD421.3 .M33 2003
    363.37'9—dc21   2002038704

Henry Holt books are available for special
promotions and premiums. For details contact:
Director, Special Markets.

First Edition 2003

Designed by Paula Russell Szafranski

Printed in the United States of America

10 9 8 7 6 5 4 3 2 1

To Danny and John Fitzroy,
who share with me
a love of writing and the outdoors

I returned and saw under the sun, that the race is not to the swift, nor the battle to the strong; neither yet bread to the wise, nor yet riches to men of understanding, nor yet favor to men of skill; but that time and chance happeneth to them all.

—ECCLESIASTES

Contents

FIRE
AND
ASHES

Introduction

WILDLAND FIRE IS a troubling partner for modern society, as fire seasons of increasing ferocity in recent years have amply demonstrated. But the relationship between humans and fire goes back to the origins of the human race. Evidence of fire dates from the time vegetation first appeared, some 350 million years earlier. Stephen J. Pyne, a historian of wildland fire, tells an anecdote about layers of fossils found on the floor of a cave in South Africa. At the bottom of the pile are bones of humans eaten by animals. The next layer up is charcoal, an indication of the discovery of fire by early man. In the top layer, the evolutionary scale tips: the layer contains bones of animals cooked and eaten by humans.

When Europeans first arrived in North America, the face of the land had already been heavily altered by deliberate burning. Indians, beginning at least at the end of the last ice age, about ten thousand years ago, used fire to clear land for cultivation and settlement and to improve grazing and hunting. They also had fun with fire. During their epic journey west, the explorers Lewis and Clark recorded evenings spent in Indian camps when the chief entertainment was lighting the woods on fire; spruce trees burned especially well, going off like giant Roman candles.

Anthropologists today believe that the Indians used fire much more extensively than previously thought, an embarrassment to those who argue that wilderness excludes any mark of humans—that Indians had only a light touch on the land—and who from that argument make the case for uncontrolled fire as "natural."

But what is natural?

"What on earth was the West's original condition?" asks Dan Flores, an environmental historian and the author of *The Natural West*. One thing is certain: nature's way includes a human component, *Homo sapiens* setting and trying to control fire. The mix of people and fire has always been volatile, especially so since the Europeans' exploitation of the American land.

Today nearly every policy that governed firefighting in the modern era is being challenged. The issues range from whether to fight a fire at all, especially if life and property are not threatened, to the degree of acceptable risk once the battle is joined. Settlement in the wildland urban interface—the WUI, or the red zone—a place where open lands and development meet, has multiplied at astonishing rates and with few controls since the 1980s, to make an already dangerous situation explosive. At the same time, almost a century of fire suppression and, more recently, reduced logging have created wildlands badly in need of more fires, not fewer.

Paradoxically, certain logging practices over the decades, such as careless disposal of slash and excessive logging of the biggest trees, have contributed to a buildup of brush and small trees and thus to a more fire-prone forest. Yet the reality of more people plus more fire guarantees conflict. While national fire policy now calls for millions of acres to be deliberately burned each year, a preliminary Forest Service study reports that nearly half the planned ignitions have been delayed by legal appeals—environmental groups seeking to curtail logging, home owners and politicians trying to minimize smoke.

Fires have grown more intense in recent years because of drought, which has been made worse by global warming. Concern about wildland fire and forest health, meanwhile, is no longer restricted to land-management agencies such as the Forest Service and the Bureau of Land Management (BLM), inhabitants of fire country, and a small environmental elite. The environmental movement has become broadly based and, together with the media, has succeeded in raising national awareness of the values and dangers at stake. Partly as a consequence, federal land-management agencies have been forced to change their focus from income-producing activities—logging, mining, and grazing—to custodianship of the land. Laudable as the change may seem to those who do not log, mine, or run cattle, the agencies have lost authority and cohesion as a result. "The Forest Service is an agency in limbo," says Gerald W. Williams, the Forest Service's chief historian.

Wildland fire, always a natural and necessary part of the North American landscape, is now seen as the way forests and grasslands renew themselves and create healthy habitat for wildlife. But try telling that to someone whose Colorado dream house and majestic view have just been turned into a moonscape. Living in fire country today is like having a grizzly bear hibernate in your backyard: it's a thrill, but at some point the bear wakes up.

Fire season can begin as early as New Year's Day and end as late as December 31. The first fires of the year occur in Florida or California; wildfire migrates to the Southwest in the spring, the Rocky Mountain West and Pacific Northwest as summer arrives, and then returns to California in the fall.

Drought and new settlements have expanded the map of fire country. Florida has become a prime wildfire state as thousands of housing developments have spread into marshes and glades. As far north as Shenandoah National Park in the Blue Ridge Mountains of Virginia, an area normally rich in humidity and rainfall, the largest fires on record scorched more than 24,000 acres of parkland during the ferocious, record-breaking 2000 fire season. The effects in the Virginia park generally were beneficial: all but a few large trees survived, no important structures were destroyed, and no one was seriously injured.

The danger is greatest when fire threatens lives and homes, not parks.

Take one popular "destination" state, Colorado: at the time of Colorado's disastrous 2002 fire season, an estimated one million people lived in the state's red zone, which is a 30 percent population increase in ten years. It's estimated that the number of Colorado's red-zone residents will double by 2020. The National Interagency Fire Center in Boise, Idaho, estimates that the nationwide population of the "interface" grew tenfold in the last quarter of the twentieth century. Only a handful of counties in fire country have restrictive zoning ordinances: no brush, woodpiles, or propane tanks near houses, no wooden roofs, and so on. Instead, most local governments allow virtually unrestricted building.

A vivid illustration of the difference can be seen during a drive between Denver and Boulder. Near Denver, where there is little control over development, housing is dense and thoughtless. Subdivisions spring up in the middle of grasslands, with little or no connection to the land beyond their presence. But near Boulder—often mocked as the People's Republic of Boulder for its left-leaning politics—much open land has been preserved, and housing must abide by restrictive zoning that includes a stiff fire code.

I can offer a personal example of how complicated the situation has become, since I share ownership of a family cabin in northwestern Montana in a stand of giant western larch trees. The biggest larches were growing before Columbus discovered America. The trees, rising hundreds of feet, form a canopy that keeps the woods cool in summer, holds snow in winter, and provides a living link to a time when North America was a wilderness by anyone's definition.

My grandfather built the cabin of logs in the early 1920s; I put a metal roof on the place a few years ago, but to preserve the structure we've been soaking the logs with linseed oil for generations, and the place could go up like a torch. When I was a boy, common wisdom taught that the trees there had been protected from fire—the cabin is on a lake and surrounded by a river and mountains. Since then, studies of tree rings from fallen larches have shown the contrary to be true. Our forest burned about every twenty-five years, instead of the normal fire cycle of seventy-five years for this kind of timber, probably because Indians who camped here touched off fires deliberately or accidentally. The frequent, low-intensity fires kept down brush and smaller trees, allowing the big larches, which protect themselves from ground fire by dropping their lower branches as they grow, to achieve their spectacular size.

During the twentieth century, the era of fire suppression, a second forest grew up under the big trees—lodgepole pine, Douglas fir, spruce. They became "ladder trees," providing access for fire to climb to the canopies of the big larches and setting the stage for catastrophic wildfire, the kind that wipes out forests, sterilizes soil, and ruins waterways. A few years ago the Forest Service—the cabin is on national forest land—decided to imitate fire by having loggers cut and clear out the small ladder trees and brush.

The first year the Forest Service failed to put out bids on time. The second year the bids went out before the deadline, but no logger responded because the trees to be cut had almost no market value. It took another couple of years before the Forest Service traded the loggers marketable timber elsewhere in return for doing the unprofitable cutting.

While chances for human encounters with wildfire have grown, the guiding myth on how to deal with fire has proved inadequate to changing conditions. No longer is firefighting seen as the moral equivalent of war, the image that prevailed for most of the twentieth century. Firefighting still looks and sounds like war: troops in uniforms of yellow shirts and green pants deploy according to tactics ordered by a military-style hierarchy. But casualties are rarely part of the bargain, which is increasingly true of American military operations as well.

After the South Canyon Fire of 1994, which killed fourteen firefighters in a haunting replay of the legendary Mann Gulch Fire of 1949, firefighters began to say no to assignments they considered too dangerous. Within a few years, supervisors were routinely pulling crews back from fires they would have once fought twenty-four hours a day.

During the horrendous 2002 fire season, which saw some of the biggest fires in modern history, another fire broke out near where the South Canyon Fire had burned—on Storm King Mountain in west-central Colorado. The Coal Seam Fire destroyed twenty-eight homes and burned six times as much acreage—more than 12,000 acres, compared to 2,115 acres for the South Canyon Fire, which was considered a large fire for Colorado when it happened. But no one was injured at Coal Seam.

"It's the gung-ho attitude we're trying to corral a little bit," said Steve Hart, the incident commander, who fought the fire, mostly with aircraft. "Sometimes there's nothing you can do about it, so you might as well sit back and have a Snickers and a Coke."

The emphasis on safety in recent decades has saved lives. But the simplest lesson of fighting fire may have become a casualty: if you're going to put out a fire, hit it aggressively while it is small. If that lesson had been applied to the South Canyon Fire, which was not fought for the first three days, it might never have grown into a killer. The lesson continues to be ignored: failure to send in smoke jumpers at once in Oregon in July 2002 allowed the Biscuit Fire to scorch a half million acres at a cost of more than $150 million.

Fire today is viewed as a necessary tool of forest management, but it remains capable of massive, unwanted destruction.

THE RATTLESNAKE FIRE
Mendocino National Forest, California

July 9, 1953

N

0   600 feet

Powderhouse Turn

Powderhouse Ridge

Powderhouse Road

Powderhouse Ridge

Firebreak

Body Recovery Road

Firebreak

Rattlesnake Ridge

Rattlesnake Ridge

Missionary Rock

Path of attempted escape

Powderhouse Creek

Alder Springs Road

Detail area

Oleta Point

Sequence of Events

1. Arsonist tosses match about 2:20 P.M. on July 9, 1953. Fire fought here first.

2. Command post established at Powderhouse Turn. Fire is fought on three sides: one arm along firebreak; one along Rattlesnake Ridge; one at Alder Springs Road.

3. Missionary Spot Fire discovered at 8:15 P.M. Twenty-three missionaries and Ranger Powers sit down to eat supper here just after 10 P.M.

4. Wind shifts downhill, starting numerous spot fires; observed at 10:03 P.M.

5. One spot explodes, threatens missionary crew. Charlie Lafferty, line boss, leaves command post about 10:15 P.M. to warn crew.

6. Nine missionaries run uphill and escape.

7. Fifteen others, including Ranger Powers, head down canyon.

8. Tools dropped.

9. Body found 220 yards from start near Missionary Rock.

10. Body found 20 yards farther on.

11. Body found 345 yards from start.

12. Bodies of 8 missionaries and Ranger Powers found clustered 340 yards from start. Wristwatch of Raymond Sherman, cleaned off nearly 50 years later, shows time of 10:36 P.M. Other watches show 10:41.

13. Body of Stanley Vote found 320 yards from start.

14. Body of Cecil Hitchcock found 515 yards from start.

1 POINT OF ORIGIN

1

The Arsonist, the Watch, and the Rattlesnake Fire, 1953

THE HOUSE IS small, white, and tidy, with a porch screened by latticework. Trees shield it from the street. Opposite the Lutheran Church on Main Street, the only residential street in the town of Artois, the house is located in northern California's Central Valley about ninety miles north of Sacramento. A few homes and businesses dot a state highway a block from Main, but the town has nothing to invite a casual visitor, no franchise motels or restaurants, not even a major oil company gas station. The town of Artois (pronounced "our toys") has few ties to the broader world, which is why Stanford Philip Pattan chooses to live here.

Pattan's house has a large living room open to the kitchen and, off to one side, an artist's studio. Pattan rises at about five each morning and begins his daylong immersion in pencil sketches, oil paints, and canvases, creating realistic pictures of game animals, Indians, and landscapes. "I paint every feather of a bird, every hair of an animal," he exclaims; the pictures bring a modest supplement to his monthly Social Security check. On a wall of the studio is one of Pattan's proudest mementos, a snapshot of him standing next to Joe Montana, the legendary San Francisco 49ers quarterback. "He bought several of my paintings," Pattan says proudly, as though this confirms his place in the larger society.

A self-proclaimed hermit, Pattan describes his lifestyle as "hibernation." Though frequently seen in town, he does not speak unless spoken to first. He has hung paintings for sale on a wall of Nancy's Airport Cafe, a hangout in nearby Willows, where he often goes to eat. One day he overheard two young men discussing the artist whose paintings were on the wall.

"He's the guy who lit the Rattlesnake Fire," one said.

Pattan remembers the moment with something like fondness. "He wasn't talking like it was a bad thing," he says. "When I got up to leave I took out one of my business cards and laid it on the table. 'You've been talking about me. I just thought you'd like to know I heard.'" He slipped away before they could react.

Pattan has been a farmhand, a hospital worker, and a well-regarded hunting and fishing guide. Retired and in his mid-seventies, having lost his second wife, Velda, a few years ago, Pattan lives today in his private world of artistic endeavor. Long hours at the easel help stave off troubling memories a half century old. Matches flaring in dry chaparral. Men and machines battling contrary flames. The sickening moment of realization when he learned that his act of desperation had gone fatally wrong. And the twilight world of remorse ever after.

In a bizarre but curiously fitting turn of fate, a third wife, Connie, lost her memory of who Pattan was after she underwent surgery for a brain tumor. She woke up looking at a stranger, her husband. Connie and Pattan divorced after her memory of him failed to come back, but they became friends; Connie is a waitress at Nancy's Airport Cafe, and they spend a lot of time together.

Not everyone connected to the Rattlesnake Fire has hidden memories. Pattan set the fire on July 9, 1953, when he was twenty-six years old; in succeeding years, the tragic event has become a teaching tool for fire behavior as well as the marker for lives lost: fifteen wildland firefighters, a total not equaled since then.

The deaths were unsettling not only for the high number but for the character of the people killed. Shockingly, fourteen of the fifteen victims were volunteers, members of New Tribes Mission, a nondenominational group of fundamentalist-Christian missionaries who maintained a training base, or "boot camp," nearby. Each summer, as a form of community service, the missionaries in training put together a volunteer crew to help fight wildland fires.

The fifteenth fatality was equally unmerited. Robert Powers, an assistant ranger for the Forest Service, found himself in harm's way because he had a concern for others: having finished one fire assignment, he volunteered to take milk and sandwiches to the hungry mission crew. The fire exploded minutes later.

The Rattlesnake Fire was started at midafternoon in a brush-filled canyon in the Mendocino National Forest thirty miles west of Artois. Firefighters were gaining control of the flames as darkness fell, but a contrary wind sprang up and scattered embers into the canyon, igniting new spot fires. For long, fatal minutes everyone forgot about a crew of twenty-four, Powers and twenty-three missionaries, who had been sent into the canyon earlier to extinguish a small spot fire.

In seconds the wind turned from blustery to a gale. The spot fires erupted into a wall of flame and hurtled *down* the canyon at speeds beyond the experience of veterans of decades of California brush fires. The enduring lesson in fire behavior is that when conditions are right, flames can burn as fast downhill as uphill.

The mission crew had cut a line around their spot fire, which burned in heavy brush, and they'd contained it. It was late, past ten P.M., and they were tired and hungry. When Powers brought them supper, they sat in a circle to eat instead of first walking the few yards out of the canyon. Their foreman, Stanley Vote, had just said a short grace when they heard a voice yelling at them from above.

Charlie Lafferty, in charge of fire-line operations, had raced to warn the crew that flames were headed their way, hidden from their view behind an intervening lateral, or spur, ridge. But Lafferty himself did not fully understand what was happening. He hollered at the men to go *downhill*—the same path the fire would take. Luckily, about half the crew misunderstood him. Nine missionaries clambered uphill toward Lafferty—and survived. Lafferty barely escaped with his own life, scrambling on all fours and losing his hard hat, but managing to stay ahead of the flames. In some ways, though, he never escaped the fire. After recounting his story several times for the official record, he told his wife, Flora, that he never wanted to speak about it again.

Decades later, when a fellow employee, J. W. Allendorf, tried to interview Lafferty about the fire for posterity, Flora Lafferty refused to let him in the door. "It would kill him to talk about the fire," she told Allendorf.

Powers apparently heard Lafferty's shouts to go downhill; he followed his superior's order to the letter. Powers formed the rest of the men, fifteen counting himself, into a line and began to march down the canyon. They followed a roller-coaster route, down the side of one spur ridge and up another, blind for most of the time to what was coming behind them. They did not see the fire turning downhill and following them until it was too late. Lafferty's order had put the men on a pathway to their deaths—enough to give anyone nightmares. But there is more.

The official fire report allows far too much time—twenty-six minutes—for the race with the fire. The report says Lafferty started out to warn the crew at about 10:15 P.M. and puts the time of death at 10:41 P.M., based on the stopped watches of the dead crew members. Trial runs conducted by myself and members of the California Department of Forestry and Fire Protection, known as the CDF, show to the contrary that the terrain can be covered in less than half that time. Even with leeway for watches being off and the start time of 10:15 being approximate, the discrepancy we discovered is great enough to be disturbing and significant.

The official fire report blames no one for the deaths, a common conclusion of fire reports, which to this day are produced by the same agencies that fight the fires: a case of the fox being sent to check on the unfortunate occurrence in the chicken coop. The Rattlesnake Fire report acknowledges that the mission crew was forgotten for a while—it allows for a delay of ten to fifteen minutes between the wind shift that started spot fires and 10:15, when Lafferty took off to warn the mission crew. On the night of the fire, many seasoned firefighters and a newspaper reporter watched the events unfold, and none at first recognized the threat to the mission crew, so the delay as described is no cause for indictment. But if the delay was substantially longer, as some reports and evidence suggest—perhaps as much as an additional fifteen minutes or so, for a total delay of a half hour or more—then negligence should be at least considered.

A half century later, a silent witness would appear literally from the ashes of the fire and give testimony to help solve the riddle of the twenty-six-minute race.

Pattan was first questioned about the fire the day after the fatalities, July 10, at the Rattlesnake Fire camp, where he had found temporary work as an assistant cook; his final wages came to twenty-four dollars. Pattan was well known to the Forest Service. His father, Philip, was a respected Forest Service engineer in charge of road building in the district. The younger Pattan had often worked as a temporary firefighter and was a bit miffed this time to be relegated to a camp job.

By today's standards, Pattan was roughly handled by the law. He was questioned without a lawyer present for thirty-six hours by a team of lawmen that included a Forest Service arson investigator, the county sheriff, and the district attorney. Pattan made two initial statements denying that he'd set the fire. The lawmen then confronted him with close-up photographs of the dead and urged him to submit to a polygraph, or lie-detector test. Pattan agreed, without the counsel of a lawyer. After sweating for an hour on the lie box, he broke down and made a full confession.

Pattan was charged with second-degree murder, but a Glenn County grand jury decided that he had not intended to harm or kill anyone, a necessary precondition for a murder indictment. The grand jury reduced the charges to two felony counts of willful burning, one for the Rattlesnake Fire and one for a smaller fire Pattan had set earlier the same day; it had been quickly controlled and had caused little damage.

Pattan remembers, during those first days after the fire, looking out of the window of his cell on an upper floor of the Glenn County Jail in Willows, the county seat. A crowd of newsmen swarmed below "like a lynch mob howling for my blood." The experience chilled any desire to defend himself in public.

During brief courtroom appearances, Pattan restricted his comments for the record to "Guilty, sir" for each of the two counts of the indictment. Asked at the sentencing a few days later if he wished to say anything on his own behalf, he stood mute. A judge sentenced Pattan to two consecutive terms of one to ten years in San Quentin State Prison.

Pattan was lucky in his prison experience, as these things go. He was young and good-looking and could have fared very badly. He obtained work as a medical orderly, though, dealing with inmate ailments at night, when no doctor was present; the job allowed him to sleep in the hospital unit, away from the general prison population. During the day, he worked as a painter.

13

"We had a lot of talented artists in the population," he says, "and they put us to work painting murals in the mess halls." Pattan developed his talent through an art correspondence course, the kind once advertised on the inside covers of matchbooks.

While he served his time, his father, Philip, moved away from Willows in shame. The younger Pattan revered his father but lived in his shadow, habitually introducing himself as Phil Pattan's son. Others sometimes addressed him as "Phil Pattan's boy." Pattan probably would not have come back to Glenn County, he says, except in those days a prisoner had to have a job before he could qualify for parole. Friends offered him work on their farm, and after three years of incarceration, he was released on probation. His civil rights were restored under an amnesty program available at that time after successful completion of probation, which took him an additional three years.

Pattan has lived a quiet, law-abiding life ever since, and had refused all requests for interviews. He was not easy to locate: his name was misspelled "Patton" in many news and court documents, which sent researchers up a blind alley. According to Pattan, one writer assumed that Pattan was dead and wrote a story that described him in florid terms as a deliberate killer stalking the mountains for prey. A threatened lawsuit resulted in an out-of-court settlement, terms not disclosed, according to Pattan.

Then one evening his phone rang, intruding on his guarded existence.

It's difficult to know how to approach someone like Pattan, a near recluse with a notorious criminal past. I, the caller, began by saying, "I'm looking for the son of Philip Pattan."

Pattan hesitated. It might have been decades since a stranger had struck that chord. When he answered, it was with a touch of pride. "That's me," he said.

I explained that I was doing research for a book and wished to interview him about the Rattlesnake Fire. There was a longer pause. At last Pattan replied, heavily, "All right, I'll talk to you about it." Fifteen minutes later I drove up to the house in Artois.

Pattan, a man of medium but sturdy build, gives an impression of suppressed physical power. He stands a little hunched, as though defending against a body blow, but he does not cower. He has white hair, combed straight back, and strong facial features—a long face, heavily creased and

Stanford Philip Pattan at his easel today. He immerses himself in the work, beginning early in the morning and sometimes not stopping until dark. Photograph by author.

marked by a prominent Roman nose, similar to a sketch he once made of a classic Indian face. He is of Italian extraction; the Pattani family, having arrived in California with the gold rush, failed at mining and took up farming.

Pattan answered the doorbell wearing a T-shirt with the word *Wildfire* emblazoned across the front. He designed the shirt for a neighbor who makes a business of screening images onto T-shirts and selling them at fire camps. After the interview, Pattan began to worry about the image the fire T-shirts might create, if it became known that he was the artist, and decided to give up the work.

At the time of the fire, Pattan said, he was overwhelmed by personal problems—heavy debts, inability to hold a job, a pregnant wife who had left him a few days earlier to live with her parents and had taken along their three children. A doctor would later testify that Pattan was having migraine headaches every other day because of "worry and nervousness."

Pattan had dropped out of high school to enlist in the navy. He had served as a cook aboard a landing ship during World War II and participated in eight island invasions in the South Pacific. The LSTs—the acronym inspired the unloving nickname "low, slow targets"—brought tanks, other vehicles, and supplies to assault beaches and often came under fire. Upon return to civilian life, Pattan obtained a job as a game warden with the U.S. Fish and Wildlife Service in the Tule Lake region of California, near the Oregon border. He loved the outdoors and took to the job. "I was trained in law enforcement," he says with intended irony. But his wife, Portia Lee, could not stand the isolation of the area.

They moved back to Willows, where the family fell on hard times. Pattan was always good for a hunting or fishing tale, but a previous employer later described him as lazy and irresponsible: "Put him alongside a pile of work and he'd never touch it unless he had somebody pushing him along. . . . He was always buying all kinds of fishing equipment and when he came back he could tell the damnedest stories you ever heard."

Pattan fell behind on rent for an apartment in a federal housing project, for which he qualified as a veteran. Portia Lee did the arithmetic and found they owed around $3,000—more than the $2,400 annual salary he had earned as a game warden. She packed up, vowing not to return until he changed his ways.

Pattan told lawmen at the time of the fire that he'd set it to make work for himself, a practice common enough that it has its own name: job fire. A half century later, he makes a different point. Pattan now says he was thinking about more than a job; what he really intended, he says, was to clear out some of the "rank brush" that had come to blanket the mountains and canyons of the Coast Ranges. The brush or chaparral, a collection of chamise, manzanita, whitethorn, redbud, Christmas berry, scrub oak, digger pine, and greasewood, had taken over vast sections of the Mendocino National Forest after the Big Blowup of 1910, the great fire of northern Idaho and northwestern Montana, which killed no fewer than eighty-five people, blackened more than 3 million acres, and spurred the Forest Service to adopt a blanket policy of suppressing all fires on sight.

The policy was a success in the Mendocino National Forest. The Forest Service began keeping fire records for the forest the next year, 1911, and from that date until 1953 there is no mention of fire at the site of the Rattlesnake Fire, which means there was a brush buildup at the time of the fire at least four decades old.

The brush was more than a nuisance. Left unchecked, chaparral becomes an interlocking spiderweb of brambles and thorns that soaks up moisture, kills grass, and forms a nearly impenetrable barrier to man and beast. Irrigation water vanishes. Game disappears. Hikers and travelers have to skirt the stuff. When dried out, chaparral can burn with white-hot intensity. Many local people came to hate the brush and the Forest Service along with it. There was much talk about burning the brush, and more than talk: incendiarism became a perennial problem in California.

The earliest support for Pattan's brush-burning argument came immediately after the fire. In a page 1 note to readers, the *Willows Journal* described the long-standing controversy: "Last week's tragic forest fire has brought to a head long held differences of opinion between a substantial number of residents in this area and the U.S. Forest Service. They center around the question of whether brush on the forest's fringe should be burned out annually or left to grow."

In an accompanying article in the newspaper, Charles Gleeson, the reporter who'd witnessed the fatal moments of the Rattlesnake Fire, described in rosy terms the practice of the nineteenth century, when shepherds and other stockmen regularly burned the hills. "The last man out each fall set fire to the forest as he went along and he returned in the spring to a country of green canyons and glades open as far as the eye could see," Gleeson wrote.

In 1953, the Forest Service believed that most fires harmed the soil and the forest, which added scientific support to the fire-suppression policy. "Heat can close the soil's pores," a Forest Service official told Gleeson. "It destroys the soil bacteria necessary for plant growth. It creates ideal erosion conditions." Whether the science was right or wrong, the Forest Service's policy was to put out all fires.

Pattan says he had no plan of action when he set out for the mountains that day. "It was kind of a spur-of-the-moment thing," he said. "I didn't preplan. I was devastated from this problem I was having with my wife and I went to the mountains to get out of the valley, just to get away from it, just to think. And then I got up there and thought about this damn brush.

"I didn't dream anybody would go down in that rank brush fighting the fire."

Overall, Pattan's explanation rings more than a little hollow. When asked why he'd broken decades of silence, Pattan replied, "You said you're writing a book. I thought this might be a good way to get my side of it out."

The most immediate effects of the Rattlesnake Fire were of a human dimension. The deaths of the fourteen missionaries tested the faith of New Tribes Mission, a fledgling group that already had suffered a series of violent deaths in their work with primitive tribes abroad. A decade earlier, in 1943, New Tribes' first full year of operations, five of its missionaries were murdered by natives in a Bolivian jungle.

A year later, New Tribes established its boot camp at Fouts Springs, twenty-five miles from the eventual site of the Rattlesnake Fire. Two years later, in 1946, a wooden dormitory at the Fouts Springs camp burned to the ground, killing the infant daughter of a missionary couple.

More deaths followed. New Tribes bought a DC-3 to fly missionaries to South America; it crashed into the top of a mountain in Venezuela in bad weather on June 9, 1950, killing all fifteen people aboard. The mission bought a replacement aircraft; five months later, on November 21, 1950, it took off on its maiden voyage from Chico, California, carrying mission personnel to foreign posts. On board were the founder of New Tribes, Paul Fleming; two widows and six children of men who had died in the air crash in Venezuela; and nine others. The aircraft ran into bad weather over the Rocky Mountains and its electrical system failed—it was seen flying without navigational lights. The aircraft struck a ridge near the 12,694-foot peak of Mount Moran in Grand Teton National Park, in sight of the popular tourist destination of Jackson Lake. It wasn't until late the next summer that the snowy, high-altitude weather tempered enough to allow anyone to reach the crash site. Some of the bodies were never found.

In the summer of 1951 another New Tribes missionary was found dead, with a spear sticking out of his body, on a riverbank in the jungle along the Brazil-Bolivia border. The long, delicate spear is included in an exhibition on a wall of the reception area at the present-day mission headquarters, an old resort hotel in Sanford, Florida.

(New Tribes Mission has continued to suffer losses: Martin Burnham, a pilot and New Tribes missionary, was killed in a gun battle in June 2002 when Filipino soldiers attacked a Muslim guerrilla group that had kidnapped Burnham and his wife, Gracia, a year earlier.)

The mounting death toll put the future of the organization in doubt. "What will people think?" was the reaction of many, including Ken Johnston, a mission director who later wrote the group's history. Indeed, after the Rattlesnake Fire one missionary survivor, Paul Turner, continued on in mission work, but with a troubled spirit.

Others found that the Rattlesnake Fire brought new light to their lives. Duane Stous, another mission survivor, looked out the next morning from a road across from the fatal site at a hazy moonscape of charred brush and exposed mineral soil. On the far slope, too far away for him to make out details, a circle of men stood around a pile of what looked like naked store mannequins, arms and legs jutting at odd angles. The sight of the body-recovery operation plunged Stous into despair.

Then a glow started from deep inside him; despair turned to ecstasy. "The Lord spoke to my heart," Stous remembers. "He was in control. I could trust Him." Stous spent the remainder of his career as a missionary and teacher in the United States and abroad, speaking often of his experience of fire, both human and divine.

"I just threw it and left."

It was sunny and warm the morning of July 9 when Pattan headed west out of Willows for the foothills of the Coast Ranges. He had not dressed for outdoor work—he wore a yellow terry-cloth T-shirt, jeans, and moccasins. For an unemployed man with a large family to support, he drove a fancy car: a green 1949 Buick with whitewall tires, for which he was one payment behind. The Buick was a memorable sight, with its elegant saloon body, sloping trunk, and distinctive grille—chrome teeth in a fat-cat smile—and it contributed to Pattan's undoing. Those who saw the Buick that day had no trouble remembering it. Inside the car was a .22 rifle, a powerboat motor, an unopened half pint of whiskey for emergencies, and several boxes of matches. (Pattan was a smoker but not a drinker.)

The view from Willows in any direction is oceanic. Six million years ago the northern end of the Central Valley of California was a saltwater bay; the flatness today is mind-numbing. Roads go on for miles without a bend. The slightest haze can obscure the Sierra Nevadas to the east and the Coast Ranges to the west, causing you to feel as if you're at sea, gazing at a limitless horizon.

As Pattan headed out, he left behind the floodplain of the Sacramento River, with its soppy rice checks, as the shallow rice-growing catchments are called. In drier fields were endless rows of walnut, almond, plum, and peach trees, their trunks painted white to prevent sunburn, and acres upon acres of grapes, beets, onions, tomatoes, and sunflowers. A dozen miles beyond town, the flatness gave way to soft hills speckled with oaks and marked by deep creases and folds, evidence of mud slides brought on in part by heavy grazing. The grass on the hillsides was short and dry.

A half hour's drive took Pattan to a bridge over Stony Creek, a sparkling river in the foothills of the Coast Ranges that runs parallel to the mountains. He immediately turned north on the Chrome road, which follows the creek. Another five miles brought him to another bridge, this one over Grindstone Creek, a tributary of Stony Creek. Grindstone Creek offered good fishing higher up in Grindstone Canyon, a funnel-shaped trench of colossal proportions extending more than twenty miles to Mendocino Pass, at the crest of that range. Thick chaparral kept casual anglers out of the canyon, but Pattan knew its hidden ways. He stopped on the bridge for a look: the water appeared discouragingly low for fishing.

Pattan considered driving on a few miles to ask again for a job at Setzer's lumber mill, where he had been turned down a few days before. There was nothing for him back in Willows except a shoddy, empty apartment. He was blocked at every turn.

He got back in the Buick and drove on, passing a roadside cemetery with weathered grave markers, some dating to the 1870s and bearing the names of early ranch families—Ellis, Millsap, Powell. If the sight triggered cautionary reflections on mortality for Pattan, they did not show up in his subsequent actions that day. A few miles farther on, he turned onto Hull Road, a dirt track that leads past ranches and fields and into the mountains.

The Buick rattled across a cattle guard marking the start of the climb into the forested foothills. The road forked a few hundred yards ahead at a bushy oak tree, which still stands sentinel a half century later. Pattan pulled into one fork and turned the Buick around. It was a few minutes past noon. He picked up a box of matches and held it and the steering wheel with one hand. With the other hand, he struck a match and flicked it out the passenger window, into grass near the oak tree.

"I just threw it and left," Patten later told Clyde Larimer, the Glenn County district attorney. He pulled away fast—he always put the car in low and stomped on the gas pedal when starting up; it was his way of marking turf. He made it back to the main road without being seen and crossed again over the Grindstone Creek bridge. At a house directly ahead a man on the porch was keeping a leisurely watch on the road. Pattan pulled off and stopped. The sky was clear of smoke.

"Any fish in this creek?" Pattan called out to the man, "Tarzan" Tankersley, a logger who, despite his nickname, was of slim build. Tankersley's wife, Irene Mae, had been picking cucumbers and squash in the garden when the Buick passed the house earlier. "I seen a boy drive it," she said later. The sight struck her as odd, such a young man in such a fine car.

As Pattan and Tankersley chatted about fishing, a siren sounded in the distance. Pattan was the first to call attention to it.

"Must be the radio," Tarzan said.

"No, that's not coming out of the radio," Pattan insisted.

A CDF pickup truck came into sight, siren shrieking, and then a fire engine with men hanging on to the back. One of the men waved and pointed toward the back of the house.

"Let's look at the fire," Pattan said. He and Tarzan walked off the porch and Pattan pointed to the foothills, where a column of smoke had materialized. Tankersley, alarmed, said he better get back to his job, because if the fire grew big enough, he and other loggers would be called to fight it.

Pattan declared he would drive to the scene. He had fought fires before, he said; his father, Philip, was in the Forest Service.

The first person to report the smoke was Richard Casaurang, an assistant CDF ranger based at the Fire Control Station in the tiny town of Elk Creek, about seven miles to the south. Casaurang sighted a smoky haze at 12:20 P.M. He called in the sighting to Thelma Miller at the Elk Butte Lookout, above the town, then jumped in his pickup truck and switched on the siren. At 12:39 he arrived at the Chrome Fire, named after the nearby town of Chrome.

Casaurang suspected arson. Burning in low grass, the blaze covered several acres and had spread slowly up an open slope. How else could it have started? There had been no lightning in the region for thirty-three days. The humidity was about 30 percent, high enough to discourage a fire. There were no campfires in the vicinity.

"Have to be a match," Casaurang said later.

He and the CDF engine crew began to dig a break around the sputtering flames.

Pattan, meanwhile, thought it might be too obvious if he showed up immediately at the scene of a fire he had set. Instead, he drove from the Tankersley place in the opposite direction, toward the Elk Butte Lookout; from there, he would have a good view of the fire's progress without incriminating himself. By the time Pattan reached the lookout, Miller was a busy woman.

She and her husband, Archie, a firefighter for the Forest Service, had been eating lunch when she'd received Casaurang's initial smoke report. Thelma looked out the window—there were forty windows in the lookout, each one requiring weekly washing—and saw haze to the north. Within thirty seconds it coalesced into a smoke column. She radioed the Mendocino National Forest headquarters in Willows and reported the fire, which appeared to be on state land.

"Roll the state," replied Harley Ripley, the Forest Service dispatcher, adding that Archie might as well go, too. As Thelma telephoned CDF firefighters, Archie left his meal behind and headed out.

Pattan showed up at the lookout just minutes after Archie had departed, offering the convenient lie that he had seen smoke while in the town of Elk Creek and had come up for a better view. He and Miller watched as the smoke column boiled and thickened. If the fire burned into Grindstone Canyon, Pattan remarked, "it'll go like hell."

When Miller asked him who he was, he said his name was Pattan. "I guess you know my dad," Pattan said.

Miller said yes, of course, she knew Phil.

As they watched, the smoke stopped churning, then thinned out and turned white. The Chrome Fire was becoming another in a long series of failures for Pattan. Over the lookout radio they heard CDF firefighters describing flames dying down after scorching a paltry 11 acres of grass. The fire burned around but did no damage to a row of scrub-oak trees. A firefighter's hand-drawn map from that day shows a string of X's for the trees, which remain in a ghostly line a half century later.

Pattan hung around the lookout for a half hour or more. The excitement drained away. At some point, he signed the lookout register, perhaps out of boredom or perhaps to say he had nothing to hide. Miller, preoccupied with her work, did not notice when he left.

Pattan drove into town, stopped at the Elk Horn Tavern, and bought himself a beer. The bartender, Edward Howard, remembered glancing at a wall clock as Pattan came in the door: it was two P.M. Pattan perked up a little when Howard recognized him. "This is Phil Pattan's boy," Howard said, introducing him around. It was such an event that the bartender bought Pattan a second beer.

Pattan left the bar without standing a round himself. The day was warm, but not hot. The mercury would reach the mid- to high eighties, far short of the record-setting temperatures of the next days, which would soar into the hundreds. A gentle breeze blew from the southeast.

Pattan drove north again, this time turning west sooner and heading back into the mountains on Alder Springs Road, which runs parallel to Grindstone Canyon along its southern edge. He drove four miles to a hairpin turn called Oleta Point, halfway up a short canyon that branches off Grindstone Canyon. The short canyon, about a mile and a half long, lies between two ridges, Rattlesnake Ridge to the south and Powderhouse Ridge to the north, the latter named for a Forest Service dynamite shed on its north side, overlooking Grindstone Canyon. Local names vary, but in this story the short canyon will be called Powderhouse Canyon.

By now, Pattan had become a seething mass of frustrations, an animal willing to bite itself. He took out the .22 rifle and fired several shots. Brush was the only target, and he poured out his venom on it. The snap of the shots echoed emptily and died away. Pattan got back in the Buick and retraced his route to Elk Creek, this time stopping for a quick milk shake at the Green Room Cafe. The mix of sugar and the unaccustomed alcohol made him feel uninhibited and mean. Back in the Buick, he retraced his route to Oleta Point, again took out the .22 rifle, and shot into the canyon, scattering more brass shell casings.

Then Pattan got back in the Buick and dug out a box of matches. He put the vehicle in low and gunned it, lighting a match as he accelerated. He went less than a hundred yards—240 feet by later measurement—before flipping the match out the driver's window. When he demonstrated the gesture in his living room decades later, his eyes took on a hooded look and his arm lashed out in alarming imitation of a rattlesnake's strike.

The flaring match landed in chaparral on the uphill side of the road, which meant the fire could burn upward, its normal path, without the road acting as a break. An observer would give much to know what passed through Pattan's mind during these seconds. Was he the coolheaded arsonist of some accounts, hoping for a paycheck and damn the consequences? This was his second try of the day, after all, so he'd put some forethought into it. When Pattan confessed, the only reason he gave for setting the fire was to make work for himself.

"And now, just tell us again, like I told you before, honestly, why did you start the fires?" District Attorney Larimer asked.

"I needed the work and the money," Pattan replied.

"Is that the reason why you started the fires?"

"That is the reason why I started the fires."

But he felt some ambivalence or reluctance about actually doing the deed. He had started the day in town clothes, not work clothes for fighting fires. He wandered around the mountain roads, stopping here and there, telling easily disproved lies, and leaving his name in the lookout register. He drove to Oleta Point twice before he struck the match.

Pattan was in a disturbed mental state. Even those who arrested and interrogated him, Sheriff Lyle Sale and District Attorney Larimer, expressed understanding for the depth of his confusion. The last words of their final interview with Pattan, after they had extracted a complete confession, were these:

Sale: Stanford, is there anything else that you might want to tell us that we have not asked you?

A: No, all I did (hesitation) I didn't (hesitation)—

Larimer: I think what you want to say is you certainly didn't intend to kill anybody. What you intended to do was start a fire and get a job on it. You didn't know that anybody was going to be burned to death?

A: Yes.

Larimer: Is that it?

A: That is it, yeah.

Is there a shred of evidence that Pattan had a moment's thought at the time, as he now claims, about burning brush for the common good? The brush offers its own mute testimony. It was a forbidding gray barrier stretching to the horizon, depriving Pattan of his most reliable pleasures in life, hunting and fishing. He literally shot the brush with his .22 rifle, transferring frustrations about his personal life onto it. He no doubt shared the common attitude, recorded in Gleeson's story a week later, that the Forest Service was acting against local interests in allowing the brush to build up.

After the shock of the fatalities and his arrest had a chance to wear off, Pattan gave a probation officer a fuller account of why he had started the fires. He had left Willows to look for work in a lumber mill, he said, but "there was none." He didn't know what to do with himself, except he had thought of "starting a brush fire."

"I had in the past heard a lot of people say it would be a good thing if Grindstone Canyon would burn off, and I knew I could get work of some kind on it. I have never started a fire and it took a lot of will power to do it, I was desperate at the time."

Pattan, then, at least mentioned brush burning as a motive at the time. As to what he was thinking during the fateful moments, the answer most probably is: not much. The fire was his attempt to escape internal terrors, a sense of being overwhelmed, for which the choking "rank brush" made a worthy metaphor.

After tossing the match, Pattan drove off without a backward glance.

The first person to see smoke from the Rattlesnake Fire was Archie Miller, who, after leaving Elk Butte Lookout and his dinner, had driven to the Chrome Fire. The CDF crew, supplemented by a few Forest Service firefighters, had matters there well in hand, so Miller drove back the way he had come, except this time he turned west onto Alder Springs Road, just as Pattan had a few minutes earlier. Miller had barely started up the road when he saw a thread of smoke rising from the mountains. He estimated that the smoke was about four miles ahead (it was 4.1 miles as measured a few days later). The fire under the smoke appeared to be small, about "three times bigger than a man's hat," in Miller's later, vivid description of it.

Miller hurriedly drove on, hoping to find a telephone at the Gillaspy ranch at the mouth of Powderhouse Canyon, a short mile below the fire. The ranch phone was out of order. Miller set up his radio, a boxy affair with a whip aerial, and tried to raise his wife, Thelma, at the Elk Butte Lookout. He received no answer but described the fire anyway, in case Thelma could hear him but not respond. Then, he says, "I just practically threw my radio back together and drove on to the scene of the fire." By the time he reached the scene, the blaze had grown considerably larger than three hats.

"I saw it was too big for one man to handle," Miller said. Flames had spread twenty-five to thirty feet up the steep bank. Miller drove on, hunting for an unobstructed place to set up the radio again. When he finally made contact with Thelma, it turned out she had monitored his earlier call and passed his report on to the Forest Service headquarters in Willows. Her call was logged there at 2:40 P.M. Two minutes later, at 2:42, firefighters on the Chrome Fire reported their blaze under control (it wasn't; the fire flared up that night and then was brought under control). As a consequence, men working at the Chrome Fire and others on the way were diverted to the fire at Oleta Point, which meant the firefighters caught the fire early. Delay was no issue.

"Yes, men are rolling," Thelma told her husband. "Men are coming to the fire."

Archie headed back to Oleta Point and the base of the fire. By then, flames had scorched an area in the shape of a massive first baseman's mitt, a rounded V with a narrow, blackened bottom at Alder Springs Road and a wide, irregular top. Two other firefighters had arrived and started up the bank to attack the fire: Julio Silva, a Forest Service ranger, and his helper, David Pesonen, at nineteen years old probably the youngest man to fight the fire.

"I'd been on the job a week—no training, just a healthy body and knew how to use a shovel," remembers Pesonen, who revisited the scene and walked the ground with me a half century later. "Here was a *huge* fire just taking off up the mountainside. We couldn't *possibly* do anything with it. We called for help."

In 1953 Pesonen was a young man on the loose. He had graduated with a forestry degree from the University of California at Berkeley, then bummed around for a while. He had taken his first real job a few days before the fire as a tank truck operator for the Forest Service, under the tutelage of Silva at the Alder Springs station several miles west of the fire site. Having driven to Willows earlier the fateful day for a job-related physical examination, he was driving back to Alder Springs—he'd passed Oleta Point minutes before Pattan set the fire there—when he saw Silva in a truck "coming around a corner hell-bent for leather."

"We've got a fire," said Silva, who told Pesonen to throw his gear in the truck, a Dodge Power Wagon with a slip-on pumper unit. It would be Pesonen's first and most memorable fire experience, though he would go on to train as a smoke jumper. After an injury on a practice jump ended that experience, he became a lawyer and antinuclear activist and was eventually appointed the director of the CDF under Governor Jerry Brown—which meant he went from grunt-level firefighter to the man in charge of California's vast firefighting corps. As CDF director, he returned to the Mendocino National Forest and had a reunion with Silva, which included an attempted joke or two about Silva having taught Pesonen everything he knew.

Pesonen and Silva had been driving only a minute or two when they came around a curve and there, not thirty years ahead, was a green Buick making a fast turn onto a little-used side road. Pesonen glimpsed the Buick's rear license plate.

"Remember these things," Silva instructed him. Two fires in the same general area on a calm day, Silva said, could mean arson. And it was unusual to see a sedan on that road, which led to Long Point Lookout and then down to the bottom of Grindstone Canyon. Pesonen scratched a few numbers on a slip of paper and stuffed it in a pocket.

The pair drove on and arrived at Oleta Point about 3:15 P.M. By then, flames had extended beyond the reach of the hose on their truck. Silva radioed for a bulldozer and more men; then he and Pesonen grabbed a brush hook and root ripper and started up the slope. Silva called a halt within minutes. The slope was nearly sheer, the brush close to impenetrable, and the fire had too much of a head start. They slid and stumbled back to Alder Springs Road.

By then, a large contingent of men and vehicles had gathered there, including Lafferty, who had driven over from the Chrome Fire. Lafferty took charge. "I talked to the boys and advised them to follow me," Lafferty said later. He led them to the head of Powderhouse Canyon, where a second hairpin turn, Powderhouse Turn, created a pullout with a sweeping view. That spot instantly became the fire command post.

The Rattlesnake Fire on the afternoon of July 9, 1953, looking east. Courtesy U.S. Forest Service

Jack Ewing, a senior Forest Service supervisor, joined them there within minutes; he had been assigned by Forest Service headquarters as fire boss and took over from Lafferty, who became number two, or line boss, in charge of operations. Ewing was "one of the most experienced brush fire men in the California region," according to the official fire report. The reputation had come at a price: Ewing was a man with a past.

A decade earlier, on October 2, 1943, Ewing had been fire boss when eleven U.S. marines were killed and seventy-two others injured while fighting the Hauser Creek Fire in the Cleveland National Forest in southern California. In the aftermath, Ewing was held partly responsible for the deaths. The fire had started from marine gunnery practice, and the marines turned out in numbers to fight it. Ewing put more than a hundred marines in the charge of Buel Hunt, a relatively inexperienced subordinate, and sent them off to attack the fire. Ewing went to attend other duties and never checked back on Hunt and his marine crew.

The wind shifted unexpectedly—exactly what would happen a decade later in Powderhouse Canyon—and flames overran the marines. They tried to hide on a boulder-strewn hillside, but the fire claimed its eighty-three victims including eleven dead. The official report cited Ewing for making a serious error of judgment when he "over-appraised" Hunt's abilities. Hunt bore the heaviest responsibility, according to the report, because he acted "imprudently" in constructing a fire line too close to the main fire. But Ewing should have kept a closer check on Hunt and his men. The report cites both Ewing and Hunt for negligence in language remarkably accusatory for the day, a time when fire deaths were considered acts of nature and fire bosses virtually beyond reproach.

"It is at least a question whether one of them might not have been spared for a time long enough to check the location of the line selected for initial attack, to check fire behavior for a longer period than that done by Ewing before Hunt's assignment to the East line, and to appraise the early results of the attack on that flank," said the report, edging close to sarcasm.

The report recommended no disciplinary action against either man. It excused them with an argument unthinkable in today's world of heightened concerns for firefighter safety and for accountability on the part of supervisors: "Few of the seasoned senior officials of unquestioned fire fighting

The area burned by the Rattlesnake Fire, looking northwest. The site of the Missionary Spot Fire is circled just to the right of center. Powderhouse Turn is just to the left above that. Grindstone Canyon is in the background. Courtesy California Department of Forestry and Fire Protection

ability have reached their present status without narrow escapes of themselves and their men, comparable in everything but tragic consequences, with Hunt's situation on this fire. *The training of fully dependable high caliber leadership demands this rather rugged and at times brutal process* [emphasis added]."

At the time of the 1953 fire, memories of the Hauser Creek Fire had blurred, or at least there is no mention of it in the official report. This fire, though, echoed the mistakes made at Hauser Creek: failing to anticipate the wind shift and forgetting about a crew placed in harm's way.

When Ewing took charge of the fire, he had about fifteen men at his command and many more on the way. Miller, Silva, and Pesonen had been the first to reach the site; Casaurang and a CDF crew from the Chrome Fire had shown up shortly afterward, as had Powers, the assistant ranger, and two others from the Alder Springs Forest Service station: Robert "Red" Werner, who would bring a lifetime of comfort to a bereaved family after the fire, and Harry Simpson.

It was about four P.M. when this group gathered at Powderhouse Turn, with its panoramic view, to plan an attack. The fire, which had been burning for an hour and a half, sent up a narrow but dense plume of smoke. Its base was nearly a mile down the canyon. The firefighters decided to start from where they were, at Powderhouse Turn, and box in the fire on three sides—considering that the fire was burning up the canyon at this point, there was no need to contain it on its lower, down-canyon side. It was a classic plan: establish an anchor point, flank the fire, and pinch it off at the head.

Alder Springs Road provided one ready-made fire break; it became the lower-flank fire line. Ewing stationed men and vehicles along the road to prevent flames from spilling into the bottom of Powderhouse Canyon, which could turn into a furnace. If that happened, the fire easily could sweep over Powderhouse Turn and into Grindstone Canyon, where no natural feature would stop it for miles and miles.

Simultaneously, a crew with hand tools was sent to construct a firebreak along the ridge top on the flank above the fire. That would keep flames from slopping into the next drainage, Rattlesnake Creek, the landmark that gave the fire its name. (The ridge where the fire occurred is referred to in Forest Service documents and court testimony as Rattlesnake Ridge, and will be so identified here, though Forest Service maps identify Rattlesnake Ridge more specifically as the next one to the south.)

Those two fire lines, along Alder Springs Road and the top of Rattlesnake Ridge, would contain the fire's flanks. Meanwhile, a third line would be cut in advance of the fire, straight up from Powderhouse Turn to a place aptly named High Point, at a peak on Rattlesnake Ridge. Together, the three lines would box in the fire.

Once the lines were well established, crews using fusees would light fires along Alder Springs Road and the line in advance of the main fire. There was no need to set fires along the top of Rattlesnake Ridge because fires do not readily burn downhill, except in the most unusual circumstances. If everything went as planned, the set fires would consume unburned fuel within the box and burn into the main fire. With nothing left to feed it, the fire would die out.

It was a good plan. A half century later thirty seasoned CDF firefighters would tour the site, taking on the roles of the 1953 firefighters, and come up with no better initial plan of attack. The plan worked, too, until darkness fell, the wind grew antic, and the men forgot the tricks fire can play—and even forgot one another. Success too often leads to forgetfulness of past troubles and of those who depend on us, and as long as daylight lasted the plan for the Rattlesnake Fire proved a grand success.

"There's a hell of a fire."

Though Pattan had tossed his match and driven off without a backward glance, he yearned to see the effect of his handiwork. The Chrome Fire had quickly died out; perhaps this second fire, too, would end in failure. Pattan drove west, into the mountains, for nearly six miles and then turned onto the side road leading to Long Point Lookout, perched on the end of a ridge that sticks like a thumb into Grindstone Canyon. A half century later the only sign of the fourteen-foot-high lookout building—it was sited flat on the ground and could hardly be called a tower—is a crumbling concrete foundation with tufts of chaparral sprouting inside. The place has an eagle's view. On a clear day you can see miles beyond the mouth of Grindstone Canyon to the east, and to the crest of the Coast Ranges to the west. Even on a calm day, wind currents here can take off your hat.

Pattan saw a curl of smoke from the Rattlesnake Fire rising over a lip of Grindstone Canyon that marked the top of Powderhouse Canyon. Firefighters would be there by now, he figured—he had seen how quickly they'd reacted to the Chrome Fire. But the fire would not be big enough yet to justify hiring temporary firefighters. The flames needed time to develop.

Pattan drove to the bottom of Grindstone Canyon and stopped at a picnic table, where he took out his .22 rifle and plinked at cans for a few minutes. Bored and restless, he got in the Buick again and drove back up to Alder Springs Road, heading for the Forest Service station at Alder Springs.

Pattan's Buick was becoming a familiar sight; Silva and Pesonen had not been the first to mark it. Lester Gillaspy, whose ranch lay at the mouth of Powderhouse Canyon, had seen the Buick earlier in the day, when Pattan had driven past for the first time. "I saw a green Buick sedan with one man in it," Gillaspy said later. "The car was gone a short time and then came back down. I went to Elk Creek and saw the green Buick sedan was parked in front of the Green Room Cafe and the man inside was sitting at the counter."

William Brown, a Forest Service firefighter released from the Chrome Fire, glimpsed the Buick at the bottom of Grindstone Canyon as he took an alternate route to the Rattlesnake Fire. The sedan headed up to the Alder

Springs Road "going so fast all I seen was a broadside of the car. . . . He went so fast I never could catch him." He noted the distinctive slope of the vehicle's trunk, but could not be certain of recognizing the car again.

As Pattan drove into the Forest Service station at Alder Springs, two women stood outside: Viola Silva, Julio's wife, and Maude Powers, whom everyone called Maudi, Robert Powers's wife.

"He seemed very friendly," Mrs. Silva said later. "He asked Maudi and I how the fire was." The women said their husbands had left moments ago for the fire.

Mrs. Silva asked Pattan who he was. Stan Pattan, he replied. Did she know his father, Phil?

Yes, she said, everyone knew Phil.

Pattan told the women he did not want to fight the fire in the clothes he was wearing, the terry-cloth T-shirt, jeans, and moccasins, so he was going to bypass the fire and go home to Willows by another route.

Lawmen later pressed Pattan about this encounter, trying to stir his conscience.

"Do you know the names of either of the women you talked to?" asked District Attorney Larimer.

"Well, I know Mrs. Silva. And I don't know Mrs. Powers."

Did he *ever* realize who Mrs. Powers was married to? they asked.

"Yes," Pattan said, he'd found out later who she was.

Pattan took a one-lane back road to Elk Creek and had to squeeze the Buick past a logging truck coming the opposite way.

"There's a hell of a fire down at Powderhouse Curve," he told the loggers. "I don't want to fight fire, so I'm going down the access road."

The loggers made a joke of it, saying maybe they should turn their rig around and flee, the fire being so big. The exchange took place at 4:05 P.M., the loggers would recall.

By then, men were converging on the Rattlesnake Fire from far and wide. The flame of a single match had raised a column of smoke that had become a guidon for battle. Men with willing arms and backs headed for the smoke from logging camps, forest stations, and the Forest Service headquarters at Willows.

At the missionary boot camp, tucked far from the temptations of the world, men and women left their chores and hastily assembled at the chapel. The motto "To Die Is to Gain" hung on a placard in the chapel, a reminder that life on earth is brief and glory lies beyond the grave. The men wore their work clothes: denim pants, long-sleeved shirts, wide belts or suspenders, and soft hats. Wives in gingham dresses came from gardens or slab-sided cabins, children on their hips and holding their hands. Girls whose faces had no makeup came to wave good-byes to friends, sweethearts, and fiancés.

The scene had the festive air of a barn raising. It was the first fire of the season and had been eagerly anticipated; fire gear had been packed and ready for weeks. The missionaries flipped a coin to decide who was lucky enough to go on the first truckload. They were glad to join together for a work of service. They had no way to see what lay ahead: natural forces with the power to turn Pattan's casual description of a "hell of a fire" into an all-too-real hell: a place of anguish, torment, and devouring flames.

"He never knew a stranger."

Harley Ripley, the Willows dispatcher, wasted no time in ordering out the mission crew. Ripley made the call to the Fouts Springs camp within the same minute, 2:40 P.M., the fire was reported to him. It was the second fire of the day, and Ripley needed every able body he could muster. Answering the call at Fouts Springs was Homer Hancock, a mission director who kept a small general store at the camp and worked for the Forest Service as a seasonal firefighter. The first truckload of twelve missionaries, plus Hancock as driver, left for the fire eleven minutes later, at 2:51 P.M., a quick start for a pickup crew even today.

The missionary trainees hailed mostly from small towns with names like Ypsilanti, North Platte, Birchdale, Ogallah, and Glendale, from across the United States and Canada. Many of the men had served in World War II and started families immediately upon their return home; they had young children galore. Most of them in their twenties and thirties, the missionaries were of various Protestant denominations, but they shared a literal interpretation of the Bible and a commitment to preach the Gospel to primitive tribes who had never seen a missionary before—the "new tribes" of the mission's name. They were seekers embarked on a quest, not adolescents out for a frolic.

The missionaries were plain in appearance, but set apart in manner. A reporter for the *Chico Enterprise-Record,* Lee Soto, spent a few days at Fouts Springs before the fire and struggled to describe them. "It is difficult for one from the 'natural world' to live among people who eat the same food you do, wear clothes like you, speak the same language and can laugh—but still consider themselves to be from another world."

When they'd first arrived at Fouts Springs, a picturesque but lonely valley far back in the mountains, the missionaries had been full of hope. The group was founded in 1942 by Paul Fleming, a missionary with a charismatic personality, or "burning heart," as Johnston, the mission historian, described him. A native of Los Angeles, Fleming had contracted malaria while working as a missionary in the 1930s in what was then the British colony of Malaya, present-day Malaysia. During his recuperation he had what he called a "vision," a moment of inspiration compelling him to preach the Gospel to primitive peoples. Fleming's vision was apocalyptic, an attempt to fulfill a passage in the Gospel of Matthew, 24:14, which calls upon Christians to witness "to all nations; and then the end shall come." He and his followers made a covenant committing themselves to reach "the last tribe with the Gospel in our generation," which for them meant bringing on the end of the world.

New Tribes Mission started with few members and little money, but by November 1942 it had sent abroad its first group, ten adults and six children; this party went to Bolivia, where five of them were killed the following year. First based in Chicago, the mission turned a vacant Rush Street nightspot, the Hi Hat Club, into its headquarters; over the years New Tribes would convert many resorts of dubious reputation.

The next year, 1943, the mission started a publication, *Brown Gold.* The title sounds patronizing to the contemporary ear, but it was brave for its day, calling on Christians to treasure souls in brown bodies. As the organization grew, it soon felt the need for more spacious administrative quarters and a place to train for the rigors of jungle life. Johnston, who was then a preacher in California, suggested Fouts Springs.

The place had known the high life early in the twentieth century as a mineral-springs resort, but that enterprise had failed with the repeal of Prohibition. During the Great Depression, the springs became a base camp for the Civilian Conservation Corps, the federal program that put the army of unemployed to work in the nation's forests and parks. The CCC camp closed when World War II turned the unemployed into a real army—of soldiers and factory workers. By 1944, the Fouts Springs facilities were vacant and falling apart; that year the Forest Service granted New Tribes Mission free use of the place—649 acres of wild country and six dilapidated CCC buildings—in return for custodial services. Johnston gave up his pulpit and led an advance party, including his wife, Lilly, and their two children, to scout the place.

The cabins were not only tumbledown, they lacked even such basics as stoves. There were no power lines for miles, let alone electrical hookups. Water came from nearby Trout Creek; the first person to fetch it returned with a big rattlesnake he had killed on the bank. "What tremendous possibilities! It looked like the perfect location!" Johnston exulted in his history, written long after this daunting introduction.

The first missionary class of about one hundred came to Fouts Springs a few months later, in January 1945, and the following year the entire New Tribes Mission moved there. A trip to the nearest town for groceries took a day. The fledgling missionaries learned to hunt jackrabbits and deer in season, keep cows and pigs, and tend kitchen gardens. After the 1946 fire destroyed the dormitory, the missionaries built their own slab-sided cabins, storage buildings, and work sheds. By 1953, there were more than sixty structures, all painted the same brownish red.

From the start, serving on fire crews offered the missionaries a chance to perform a community service in lieu of rent, a welcome diversion, and an opportunity to earn hard cash. The volunteers quickly established a name for themselves as firefighters; in fact, they were known by several names: the missions, the mission boys, or, more commonly, the mission crew. At the time of the Rattlesnake Fire, New Tribes Mission had a contract with the Forest Service to provide, day or night, "all or a portion of its employees as may be determined by the fire emergency."

The mission crew was used to supplement the better-trained state and federal units; the mission crew was supposed to be the last called out, the first relieved. But the missionaries proved to be so eager and reliable that they were often summoned at the first sign of trouble, as happened on the Rattlesnake Fire. Leon Thomas, supervisor of the Mendocino National Forest, often sang their praises. "They are the tops," he told public gatherings.

The contract for 1953, signed for the government by Lafferty, who became line boss on the fire, fixed pay rates at $1.30 an hour with board for unskilled firefighters, and up to $2.48 an hour without board for the most highly skilled workers, those who packed airplane cargo. The money made a difference: at the time New Tribes could keep a missionary in the field for $60 to $90 a month, a few days' wages with overtime for a firefighter.

"We were kind of a hotshot unit," said Stous, the survivor who recommitted himself to missionary work after the Rattlesnake Fire. "All the men went. It was a good deal. They paid us good, fed us good. It was exciting." The term *hotshots,* which was in casual use in those days, now applies to highly trained, interregional twenty-person federal crews who fight big fires anywhere they happen, from Florida to western Washington.

The mission crew was nothing like contemporary hotshots. Its members were "above average" in training for the day, the official fire report says, because "half of them had fire training or experience or both," which means half of them had no training and no fire experience. "Back in those days, everything was pretty loose," Stous remembers. The Forest Service ran a rudimentary fireguard school in the spring, which some missionaries attended. But Stous had joined the mission three days before the Rattlesnake Fire and had never fought a fire in his life. One mission crew member had been at Fouts Springs for only a matter of hours—Paul Gifford, a supporter of New Tribes who was visiting from Vancouver, British Columbia. He joined the fire crew on the spur of the moment and paid the highest price for his decision.

The missionaries had a few experienced fire hands. Stanley Vote, who said the crew's final grace, had risen to the rank of foreman as a regular "seasonal" firefighter. He had attended fireguard school and had fought fire for two seasons. In recognition of this, the twenty-four-year-old wore a nickel-plated badge, while regular Forest Service employees wore solid bronze badges; the difference would matter after the fire. Vote, whose parents were evangelical pastors in Minnesota, was a popular figure at Fouts Springs, where he was engaged to another trainee, Ramona Briggs; the couple planned to go to Thailand together as missionaries. He had a cheerful spirit and a talent for singing and playing the accordion. "He never knew a stranger," said his brother-in-law, Gerald Hosterman.

Among those clambering aboard the fire trucks was Benjamin Dinnel, twenty-six, a native of Chico, near Willows. Dinnel had arrived at Fouts Springs four days earlier, on a Sunday. A navy veteran with service in the South Pacific, Dinnel had spent months considering his decision to join the mission. He hoped to be sent to Africa. Dinnel's father, Glenn, described him as a faithful member of the Grace Baptist Church who frequently attended Youth for Christ meetings. "We wanted him to do just whatever he wanted to do," the elder Dinnel said of his son's decision.

Others had more involved personal histories; the fire would act as leveler, bringing them together. Don Schlatter and his wife, Janet, had gone through boot camp at Fouts Springs two years earlier. The course lasted a year and included language, geography, and religious studies as well as rigorous hiking and camping expeditions; it has since been expanded to four years with added training in linguistics, culture, aviation (missionaries often pilot their own planes), and electronic communication. "I had been a schoolteacher in Indiana before going to Fouts Springs Boot Camp in July of 1951 with my wife, Janet, and six-month-old daughter, Rachel, and while I was there taught in the little government school on the premises to some of the children whose parents were in the training," Schlatter recounted years later. After Schlatter and his wife completed the course, they returned to Indiana, where he taught school for another year before they headed back to Fouts Springs to await visas to Thailand. While at camp, Schlatter often joined the mission crew on fires.

"I had experience fighting various fires during the time I was at Fouts Springs, but the specific training we had was very elementary. We were just told to follow the orders of our supervisors."

Schlatter and Dinnel would find themselves in near lockstep, one behind the other, at the key turning point in their lives and then would part forever. One step made the difference. They took different paths, one leading to fulfillment of lifetime goals and the other to eternity in minutes and yards.

The same thing happened with different results to another pair: Duane Stous and Ken Etherton, who was the mission dentist. They raced flames side by side until Etherton collapsed in exhaustion, telling Stous to keep going and save himself. "I was nearly dead; I couldn't have gone another step," Etherton said later. Stous urged him to his feet and helped him to safety.

Some missionaries were made of sturdier stuff. Cecil Hitchcock, a twenty-year-old farm boy from eastern Colorado, had ridden horses, fed stock, and pitched hay from the time he was nine years old. "He was an excellent climber and hiker in the mountains and had an uncanny sense of direction," said his sister, Mavis. Cecil was active in the First Christian Church of Englewood, teaching youth classes and singing in a quartet with Mavis, with whom he sometimes also sang duets. "He was outgoing and friendly and well liked," Mavis said. "He was my best buddy all through our lives together." When the test came, Hitchcock's strength and sense of direction would carry him farther than any of the others and to within yards of escape.

It is not too early at this point to begin asking the question that haunts every step of this narrative, from Pattan's troubled act of arson to the turning points in the race with fire and to the eventual tragic climax: Why?

For Pattan, it is the sad "Why?" of human catastrophe: why did he chose that place, time, and way to vent his frustrations, and why were the consequences so terrible? By improbable coincidence, arsonists with far more malicious intentions than Pattan were touching off fires all across California that same day. None of the other fires had fatal results. Six grass fires believed to have been set by firebugs burned 1,200 acres and threatened homes near Oroville, which is about thirty miles east of Willows.

More spectacularly, a "ring of fire bugs," according to newspaper accounts, simultaneously touched off a dozen building fires in downtown Fresno on July 9, causing officials to declare a state of emergency. The National Guard was called out to protect public buildings and restore calm. The fires caused $1 million in damage; twenty-five firemen and two volunteers were overcome by smoke, but no lives were lost.

Pattan, by contrast, started his fire in nuisance brush more than a mile from the closest human habitation and with no intention of harming anyone. Yet his fire caused the greatest loss of life among wildland firefighters since the 1933 Griffith Park Fire near Los Angeles, which killed no fewer than twenty-five firefighters.*

---

*The Griffith Park Fire is an oddity in the history of wildfire because the park is in the middle of an urban area and those who fought it were a Depression-era work crew, not designated firefighters. Records of who was on the crew were poorly kept, and the account of the dead and injured became controversial. The fire broke out on a hillside below a work crew building a road in the park, which is directly east of Beverly Hills. Many of the crew regarded fighting the fire as "a lark" and went willingly to work. But the wind shifted, turning the blaze into an inferno. Afterward, the foremen claimed they had not ordered anyone to fight the fire. Survivors remember foremen yelling at them to "get the hell back in there" and battle the flames. The National Wildfire Coordinating Group, which is charged with keeping wildfire fatality records, today puts the death toll at a very conservative 25; at least 125 were injured. At the time, survivor and pro-labor groups put the death toll above 50, which is almost certainly too high. Today the site of the fire, near the Los Angeles Zoo and a municipal golf course, is a picnic area sometimes used as a movie set by film companies from nearby Hollywood. A memorial plaque was erected in November 1933, but it has long since vanished. There is no marker anywhere in the park to commemorate or recall the event.

The 1937 Blackwater Fire on the Shoshone National Forest in Wyoming killed the same number, fifteen. The greatest loss of life among wildland firefighters since the Rattlesnake Fire was a lesser number, the fourteen killed in the 1994 South Canyon Fire.

For the missionaries, the question "Why?" goes beyond bad luck and enters the theological dimension: why did people who believed they were acting in harmony with a divine and benevolent will come to such bad ends? Schlatter and Dinnel, men of similar commitment under identical circumstances, wound up with fates as different as they could be—one lived, one died. Was it by mere chance, blind luck, or their own judgment calls? Or did it go beyond that, as many of the missionaries came to believe, and involve an act of divine will beyond human understanding but ultimately working for the good? "They were fine fellows," Joe Knutson, a mission official, said at the time, "and we know they were willing to die if God willed it."

Questions such as these can be put aside by those who feel no need to include a divine actor in their explanation of the universe. But the missionaries had dedicated themselves to a quest to reach the end of time by bringing godly fire to the souls of primitive tribesmen. For the thirty mission volunteers who filled the trucks at Fouts Springs that day, the fire promised an interlude, a welcome break from the rigors of their training. Instead, the fire would bring fulfillment to their quest, though not the one of their hearts' desiring. In a few hours they would confront savage forces with not a care for them or their message, and for fourteen of them it would mean the end of time on earth.

"Go downhill, downhill!"

The road from Fouts Springs winds through endless switchbacks and over steep mountains, seemingly ready in spots to slide into oblivion. It took Hancock an hour to drive to the fire, but because the summons had been immediate, he and the crew of twelve arrived at Powderhouse Turn at 3:55 P.M. as Ewing, Lafferty, and the others gathered to set strategy.

Many hours of daylight lay ahead, plenty of time to catch the fire. True, the smoke had turned heavy and flames were expanding. But the fire was confined to the slope of Rattlesnake Ridge above Alder Springs Road. Flames would pause when they reached the crest of the ridge and were no longer driven by the slope. If the firefighters hurried, they could establish a fire line along the crest to keep flames from lapping onto the other side.

The firefighters separated into groups to construct and defend the three sides of the box: the line along the ridge crest, the second line in front of the fire, and the third, which was Alder Springs Road. There was intermingling of state, federal, and private firefighters, but in general, assignments broke out like this:

Vote, with most of the mission crew and several loggers, went to cut the line along the crest of Rattlesnake Ridge. They nearly lost the fire before they started. As the head of the fire reached the crest of the ridge, a tongue of flame licked over the top and ignited brush on the far slope. Vote's men quickly slid down below the finger of fire. They had to brace themselves against the steepness of the slope as they hacked out a quick firebreak. They not only stopped the finger of fire, but the line they subsequently constructed along the ridge crest held for as long as the fire burned.

Another mixed crew constructed the line from Powderhouse Turn up to High Point on Rattlesnake Ridge. Red Werner, who would play a healing role after the fire, was in charge here, along with Ranger Powers.

Richard Casaurang of the CDF volunteered to take charge along Alder Springs Road, supervising his state crew and whoever else had a vehicle, which included Silva, Pesonen, and their Dodge Power Wagon. Casaurang posted trucks, engines, and crews in a staggered line along the road, ready with hoses and pumper units if flames threatened.

Lafferty, the line boss, was everywhere. "I was up on the ridge above, and back and forth on the line-duty job," he said later. "Fire control was progressing nicely." Lafferty optimistically reported to the dispatch office in Willows that he expected early control of the blaze, unless an "adverse change in weather" came along, a caution that would prove prophetic. He felt confident enough of success to leave the flames and go in search of a fire-camp location; Powderhouse Turn was becoming overcrowded with bulldozers, tractors, a food truck (or "candy wagon"), and crews to run the equipment.

At the wheel of one truck coming around the turn was Pattan, who had found employment at last. After driving away from the mountains in midafternoon, Pattan had wandered around Willows for hours, hoping for the Rattlesnake Fire to become big enough to require extra manpower. He stopped by Al Johnson's service station, where he had once worked, and asked Johnson's partner, Jack Ferguson, if he knew "there was a fire up in the hills." Ferguson said no, he had heard nothing. Perhaps to give himself cover, Pattan suggested they drive together to Forest Service headquarters and inquire.

There, they were told the Rattlesnake Fire was nearly under control and no more men were needed, a keen disappointment for Pattan. He dropped Ferguson back at the service station and went on to visit his estranged wife, Portia Lee, at her parents' home. He didn't like being there, he said later, because it made him feel beholden to his in-laws. But he had cake, ice cream, and a cup of coffee. In a show of bravado, he told Portia Lee at some point— the timing varies in his accounts—that he expected to be gone for ten days or so fighting fire. After eating with his in-laws, he drove back to Johnson's service station and killed time washing the Buick.

In early evening, unwilling to admit utter failure, Pattan returned to the Forest Service office. He hung around for an hour and was about to give up when, shortly after eight P.M., reports came in of flare-ups on the Rattlesnake Fire; it was going to be an all-night campaign, and the crews would need a hot breakfast. Pattan could have a job, he was told, if he didn't mind setting up a kitchen.

Pattan jumped behind the wheel of a Forest Service truck and retraced his route to the mountains. He reached the fire at about nine P.M. and drove on to Camp Ellendale, a picnic ground in a grove of ponderosa pines four and a half miles west of the fire, which Lafferty had chosen as a fire camp; it is a picnic ground to this day.

As Pattan made Powderhouse Turn, standing there were Thomas, the forest supervisor, and Gleeson of the *Willows Journal,* who had driven up from town together. Thomas had telephoned Gleeson in early evening and invited the reporter to drive with him to the fire. "We've got a fire, first one of the season," Thomas told Gleeson. "Thought you might like to see it." Gleeson's account of subsequent events, contained in several articles in the *Willows Journal* and in interviews with other newspapers, has the freshest memories of what was said and done during the fire.

On the drive out from Willows, Thomas told Gleeson that circumstances indicated that the fire was an arson job; two fires on the same day with no recent lightning or nearby campfires raised everyone's suspicions. Thomas had followed the progress of the Chrome Fire, and he hoped the Rattlesnake Fire would be as easy to control.

"We think we've got it hemmed in on three sides," he told Gleeson.

As they drove up Alder Springs Road, the flames were close enough for someone to "rush out and grab a burning bush," Gleeson noted. But the overall situation appeared favorable. There was an abundance of men and machines, and backfires were burning into the main fire. "Given any kind of a break, it seemed, and the blaze would be under control within an hour or two," Gleeson estimated.

As the only passage across the mountains for many miles, Alder Springs Road remained open to traffic. Every now and then a logging truck would worry its way through the fire vehicles and around Powderhouse Turn—no minor feat. Logging trucks tipped over at the hairpin turn with such regularity that dumped logs had scraped a wide chute down the side of Powderhouse Canyon, a feature that would play a role in the minutes ahead.

As Gleeson and Thomas pulled up at the turn, they heard Lafferty sign off "ten four" on his radio. Lafferty had just received the latest weather report, and it was a good one. The southeasterly breeze was holding steady at about fifteen miles an hour. "Let 'er blow," Lafferty commented. "Just what we want." The wind was pushing the main fire into the backfires, just as they'd planned.

As dusk settled down and the drama began, Thomas and Gleeson would play the role of constant watchers from their post at Powderhouse Turn. Lafferty and Ewing witnessed snatches of the evening's events, but their duties had them running from place to place. Thomas would see disaster in the making and raise the alarm, not once but several times. Gleeson would become eyewitness to the biggest story of his career, a national scoop, and he would have it alone. Living a newsman's dream would inspire him to touches of poetry:

> It was still light and a bulldozer crew was silhouetted atop one ridge about a mile away. Flames were burning on three sides, but the road was the fire line. As darkness fell the blaze took on its full beauty in a dozen shades of rose, red and orange, crawling, reaching out long fingers to catch the tops of digger pines, boiling up in pools that changed colors with each new puff of wind.

Black areas suddenly took on light that turned into acres of jewels. As these burned out they took on the appearance of a city, dazzling with golden lights.

It was 8:10 or 8:15 P.M., a few minutes after Thomas and Gleeson had reached the scene, when an evening breeze started up, blowing an occasional cluster of flaming brush over Alder Springs Road. The fire wasn't going to lie down and die, after all. Firefighters scrambled from one burning bush to another, squelching the new flames. After a few minutes, Thomas saw trouble: a spot fire was developing in the depths of Powderhouse Canyon, too far down the steep slope to be attacked from the road.

Thomas walked a few steps into the thick chaparral for a better look. He had fought more than a hundred big fires in his career and had no qualms about making tactical decisions, especially with Lafferty and Ewing busy elsewhere. The spot fire did not appear to be very threatening. If it made a run, Thomas figured, it would burn to the top of Powderhouse Ridge, opposite Rattlesnake Ridge, where it would be easier to stop.

"Our calculations at the time were that it would run up the hill," Thomas said later. "There was no reason why we should send anyone into the spot fire if it was going to."

The rest of the spot fires were not particularly troublesome. They glimmered and sparkled along the down-canyon side of Alder Springs Road. Emergency lights flashed. Men shouted. As firefighters scrambled after the spot fires, hauling hoses and long-handled tools, firelight danced off them and their equipment. Silvery streams of water arced from the road onto the fires, which shone ever more brightly as the sky and canyon darkened. When water hit the flames, puffs of white smoke shot upward. Then a new spot fire would sparkle into being a few yards away, and the sequence would repeat itself.

It must have been a mesmerizing sight: firefighters battled flames that danced and died in parody of war, and no one got hurt. An hour ticked by. The light of day slowly extinguished itself, as though the houselights in a theater were dimming in anticipation of the main feature.

Lafferty and Ewing checked in at Powderhouse Turn, and Thomas drew their attention to the untended spot fire deep in the canyon. It had not grown since Thomas had first seen it, but it continued to sputter.

The wind, meanwhile, had died out completely. Flame lengths shrank from feet to inches; the fire lay nearly flat on the ground. The spot fires that had started an hour earlier had been extinguished, except for the one deep in the canyon.

Once again, it looked as though the fire would be under control in an hour or two, after that final spot fire was extinguished. As Lafferty, Ewing, and Thomas talked, four members of the mission crew appeared at Powderhouse Turn and asked for a new assignment, having finished their work along the crest of Rattlesnake Ridge. Lafferty recognized one, David Johnson, as an experienced firefighter. Johnson had attended fireguard school that spring and had fought fire for several seasons in the Klamath National Forest before that. Lafferty extracted a promise from Johnson to not "take any undue chances." Johnson said "that he would be careful and cautious," as Lafferty remembers it.

Johnson and the others became the first of three contingents of firefighters to be sent to the spot fire, which came to be called the Missionary Spot Fire.

"We saw this fire down in the valley, a little bitty fire," remembers Stous, who was with Johnson. "We didn't know there was any danger."

The Missionary Spot Fire covered no more than an acre when Johnson, Stous, and the others started toward it. It lay just off the crest of a spur ridge extending down into Powderhouse Canyon: it was about 100 yards off the crest of Powderhouse Ridge and 150 yards above the bottom of the canyon. Initially this spot fire had escaped attention because most of it burned on the down-gulch side of the spur ridge. The men at Powderhouse Turn had trouble seeing it, and once the missionary crew got down to it, they couldn't see back to the turn, either. Those poor sight lines brought on disaster.

Four missionaries were too few to handle the acre-sized blaze. The slope was steep—much steeper than it looked from above—and the brush miserable to chop through. Digging was a backbreaker, with hardpan a few inches below the surface of the mineral soil.

"We weren't doing too good and Charlie sent more guys down," Stous said.

When a second, larger batch of missionaries—fifteen this time—showed up at Powderhouse Turn, also having finished their work on the crest of Rattlesnake Ridge and looking for a new assignment, it was natural to send them on as reinforcements. Another experienced firefighter, Vote, led this group. Before dispatching them, Lafferty made certain they had headlamps. As he remembers it, he told Vote to be "very careful and watch for any change of weather and be sure he had his escape planned."

The time was about 9:30 P.M.; there was still light in the sky, July 9 being one of the longest days of the year, as the fifteen missionaries marched off Powderhouse Turn and disappeared into the chaparral.

A hush fell over the canyon—the official report calls it "a definite lull."

"The fire was just about out, it was fizzling," remembers Werner. He had tried to get a backfire going along his section of line, the one in front of the main fire, but without wind to stoke it the backfire refused to burn. Werner gave up and joined the trickle of firefighters drifting toward the magnet of men and machines at Powderhouse Turn.

Powers, too, headed off that fire line for the rally point. Upon arrival there, he discovered that the firefighters sent to the Missionary Spot Fire—a total of nineteen now—had not been fed; one of them had complained before leaving about not having eaten since his arrival on the fire.

With nothing else to occupy him, Powers offered to pack supper down to the crew; by then a candy wagon with sandwiches had parked at Powderhouse Turn. Powers, a man of generous spirit, had a way of making the best of bad circumstances. He had been shot down in Southeast Asia, over Hanoi, during World War II while on an unlucky thirteenth mission as a navigator on a B-24 bomber, based in China. He was captured, then beaten and denied medical treatment while in a Japanese prison camp. Afterward he shrugged off the experience. "What's there to be bitter about?" he said in an interview following his release. "Life was never as good as it is now." Powers had been assigned to the Forest Service station at Alder Springs a few weeks earlier, in May, along with his wife, Maude, and their children, Bob and Sue.

At the time Powers offered to haul the meals, the Missionary Spot Fire had become nearly invisible—only an occasional flicker was noted. Four more missionaries at Powderhouse Turn volunteered to help Powers— probably more than were necessary and probably because they, like Powers, took pleasure in being of service. Every one of the twenty-four men who went to the Missionary Spot Fire volunteered for the assignment.

Lafferty made sure that Powers and the others had headlamps and sent them on their way; he had other problems demanding his attention. With the fire dying down, Bill Randrup, the owner of Taylor and Randrup Logging Company, was asking when his men and heavy equipment would be released.

And then the world turned. One minute the wind was nonexistent and the fire on its way to extinction; in the next, the wind sprang to life. It struck flames, which sprouted several feet high and began to boil. The lights went up on a living nightmare.

Powderhouse Canyon is a natural amphitheater, with Alder Springs Road forming a gallery along one side. The canyon has a narrow head, a slot in the shape of a V, at Powderhouse Turn. Below that, the canyon widens some, but it is remarkably narrow and steep along its length of a mile and a half, until it fans out just above the Gillaspy ranch. The sides of the canyon ripple with spur ridges; no one who did not have to would walk the place, but the rolling terrain means a hiker would cover much more than a mile and a half going from top to bottom. Adding to the difficulties, the canyon is blanketed, as it was then, by unbroken chaparral waist to head high and higher. The only outstanding feature along its entire length is a large outcropping of rock, which came to be called Missionary Rock, about a quarter mile as the crow flies down the canyon, on the north slope opposite Alder Springs Road.

In the unfolding drama, Powderhouse Turn became the best seat in the house for the tragedy, the box seat over the stage. A common characteristic of fatal wildfires is an absence of witnesses to the final act. There may be spectators during early parts of a race with wildfire, but the last moments, virtually by definition, are hidden from sight in a fury of smoke and flame.

The final, tragic act of the Rattlesnake Fire, however, played out before a rapt and horrified audience. Darkness was no mercy. Instead, nightfall turned the last act into a living theater of lights and shadows, complete with sound and motion. The human characters played their roles as pinpoints of light—the headlamps of the firefighters—sometimes stationary, sometimes scrambling, sometimes lined out in purposeful formation.

The fire wore many masks. It started out on more or less equal terms with the humans as pinpoints of light—the spot fires that wavered, winked, and mostly snuffed out along the canyon wall below Alder Springs Road. Then a new spot fire, deeper in the canyon than any other, transformed itself into a climbing wall of cherry-red flame; it took off after a handful of the tiny, bobbing human lights, the headlamps of nine members of the mission crew. The wall of flame was about to overtake those headlamps when for a second time everything changed, this time in defiance of common sense or any notion of divine or human justice, mercy, or fair play.

In a moment of diabolical contrariness, the wall of flame, terrible enough in itself, transformed into a swirling cauldron of fire. A gale wind coming over the lip of Powderhouse Canyon whipped the fire to a frenzy. The cauldron of flame tipped and poured *down the canyon,* changing direction ninety degrees, abandoning the chase the flames were about to win with the nine headlamps. Denying the principle that fire can race uphill but not down, the boiling mass of fire plunged downward, dead on the track of a second, larger batch of headlamps—the fifteen remaining members of the crew—which until that moment had been bobbing along in single file on a secure down-canyon path to escape. Suddenly the fifteen headlamps had nowhere safe to go. The canyon below them was deep and tortuous. The slopes on either side were long and steep. Behind them flames lunged toward their headlamps in an arcing wave. The drama of lights, of flames thundering down the canyon in pursuit of the tiny, all-too-human headlamps, etched its way forever into the minds of those who saw it.

The lull of early evening had ended at about ten P.M. when the wind returned, but no longer was it the gentle southeast breeze; no longer did it nudge and worry the main fire and creeping backfires together. The wind reversed track and blew from the northwest, pushing a new crop of embers over the lip of Alder Springs Road.

This was no ordinary evening breeze. The northwest wind blew unobstructed from the crest of the Coast Ranges, down the long funnel of Grindstone Canyon. It compressed at the narrow V at the head of Powderhouse Canyon in a venturi effect, gaining momentum by constriction, and then gushed unabated into the canyon.

The first puffs fanned old embers to life. Wispy clusters of flaming brush rose in the darkened sky and cartwheeled over Alder Springs Road. The watchers at Powderhouse Turn could see every stage of the advance. "Within a very few minutes there were two or three little spot fires that developed immediately below the road and got not more than twenty-five yards or so from Powderhouse Turn," Thomas recalls.

Lafferty remembers "a sudden change . . . and the fire livened right up."

Flames and shadows once again made antic figures of fire trucks and firefighters; again, shouts arose; again, men dragged hoses and sent cascading streams of water, glittering with the reflection of yellow and red flames, into the canyon.

"I think we can get it," Thomas told Gleeson.

This time, though, the wind did not die out. This time, it erupted.

"I've seen this kind of wind change in southern California, but never up here," a worried Thomas told Gleeson. "Ever hear a fire explode? Well, watch this one."

A blowup on a fire is an unforgettable event, comparable in violence to a hurricane, volcanic eruption, or flash flood; it's one of nature's most volatile and destructive moments. In the dry terms of fire science, a blowup is nothing more than a sudden increase in fire intensity strong enough "to prevent direct control or upset control plans." But a true blowup is worthy of legend: a swift, thunderous event engulfing everything in its path in a tidal wave of white-hot fire. A blowup occurs when a fire receives a sudden, massive injection of oxygen from a fresh wind and explodes into a ball of flame, consuming everything from ground litter to the tops of forest giants. The effect is greatly magnified by slope; a blowup is most intense when confined to a narrow canyon. As long as no one is standing in its way, a blowup is a natural event. Put people in front of it, and it becomes the stuff of tragedy.

Blowups are common enough to have been familiar to the secretary of the Glenn County grand jury, Earl Vail. After the fire, during testimony on Pattan's arson case, he asked Lafferty whether a blowup had occurred on the Rattlesnake Fire.

"Charlie, was there an explosion when the fires came together, like there generally is?" Vail asked. "Could you hear it?"

Remarkably, Lafferty had trouble remembering.

"Well, yes, perhaps," Lafferty said, groping. "I imagine there was."

By the time the Rattlesnake Fire blew up, Lafferty was preoccupied by matters more pressing than the sound of the fire.

As the rash of spot fires along Alder Springs Road came under control, Thomas saw tips of flames fingering up from near the bottom of the canyon behind a spur ridge, just as the Missionary Spot Fire had done more than an hour earlier. This new spot fire, too, had grown unnoticed. But it was lower in the canyon than the Missionary Spot Fire, well below the chute carved out by sliding logs. By the time Thomas saw this spot fire, it had grown to an alarming size.

on's later calculation, a quarter hour passed between the time the
oke out along Alder Springs Road, at about ten P.M., and the time
Thomas noticed the big spot fire in the bottom of the canyon. During those
fifteen minutes, no one gave a thought to the twenty-four men on the Missionary Spot Fire. There wasn't much to remind anyone: nothing remained
of the Missionary Spot Fire except a few embers. The crew had turned on
their headlamps, but they were hidden away in an isolated spot.

The collective amnesia would haunt Lafferty and others.

During this time, the fresh spot fire began to make an uphill run on a
course straight for Powderhouse Turn. The log chute, because it was scraped
somewhat free of brush, made a natural fire barrier, but it needed more clearing out if it was to stop the uphill progress of the fire. Bulldozer operators
asked to perform the job simply refused; the slopes were too steep for their
machines, they argued. CDF firefighters who toured the site fifty years later
agreed with that judgment. "Easy to get in, hard to get out" was the wisdom
of hindsight. But that did not stop the refusal from becoming a public and
nasty controversy directly after the fire.

The log chute, nonetheless, had to be cleared. A fire truck was backed to
the head of the chute, and two men started down the side of the canyon, one
uncoiling a fire hose from the truck and the other wielding a torch. The plan
was to burn out a little V, as Thomas later described it, a wedge down the
side of the canyon to block the advance of the spot fire. The man with the
torch began burning one side of the chute, while the other used the hose to
control those flames. Once the men reached the bottom of the chute, they
were to work back up the other side, firing along the way, and thus create a
scorched V.

The scheme nearly got both men killed.

The spot fire unexpectedly picked up speed and threatened to cut off
their retreat. They abandoned firing and started a mad scramble back to the
road. The footing was loose and the slope nearly sheer. The shale came away
when they grabbed it. With desperation growing, they had the crazy idea to
climb the fire hose. Amazingly, it worked. They grappled their way upward,
hand over hand, like monkeys. The hose was firmly attached to the truck,
and it held. The men came out of the canyon with flames on their heels, and
inspired the false rumor—current to this day—that some of the missionaries
had climbed a fire hose to get out of the canyon.

The spot fire's threat to Powderhouse Turn had one good effect: it at last triggered fears for the twenty-four men on the Missionary Spot Fire.

"It was then that several of us realized the possibility of [the spot fire] jumping the log chute and burning in the direction of the low saddle on Powderhouse Turn," Thomas recalls. "And there were several of us that mentioned the necessity of warning these people here if they had not already known about it."

Thomas's description sounds like a good bureaucrat writing a report. What actually happened was a moment of stark realization followed by near panic.

"Has anyone warned the missions, the boys on the spot?" Thomas asked.

Without a word in response, Lafferty took off at a dead run. He sprinted up the road toward Powderhouse Ridge and turned off after a few dozen yards, into a bulldozer line cut earlier in the day as a firebreak. He ran along the cut until he could see headlamps below him, then dropped down into the brush.

"I started calling for the boys to get out. I yelled, 'Get out, hurry out.' And went down the ridge as I was calling them."

Farther down the slope, below the lights of the headlamps, Lafferty could see cherry-red flames lunging upward.

"The fire was rolling toward me at, I would say, a very fast clip," Lafferty recalled. "And I noticed the lights spreading. And some lights coming up toward—to the ridge." He recalled a "terrific roar," though not exactly an explosion.

"And then the lights just came on with a terrific force, like a—numerous floodlights from the main fire, coming at me. The light from the sky was illuminating the whole thing for me."

Waves of heat buffeted Lafferty.

He shouted a second time, now telling everyone to go downhill. It was the only safe place. Fires almost never burned downhill, and this one, true to logic, was burning uphill, toward him. He waved and shouted over and over: "Go downhill, downhill!"

The headlamps, which at first had formed a stationary circle, began to swirl about as Lafferty yelled. When he hollered for the men to go downhill, the headlamps divided into two groups: nine lights continued up toward Lafferty; fifteen others strung out in an orderly line and headed down the canyon, following his order. Referring to the larger group, Lafferty would later say in an agony of self-justification, "I feel in my own mind and heart, had the boys tried to make their escape by coming to the top of the ridge they would not, could not possibly, have done so. I felt at the time they were making the best possible route of escape."

The heat became too much for Lafferty.

"I realized I had to leave immediately in order to save my life," Lafferty recalled. He headed straight back, not retracing his steps up toward the bulldozer line but taking the quicker route to the road across the slope and through the brush. The chaparral was impenetrable; Lafferty fell to his hands and knees and scurried "like a rabbit would do." The brush tore off his hard hat, but he didn't dare stop to retrieve it. Thorny branches whipped his face and bare head. The shale cut his hands and knees. He broke free of the brush at last, but it was a personal reprieve, not freedom. He would wander Alder Springs Road the rest of the night, begging men to give him hope for the lost crew. Right now, though, he ran as hard as his legs would take him to report to Thomas at Powderhouse Turn.

"I saw the doomed men's lights."

The crew at the Missionary Spot Fire had taken the first bites of their sandwiches after Vote's grace when they heard Lafferty shouting. They had picked a peaceful spot for supper, on the low, down-canyon side of their fire, now controlled, and seated themselves in a circle for fellowship. The brush around them was so tall that they could not see out even when they stood up. But they set no lookouts. Vote and Powers talked about lookouts, survivors would recall, but with the Missionary Spot Fire virtually dead out, they thought they were perfectly safe—the main fire, with its active flames, was on the opposite slope of the canyon.

Darkness was everywhere around them.

Lafferty's first shouts were unintelligible; Schlatter, the Indiana schoolteacher, could not make out what was said, but he got to his feet with the others and began walking uphill. "My understanding at the time was that the rangers on the hill were calling us to come up to them, and I assumed they had other responsibilities for us," Schlatter recalls. "I don't remember being in a panic or extremely fearful, because I had not heard the details of what was apparently said."

Some of the men were in a hurry, though, and dropped their tools; Schlatter stopped to pick them up.

As the missionaries started the climb, Dinnel was directly in front of Schlatter, but after a few steps Dinnel unaccountably veered down the canyon, joining the group heading that way. Perhaps he heard Lafferty yelling to go down; perhaps he was trying to get out of the path of the fire coming up from below. Schlatter had walked out in that direction earlier and remembered the brush being exceptionally thick. The downhill route was not for him; he continued straight up, and he never saw Dinnel again.

"When I got to the top I expected to find the other fellows up there, too, and was surprised that so few of us were at the top of the ridge," Schlatter remembers.

Emerging from the brush behind Schlatter were Stous and Etherton, the mission dentist. Stous had started out in the lead but had turned back when Etherton began to struggle.

"Charlie hollered down to us, 'Get out of there' and we took off up the side of the mountain," Stous remembers. "It was pretty steep, the manzanita was shoulder-high. I wasn't scared, I just happened to be in the lead. We got about halfway up when Charlie called, 'You're not going to make it; run down, away from the fire.' I looked down and thought, That's stupid. I'm not going to run back down there.

"I don't think the other guys would have made it, anyway; some of them may have been slow pulling their stuff together. We didn't realize the danger. We never could see the fire until later."

A few yards behind Stous, Etherton fell to his knees.

"Ken was totally out of shape," Stous remembers. "I was in excellent shape, real athletic. About halfway up Ken was absolutely petered out. He said, 'I've got to rest, I'm going to lie down.' I just kept after him, encouraging him, helping him along. He hit that firebreak and was sick the rest of the night from exhaustion."

Once the nine missionaries reached the bulldozer line, they were still not out of danger. The spot fire, which had crossed the log chute by then, threatened to cut off their escape. It looked as though the fire would sweep the bulldozer line and Powderhouse Turn itself, and carry into Grindstone Canyon. The men on Powderhouse Turn had many options for retreat, but the nine missionaries could be caught in the brush.

At this point, Ewing, the fire boss who'd forgotten a crew and lost eleven men on the Hauser Creek Fire, had a redemptive moment. He ran from Powderhouse Turn toward the flames and the nine missionaries, hollering at the nine to come out to Powderhouse Turn. The men stumbled into the turn like souls escaping purgatory: ashen-faced, goggle-eyed, and shaking like leaves. But they gave morale there a boost.

"When I saw the nine men come out, at first I did not really think it was them," Thomas recalled. "I heaved a sigh of relief because I figured that was all there were. The boys got out."

The situation at this point was recoverable. Grindstone Canyon might well burn out, a spectacular embarrassment to the Forest Service and its policy of putting out all fires on sight. But no one had been seriously injured. The nine missionaries were safe, thanks to fast and courageous action by Lafferty and Ewing. The fifteen others were headed in the safest of directions, down the canyon.

At this time, between 10:20 and 10:30 P.M., the wind changed direction so suddenly and with such violence that it bewildered veterans of many a nighttime fire. Winds normally switch direction after dark, changing from uphill currents, caused by land heating during the day, to downhill currents, as the land cools and draws the air down. This radiation effect was well known in 1953, and it explains the initial downdrafts on the Rattlesnake Fire.

Nighttime winds, however, normally do not cause blowups. They do not send fire crashing down canyons. They are not killers. Nighttime fires tend to be slow-moving "creepers"; temperatures are cooler, the humidity is higher, winds generally are more moderate. The explanation for the dramatic wind shift on the Rattlesnake Fire would be a while in coming; no weather observations were taken at Powderhouse Canyon the night of the fire. Meteorologists were sent to the site the next two nights, however, and their observations provided raw data for a theory about the cause of the fatal downdraft, an explanation that has stood the test of time.

On the evening of July 9, however, no one understood what was happening. The wind action seemed to defy science. An enormous mass of air swept without warning over the lip of Powderhouse Canyon, as though a dam had burst and loosed an unstoppable torrent. Flames turned from cherry red to intense yellow and incandescent white. Embers showered into the lowest reaches of the canyon, where they ignited new spot fires, which melded into the existing fires, multiplying in power many times. The flames leaped a hundred yards and more on the wings of spinning embers.

Perversely, the fire went downhill faster than some firefighters had ever seen flames go uphill. Powderhouse Canyon turned into a raging nighttime inferno. It flouted the common wisdom about fire intensity, which is that fires move fastest and burn hottest when traveling uphill during the day, with sun and slope in their favor.

The sight rattled Gleeson, who wrote a jittery but vivid description of it: "By now the entire canyon was a sparkling mass of red jewels, sparking in the night wind, as you looked down from your secure spot along the point where you knew nothing could live more than a few moments in that inferno."

Thomas would be struggling weeks later to paint a coherent word picture: "The wind suddenly shifted and came up the 'V' slope, in a northwesterly direction," he told the Glenn County grand jury. "The whole side of that fire [the downhill flank] then became a front and it was just a matter of minutes until the whole thing just swept right down the canyon. In other words, the whole smoke and everything just laid down. And from that time on, it just burned very rapidly down the whole canyon."

For the men on the Alder Springs Road, the fire was more than engaging spectacle: it threatened them. Flames blasted across the road, scorching their trucks. The youngster Pesonen found himself alone with the Power Wagon near Powderhouse Turn; Silva was off on another assignment. As flames licked at the truck, Pesonen asked someone what to do. Use your hose, he was told.

"I sprayed myself and the fire truck—all of us were doing that—while the fire leaned over the road," Pesonen remembers decades later, standing in the place where it happened. "It didn't take long before someone said, 'There's been a bunch of people down there.' I hadn't seen them go down there . . . but I had a feeling."

Werner watched from Powderhouse Turn as flames came to life along the fire line he had walked away from minutes before, the one from Powderhouse Turn to High Point. A tongue of fire darted downhill and threatened the turn. Werner grabbed a hose and ran toward the flames, shooting a jet of water. He quenched the fire and turned to look for others.

Behind him, on the opposite slope of the canyon, he saw a circle of tiny lights, each burning with equal intensity, a phenomenon that had to be of human design, not nature's random work. The circle broke apart; about half the lights headed up the side of the canyon, some haltingly, some quick as squirrels.

The fire hesitated as though taking a deep breath. "You could see it coming," Werner said. In seconds "it" arrived, a mighty wind that turned the fire ninety degrees and sent it plunging down the canyon. The change was so decisive that flames that had been racing uphill fast enough to nearly overtake Lafferty and the nine others instead took more than a half hour to creep the last hundred yards to the top of Powderhouse Ridge, edging up the slope, nibbling through brush against the downslope wind. In less than half that time, about twenty minutes, the fire ripped more than a mile downhill, to the mouth of Powderhouse Canyon.

Moments later Lafferty staggered back up to Powderhouse Turn. Werner overheard him say nobody behind him was going to make it out: he had ordered the crew down the canyon, the only safe direction. "And he was right," Werner remembers—or right as long as the fire ran uphill.

Headlamps appeared behind Lafferty. "I was standing right there, not over a hundred yards from where they come up, and I counted them and there was nine," Werner said. "The fire at this point was howling. I can't quite describe what it sounded like; like Niagara Falls, and making an awful lot of noise."

Curiously, others too remembered the wind as the rush of a watery torrent. Pesonen described it as "a heavy rain."

Then a new sound came on the wind, a curious siren wail too sweet for a scream, not desperate enough for a yell. It sounded to Werner like singing voices. Werner asked one of the missionaries standing nearby, "Did you hear that?"

"Yes," the man replied.

The singing sound went on for what seemed an eternity—two or three minutes. Perhaps more men had escaped and were singing in jubilation, Werner thought. He started to run along the road looking for them, but he quickly met a missionary on the same errand.

"Did you see anything?" Werner asked.

"No, they're not down here," the missionary replied.

By the time Werner returned to Powderhouse Turn, the sound of singing voices had stopped—never to return, never to be explained. Nature was out of joint; nothing was as it should be. Fires became watery torrents, raged downhill, and sang songs about it.

Halfway down Alder Springs Road, Hancock, who'd driven the mission truck, found himself and his vehicle blocked by the fire. Flames licked into the cab of his truck and scorched the seat.

"Never have I seen a fire travel so fast," Hancock said afterward.

On the opposite slope, a line of lights moved steadily in single file down the canyon. The lights flickered in and out of sight as the men underneath the headlamps followed the dips and rises of the spur ridges. Behind the lights, the onrushing fire rose in a wave more than one hundred feet high. Flames fanned out across the width of the canyon, from Powderhouse Ridge to Alder Springs Road. Nothing was to be spared. The fire sent ahead a vanguard, a spume of embers igniting instant blazes in its path. Bounding, howling flames gained on the headlamps with the ferocity of hellfire.

Hancock watched, transfixed.

"It was evident that there was no chance of escape for all of those who were headed down, as the flames were jumping forward at an unbelievable rate of speed—more like an explosion than the normal travel of fire," he said later.

The fire caught up with and washed over the last headlamp in line on the slope heading up to Missionary Rock. That light disappeared under a tidal wave of flame, and then another was engulfed. The flames never paused. Some of the headlamps in front of the flames broke out of line and scattered in different directions. One lonely light struck out on its own for the crest of Powderhouse Ridge, hundreds of yards away. A second broke in the opposite direction, down into the bottom of Powderhouse Canyon. This second light made it across the bottom of the canyon and up the opposite slope, nearly to Alder Springs Road. It traveled farther, lasted longer, and came closer to escape than any other, but the outcome did not change, and it was overwhelmed in its turn.

Most of the lights remained together, but the farther they went, the closer they got to a sheer drop-off, a ravine steeper than any they had encountered so far. As the lights neared the drop-off, they collapsed in a heap upon themselves.

"I saw the doomed men's lights," Hancock recounted. "Suddenly there were flames behind them, then a puff of smoke. I actually saw the flames envelop the lights and go over their heads and then all I could see was smoke, and then all was black."

The heat drove most men back along Alder Springs Road, but not Hancock. He held his ground next to his scorched truck. After the fire had passed, the others asked him for news. Swirling dust, soot, and ashes made it difficult to see into the canyon. Hancock said what he could:

"The boys are down there. The boys are down in that fire."

"I couldn't see any bodies . . . but they were there."

The fire left in its wake a bed of throbbing red and yellow embers. The scene reminded one firefighter of a lighted city at night, but if so the city had been evacuated—the embers were the only sign of life. Lafferty called Hancock on the radio and asked if any of the lost crew had shown up near him. No, Hancock replied, he had seen no one.

The embers sent up waves of heat that made an immediate search impossible—it would be many hours before anyone could set foot in the canyon. Lafferty detailed men and trucks to patrol the road for survivors. Worried about the continuing threat to Grindstone Canyon, he remembered that a side road, which led from Powderhouse Turn to the dynamite shed, made a big circle and connected to Alder Springs Road below the mouth of the canyon. Backfiring Powderhouse Ridge up from the side road would create a buffer to protect Grindstone Canyon.

Lafferty sent a bulldozer, a water tanker, and a crew to clear the side road, which was overgrown with brush. He delayed the firing operation until the lost crew had had every chance to escape. The backfiring operation commenced about midnight and was a success: Grindstone Canyon was spared.

Pesonen and his Power Wagon were among those assigned to overnight patrol duty. "It was quite an initiation for me," Pesonen says. At one point, two missionaries stumbled into the beams of his headlights near the dynamite shed, and he hit the brakes. "They were exhausted and almost hysterical," Pesonen remembers. They must have just escaped the flames, he thought; a following Jeep took the men to the fire camp for a much-needed rest.

Touring the site decades later, Pesonen still thought the two men had run out of the fire, directly into his headlights. But the nine survivors had made their escape hours before this incident happened. Today, firefighters who have close calls are whisked away for a stress debriefing. Not so in 1953. After their escape, the nine survivors were ordered to help with the backfiring operation. The men in Pesonen's headlights could have been part of this group, which would account for their position on the road and for their haggard appearance.

Pesonen patrolled through the night, without food or rest, and decided at daybreak to call it quits. He drove along Alder Springs Road past the remains of the fire, heading for the fire camp. The first rays of daylight illuminated a grim, gray scene. "I couldn't see any bodies in the ashes, but they were there," he remembers. "I began to hear over the radio that people on foot had discovered the bodies."

A shout had gone up at 4:45 A.M., when men with flashlights found the first body. Sheriff Sale and the Glenn County coroner, Frank Sweet, had been summoned during the night. With the help of daylight and other hands, they located fifteen bodies within an hour, by 5:45 A.M.

One band of missionaries, meanwhile, had spent the night along the top of Rattlesnake Ridge, sleeping fitfully on the ground. Paul Turner, the missionary who was crew boss for this group, remembers waking up not knowing exactly what had happened the night before. When fire swept the canyon, he and the others said a prayer for the men below. Surely God would watch over and protect his own, Turner thought.

As he came awake in dawn's half-light, he looked across the canyon and saw a handful of small, intense lights pop and then quickly fade out on the opposite slope. It took Turner a moment to realize that the lights were from flashbulbs. That meant serious trouble. Shortly thereafter, a Forest Service ranger found Turner's group, told them what he could about the lost crew, and escorted them off the fire line to Powderhouse Turn, where they had a silent breakfast at the candy wagon.

The question "Why?" rang in Turner's mind. Why had the God of his faith and understanding, a God of goodness and mercy, allowed this horror to occur? The men who died had been His servants, doing His will.

"I had real trouble resolving this in my mind," Turner said years later in a Forest Service interview, after he had served as a missionary in Venezuela and then taught anthropology at the University of Arizona in Tucson. "The biggest problem I had was understanding how the kind of God that I thought I knew would allow this to happen. These fellas were giving their lives to go out as missionaries and this was something that was close to God's heart; He wouldn't allow that to happen."

Pattan had been free to exercise his will and set the fire, Turner thought. But God should have controlled the wind. "Why didn't God intervene, or at least why didn't He control the elements? I have never resolved that dilemma to this day."

Turner, an elder for New Tribes Mission at the time of the fire, began to wonder whether he should continue on with missionary work. "It was obvious I didn't know anything about God," he said. "The kind of God I believed in wouldn't let anything like this happen. And I began to talk that way." Turner was counseled to keep such views to himself, especially considering that he was an elder. "I told my wife we should just turn around and go back where we came from and forget about missionary work. Once you're into something like this it's difficult to stop, to admit you made a mistake and that you ought to quit. So we went on."

As Turner and the others trudged off Rattlesnake Ridge, daylight brought to a close the drama of lights and shadows. The fully lit scene was one of unrelieved desolation. The drab brush had been replaced by low, blackened stubs, which formed a broken web pattern on the exposed mineral soil. Thin blankets of smoke drifted over the canyon. Deep shadows filled the ravines.

As the sky lightened, Sheriff Sale, Coroner Sweet, and others could be seen standing around a cluster of soft, horizontal shapes—they could have been gear bags or charred logs. A careful observer, though, would note that the objects were echoed in smaller bundles nearby, maybe two or three more.

"Some of the bodies could be seen easily from the road about 300 yards across the canyon," Gleeson wrote. "But if you didn't have glasses, you might have taken them for small clumps of dark green brush surrounded by gray ashes."

Hancock and others tried to identify the dead, but the bodies were too badly burned. It took until 8:30 A.M. the next day, July 11, before all the victims were positively identified. They were:

- Allan J. Boddy, thirty, married, with three children, of Salem, Oregon.
- Sergio Colles, forty, married, of Lancaster, Pennsylvania.
- Benjamin O. Dinnel, twenty-six, single, of Chico, California.
- Paul Gifford, thirty-four, single, of Vancouver, British Columbia.
- Harold Jesse Griffis, thirty-seven, married, with seven children, of North Platte, Nebraska.
- Glenn Cecil Hitchcock, twenty, single, of Littleton, Colorado.
- David A. Johnson, twenty-seven, married, with four children, of Oakland, California.
- Robert James Mieden, thirty-five, married, with two children, of Glendale, California.
- Darrell Kent Noah, thirty-one, married, with four children, of Ogallah, Kansas.
- Robert F. Powers, thirty-five, assistant Forest Service ranger, married, with two children, of Alder Springs, California.
- Howard Fred Rowe, twenty-five, married, with three children, of Chicago, Illinois.
- Raymond Sherman, twenty, married, of Seattle, Washington.
- G. Daniel Short, twenty, single, of Ypsilanti, Michigan.
- Stanley L. Vote, twenty-four, single, of Birchdale, Minnesota.
- Hobart Stanley Whitehouse, thirty, married, with four children, of Denver, Colorado.

The men had fallen far from any road, so a bulldozer was called in to cut a trail across the slope to the site. Clint Hensley, the bulldozer operator, kept a searing memory of the experience: one body, that of the firefighter who had struck out alone for the top of Powderhouse Ridge, was found with its fingers broken backward, as though from frantic digging.

It took most of the day to recover the bodies. For Stous, watching from Alder Springs Road, the sight seemed to confirm the judgment of those who had warned him against joining New Tribes Mission. Stous had enrolled in Bible school in Los Angeles a year and a half earlier, after his wife, Ladene, was killed in an auto accident, leaving him to care for their three children. He'd felt restless, however, and before graduation he'd begun to consider joining New Tribes Mission, though friends had cautioned him to avoid the group because of its record of violent death. Stous had packed up the children anyway and headed for Fouts Springs, arriving three days before the fire. As he stared at the ruins of Powderhouse Canyon, his dreams turned to ash.

"That morning when I saw those fellas dead, I hit bottom," Stous remembers. "I walked off sick to my stomach. There's something wrong with this organization, I thought." As he wandered off alone, his thoughts turned to his dead wife, Ladene. He could have been killed in the auto accident with her, but he had lived. He could have been killed the night before in the fire, but once again he had survived. Coming that close to death and escaping twice could not be happenstance. It must have meaning. God must be saving him for a purpose, he thought.

"I've been in this outfit fifty years and I've never doubted since."

Stous, Schlatter, and Etherton were chosen to carry the bad news to Fouts Springs. The scene at the mission camp was a terrible one, made worse by premature radio reports announcing the names of some of the dead. (Similar episodes over the years have led responsible fire agencies and news organizations to condemn this practice and agree to a policy of withholding the names of victims until their next of kin have been notified.)

Stous felt guilty and embarrassed walking through the camp. If only he had died, he thought, a married man might be alive in his place. As a widower, he understood all too well the suffering around him. At the very least, he could offer the widows heartfelt sympathy and understanding.

He sought out Mary Rowe, whose husband, Howard, had befriended him during his few days in camp. Howard had introduced him to Mary and their two children; Mary was pregnant, which would make three for her, the same number as for Stous. Over the next weeks, as Stous prayed for the widows, he found himself praying especially for Mary.

"I went and talked with her about it and we became friends," Stous says. They married the next May and bravely took their joined families—six children, all aged six or younger—to a jungle mission in Paraguay, where they remained for the next twelve years and produced a seventh child, Juanita. In semiretirement now, Stous teaches part-time at the New Tribes Bible Institute in Waukesha, Wisconsin.

When Schlatter returned to Fouts Springs, he conferred with the camp director, Macon Hare, and they decided not to pass on what little they knew about the identities of the dead; a truck carrying the survivors was due in camp at any moment, and the fates of the firefighters would become clear then.

"At that time we weren't sure how many had actually perished," Schlatter said. "Everybody was in shock."

Word spread anyway, and by the time the Forest Service truck arrived the names of all but one of the victims were known. Turner remembers riding the survivors' truck into the camp and seeing an assembly of women, anxiously waiting. He caught sight of his wife and his mother-in-law, who was visiting from Illinois. The three of them embraced, weeping.

"And other wives were there to meet their husbands, and of course one of them didn't have a husband coming back," Turner said. "When everyone got off the truck and she realized her husband wasn't coming back, she collapsed."

Schlatter began to act as a liaison with the Forest Service and the coroner, taking objects found on the bodies and showing them to widows to aid in identification—a bronze badge, a belt buckle, a metal credit card, a swatch of cloth. There was very little left. Grisly as this errand sounds, the act of seeing and touching objects belonging to their husbands brought comfort to the widows—and to Schlatter. "I experienced at that time a distinct sense of God's presence," Schlatter said. "That fire was a most tragic event and created terrible suffering, but for those of us who survived it, the event was something very special in our lives."

For Schlatter, the sense of being called to a renewed purpose in life came gradually, not in a rush as it had for Stous. But it was equally strong. Schlatter knew he could have died with the fifteen others, and he could not explain why his life had been spared. There had to be a reason, though, he thought. Everything happens for a reason.

"It was God who determined my steps," Schlatter says years later. "That's why I feel God had a purpose in it for me. I was only alive because of God's providence."

A month after the fire, Schlatter and his wife left for Thailand, where they have served as missionaries ever since. They have two sons, Philip and Tom, and a daughter, Mary, all of whom were born in Thailand and have become missionaries, and an adopted daughter, Joanna. Schlatter told his story in an exchange of e-mails with me in which he made only one request: that his views be presented, if at all, in context.

"It was a time in my life that was very sad," he wrote, "and yet I believe it was something that brought a sense of assurance that life does have meaning and purpose, and I trust it has caused me to desire a closer walk with God. The answer has to be not just faith as such, but faith in a God who is truly good. I praise him for his faithfulness through all these years!"

Observers at Fouts Springs that day took away near-psychedelic impressions of the impact of disaster. Tim Adams, a reporter for the *San Francisco Chronicle,* was struck by the bleakness of the surroundings: primitive cabins stuck in the heart of brush country. Asking directions of a pretty girl wearing a gingham dress, he mentioned the horror of the fire.

The girl smiled.

"God's will is all sufficient in all things," responded Gerry Sherman, twenty-one. She had married one of the victims, Raymond Sherman, a scant five weeks earlier; the couple had come to Fouts Springs just a few days before the fire. When word of the disaster first trickled back to the camp, Mrs. Sherman told the reporter, the group held a prayer meeting. "All the wives or sweethearts whose husbands didn't come back seemed to know it. The others weren't worried. The Lord showed me what would happen."

Then she abruptly walked away, smiling.

Meanwhile, it fell to the Forest Service to notify Maude Powers of the death of her husband, Robert, whose body was one of the first to be identified. He had been carrying a metal Standard Oil Company charge plate (these were the days before plastic cards), and he'd worn a bronze Forest Service badge and a metal Oklahoma A&M belt buckle, all of which survived the flames. (Vote's nickel-plated fire badge did not survive.)

Shortly after daylight Thomas approached Werner and asked if he was friendly with the Powers family. Werner said he didn't know them well because they were new to the district, but he agreed to accompany Thomas to pass on the news to Maude Powers. She was making sandwiches and coffee for the fire crew when the two men arrived. When she heard that Robert was dead, she started to collapse. Werner caught her and she quickly recovered, ready to discuss with Werner whether to tell the children—Robert, nine, and Susan, seven—right away. They decided it was better to do it before the children heard it from someone else. Bob and Sue took the news solemnly. Werner stayed with the family until relatives showed up.

Within a few months, Mrs. Powers and the children moved back to her family home in Oklahoma City, but she and Werner kept in touch by letter. Eventually he made a trip to Oklahoma to see her. One thing led to another, and they married in January 1954.

"It was the best thing that ever happened to me," Werner said many decades later. The family tried living in Willows, but the place had too many ghosts. Werner talked it over with Thomas, who arranged a transfer for him some three hundred miles away, to the Sequoia National Forest in southern California. Red and Maude Werner were together for forty-five years, until her death in June 1999.

Bob Powers followed in his father's footsteps. He joined the Forest Service in 1962 as a firefighter in California, served as assistant foreman on the Oak Grove Hotshots, and went on to other fire and dispatch posts. A close call on one fire brought back a rush of memories of the Rattlesnake Fire. The younger Powers was leading a crew of twenty when a fire roared out of a canyon, crossed fire lines and roads, reduced twenty-foot-high brush to stubble in seconds, and headed straight for his crew. Powers shouted for everyone to run for it. "I thought, It's going to happen to me like it did to my dad," Powers remembers. But they made it to a cleared safety zone and watched as the flames passed by.

On the morning of July 10, the fire lines were holding, but there were things to sort out on the fire. Thomas decided to relieve Lafferty, who had worked through the night and was emotionally drained. By the time Lafferty arrived home, after a stop at Fouts Springs, he had become a shadow of himself. "He was a kind man, everybody's friend," said his wife, Flora. "He tried to get it out of his mind, but I don't think he ever did."

Lafferty told his story to the Forest Service and the Glenn County grand jury, and that was enough for him.

"He went through all those emotions and then one day he said, 'Let's not talk about it anymore.' And he just didn't talk about it," his wife remembers.

Lafferty fought fires again, but he had become overcautious and unable to take the necessary risks. He was transferred to the dispatch job at Willows, replacing Ripley, who was given a good posting elsewhere. The rumor persists that Lafferty "got religion" after the fire, but Mrs. Lafferty said Charlie always had a religious side. Because they had lived mostly in isolated, rural places, it was difficult to attend services, but they became regular church-goers after Charlie transferred to Willows.

In a lengthy oral history for the Forest Service, Lafferty describes the highlights of a long, eventful career—without once mentioning the Rattlesnake Fire.

"That was my car."

Henry Erhart was having breakfast at home in Dunsmuir, California, about 130 miles north of Willows, when his phone rang with an urgent call. Erhart was an arson detective for Region Five of the Forest Service, which covers eighteen national forests lying almost entirely within California. A handful of Forest Service arson specialists are situated around the country, but California has its own squad, set up to handle the perennial troubles with incendiaries. The unit, established in 1918, was modeled on the Royal Canadian Mounted Police. Within a few years of its inception, the detectives had cut losses from arson by 80 percent. By the time of the Rattlesnake Fire, though, their success had reduced the number of detectives from squadlike proportions; Erhart, fifty-six, a man of studious appearance and dogged tenacity, was one of three left in California.

Erhart arrived at the Rattlesnake Fire camp at about two P.M. on July 10 with little doubt that he was on a manhunt. Almost nothing could explain the ignition except arson. Not only had there been no lightning or campfires nearby, but there were no railroads or power lines for miles around. A carelessly tossed cigarette can start a fire in matted duff or crushed grass, but those sorts of fuels were not present.

He was greeted at fire camp by Sheriff Sale and G. P. "Doc" Harper, a fire-fighter who had spent the night playing amateur sleuth—to good effect. Harper, a lowly "fire-prevention aid" but no fool, had had his suspicions aroused while chatting with Silva, who'd told him about sighting the green Buick minutes after the fire began. Harper sniffed around for more clues and learned that Brown had also sighted the Buick, in the bottom of Grindstone Canyon. Passing along his gleanings to Erhart, Harper pointed out Silva and his helper Pesonen in the chow line—being waited on by none other than Pattan.

"We were going through the chow line being served steak or scrambled eggs or something," Pesonen recalls. "A Forest Service investigator came up to me and said, 'I understand you may have written down something about a car.' I still had the note in my pocket with a description of the car and a number or two of the license plate."

Pattan overheard the conversation and became visibly agitated. In Pesonen's telling, when Erhart took him and Silva out of the chow line to question them in private, Pattan followed and volunteered the information that the Buick they were talking about was his.

"I think this fellow is describing my car," Pattan said. "I was up here yesterday squirrel hunting."

Erhart and Sheriff Sale told a slightly different version of the incident, in which Silva, the senior man, played the lead role and there was no mention of Pesonen or his crumpled note. The essentials, though, are the same: Pattan overheard talk about a green Buick, became visibly nervous, and volunteered the information that he'd driven a similar vehicle through the area the day before. Erhart, in a believable variation on Pesonen's account, quoted Pattan as saying, "That was my car, I'm Stanford Pattan—Phil Pattan's son."

Pattan offered a hodgepodge of clumsy lies to explain his movements in the area the day before. He said he'd driven out from Willows and made a single loop up the Alder Springs Road. He'd stopped along the way to shoot his .22 rifle, had visited Long Point Lookout and the Alder Springs guard station, and had then driven home by a back road. Erhart thought Pattan appeared "very anxious to have us believe he was telling the truth"; he sent Pattan back to the chow line while he and Sheriff Sale talked things over.

Pattan, writhing in the first pangs of remorse, was overheard to say, "Damn it, they sent me to cook and what am I doing?"

It took Erhart and Sale less than five minutes to conclude that they very likely had their man, but as yet no proof. They then asked Pattan to take them along the route he claimed to have traveled the day before, and he agreed. The tour became black comedy. Every time Pattan said he was somewhere that would support his claim of innocence, there was no evidence to back him up. Every time he acknowledged he had been in a place implying guilt, the evidence of his presence was plain.

"I tell you I had nothing to do with starting that fire," Pattan declared. He told the investigators he had never been in the bottom of Grindstone

Canyon, where the green Buick was seen. But the team found a freshly shot-up picnic table and coffee can there.

Pattan showed them a place along Alder Springs Road, above Powderhouse Turn and far from the scene of the fire, where he said he had fired his .22 rifle, but no shell cases could be found there. He admitted he had fired some shots from Oleta Point, a few yards from the origin of the fire. Harper, the amateur detective who accompanied the investigation team, picked up five .22 shell cases at Oleta Point. Pattan acknowledged that they could be his. Remarkably, Erhart and Sale treated Harper, who dogged their steps for days, as a full-fledged member of the investigation team. They allowed Harper to interview witnesses, take notes, and have a turn or two questioning Pattan. Erhart later made a favorable reference to Harper in his written report, citing his handwritten notes as a source to make a point. The cooperative spirit was noteworthy and contributed to the speed of the investigation, though not the outcome—Pattan was a marked man from the start.

The investigators returned Pattan to the fire camp and left him under the eye of a deputy while they went to further check his story. Pattan had claimed that he'd learned about the fire from Mrs. Powers and Mrs. Silva when he'd stopped at the Alder Springs guard station. When interviewed, the women said to the contrary that Pattan had known about the fire when he'd arrived.

Pattan said he had two beers at the Elk Horn Tavern around noon. The bartender told the lawmen about his glance at the clock at two P.M. when Pattan was in the place. Pattan left shortly thereafter, the bartender said—just in time to start the fire.

The investigation team returned to the fire camp, had dinner, and took Pattan back to the Glenn County jail in Willows. By all reports, including Pattan's, he was not roughed up physically. The questioning, though, continued through the night. The lawmen told Pattan about the eyewitness testimony contradicting his story and flatly accused him of setting the Chrome and Rattlesnake Fires. By four A.M., Pattan had begun to hedge.

He admitted for the first time that he had stopped at the Tankersley house and had seen the Chrome Fire from there, not from the town of Elk Creek, as he had claimed earlier. And yes, he had told Mrs. Powers and Mrs. Silva he had seen smoke; he had lied when he'd said he'd learned about the fire from them. Again yes, he had been in the bottom of Grindstone Canyon. But he insisted that he had not set either fire. He'd told those lies, he said, to explain away the reports about a green Buick, which made things look dark for him.

The interview concluded at 5:30 A.M. on July 11, by coincidence ten minutes after the Rattlesnake Fire was brought under control. The fire had briefly come back to life at about seven P.M. the previous evening, July 10, when a downslope wind started up, repeating the wind action of the night of the fatalities. The wind the evening of July 10 was not as strong, but it pushed flames across the southern edge of the fire line, which scorched an additional 80 acres. The fire lasted a little more than a day and a half, burned 1,200 to 1,300 acres, and was fought by 333 to 525 men (accounts of acreage and manpower vary). The cost to suppress it came to $50,000 and the lives of fifteen men.

At daybreak on July 11, the investigation team, Harper included, took Pattan to breakfast. It must have been a bleary, silent meal. Pattan's story was breaking down, but there was no physical evidence to tie him to the fire. The lawmen thought they had the right man, but as yet their case would not stand up in court, and they knew it. They needed something more, a confession or physical evidence tying Pattan to the fire.

Everyone drove back to Oleta Point, where Erhart put on the pressure.

"Here, I'll show you how you did it," Erhart told Pattan. He flipped a lighted match out of the car window into the gray ash of what had been thick brush.

"You didn't even get out of your car, did you, Stan?"

Pattan again denied his guilt.

The investigation team had other people to interview, so they sent Pattan back to Willows, where he caught a couple of hours' sleep in the sheriff's office. Erhart returned to town by late afternoon and held a strategy conference with District Attorney Larimer. They decided to try to break Pattan's story with a polygraph machine; Pattan "readily agreed," according to Erhart. Harry Cooper, a state agent who specialized in lie-detector examinations, was summoned and arrived in Willows by nightfall.

The investigators, meanwhile, obtained a set of photographs from the *Willows Journal* of the bodies on the hillside. They spread the brutal images in front of Pattan. Fifty years later, Pattan recalled the moment as though it had happened yesterday. "Yes, they showed me the pictures," he said without hesitation, one of his few clear memories of those days.

The most imposing image was not immediately recognizable as a group of bodies; the subject looks instead like a blackened pile of logs with branches sticking out every which way. Even once the forms are recognized as bodies, it is difficult to make an accurate count, because they are in such disorder. In shots from a distance, the ridge top is seen hundreds of yards away.

"Why? Why did you do it?" Erhart pressed Pattan. The missionaries were not the only ones asking the question "Why?"

Pattan, smoking cigarette after cigarette, was haggard from lack of sleep and distress. But he said nothing to incriminate himself. Cooper sat him down next to the lie-box machine and attached tubes and wires to his chest, arm, and fingers; the monitors checked his respiratory rate, the sweatiness of his fingertips, and his pulse and blood pressure. Today's polygraph machine is more technically sophisticated, but it monitors the same bodily reactions to stress.

It was like a scene from an old detective movie. Every time Pattan was asked if he'd set the fires, the needles skittered across the scroll paper. "The reaction of the lie detector thoroughly indicated that Pattan had been telling untruths and that he did set the fires," Erhart wrote in his report.

None of this was admissible in court. In 1953, the courts operated under a landmark ruling by the U.S. Court of Appeals in the District of Columbia that scientific evidence to be admitted must first be accepted by the scientific community. In 1923, in *Frye v. United States,* a murder case, the court of appeals had ruled that results from a unigraph (a precursor of the polygraph) could not be admitted as evidence because the scientific community did not agree that it gave reliable results.

The legal and scientific situation is little changed today; only New Mexico recognizes the results of polygraph tests as admissible. Other states and the federal government use a range of criteria, but all require some kind of agreement, by both parties or a ruling by a judge, as to the admissibility of test results. The scientific community is divided on the level of accuracy of the tests, but virtually no one claims that a machine can always spot a lie. Lying is a question left for human judgment.

After a little more than an hour on the polygraph machine, Pattan sent word that he was ready to tell everything.

Stan Pattan and Sheriff Sale examine Pattan's Buick, a luxurious auto for an unemployed young man with a family. Courtesy *Sacramento Bee* Collection, City of Sacramento, Museum and History Division

"The pictures certainly helped break him," Sheriff Sale said afterward. "When he saw those, I believe he realized for the first time what he had done."

Pattan's first confession, beginning at 10:30 P.M. on July 11, was taken down in shorthand by a sheriff's deputy. He went over the same ground again, beginning at a little later, at 11:10 P.M., as a court reporter made a verbatim record. The investigators were taking no chances: without Pattan's confession, they had no case. Pattan had been seen driving through the mountains, but that is no crime, and no one could place him within a mile of either fire. If Pattan retracted his statements, he had a plausible defense even by 1953 legal standards. Sheriff Sale later told Pattan that he had put himself in jail with his confession. Sale meant it as a compliment, and a half century later Pattan regards it in that light. He seems relieved to this day to have gotten the thing off his chest.

Erhart, ever the bulldog, desperately wanted to lock up the case by establishing a physical link between Pattan and the fires. The detective got some much-needed sleep on July 12 and went back to the mountains the next day to take photographs, measure distances, and do mop-up interviews with witnesses.

He also recruited a posse of sorts—three deputy sheriffs—to hunt for a piece of evidence he thought might have survived the fire: the single wooden match Pattan used to start the blaze. It seemed a fool's errand; the proverbial needle in a haystack should be easier to find than a burned match in the debris of a wildfire. But Erhart's posse looked first at the site of the Chrome Fire and, surprisingly, turned up not one but three burned matches. Granted, the Chrome Fire had not been nearly as intense as the Rattlesnake Fire, but the discovery of the matches there raised hopes.

Erhart went to the spot where Pattan said he had tossed the single match to start the Rattlesnake Fire—240 feet up the Alder Springs Road from Oleta Point. There, Erhart staked out a rectangle ten feet by six feet and used white string to divide it into a checkerboard of roughly three-foot squares. Each man was to search two squares. The posse completed an initial search without finding anything. Erhart had them switch squares and repeat the exercise. Again, no results. This went on for two hours.

It was Deputy Sheriff Dan Ellis who finally announced, "Here it is!" and held up the charred remains of a wooden match. Almost fifty years later, a DNA sample from a chewed hotdog in a campfire would start arson investigators on a search for those believed responsible for starting a fire that killed four firefighters, the Thirtymile Fire in Washington, but in 1953 there was no way to link the match to Pattan. Still, the match at the scene of the Rattlesnake Fire backed up the details of Pattan's confession. "This evidence was all carefully preserved and is now in possession of the District Attorney, Glenn County," Erhart wrote at the conclusion of his report.

Like the mounties, Erhart had his man.

While the arson investigation had been proceeding, fire-weather meteorologists had conducted a separate inquiry into the causes of the fatal downhill wind shift. Two researchers from the California Forest and Range Experiment Station of the Forest Service came to the scene the day after the fire. For two nights in a row, July 10 and 11, they took wind readings at more than a dozen spots along Rattlesnake Ridge, Alder Springs Road, Powderhouse Turn, and the side road leading to the dynamite shed.

On both nights, the wind shifted in the evening exactly as it had on the night of July 9, from upslope to downslope. The winds were not terribly strong—the highest velocity recorded was twenty miles an hour. But they were the right direction, over the lip of Powderhouse Canyon and down the canyon.

Though no weather observations were taken the night of the fatalities, many witnesses estimated the wind at the lip of the canyon to be far stronger than twenty miles an hour. Normal downslope winds after dark are weak, from two to five miles an hour, inadequate to explain the magnitude of what had happened. Was it possible that two wind events occurred, a normal evening downslope wind followed by something more powerful?

The official fire report, using the data collected by the researchers, discounts a two-event theory. The report describes the wind on the Rattlesnake Fire as part of a normal pattern for the terrain and time of day. Because hot air rises, daytime heating caused the fire to move uphill. At about nine P.M. the winds subsided "because the sun had dropped behind the ridges to the west and surface heating had thus stopped." The lull that occurred at about 9:45 P.M. came about "as a result of a give and take process between the last passage of upslope thermal currents and the first downward movement of heavier, cool, evening air."

The downslope wind took over at ten P.M. because cool air descends. "This downslope movement of air is a normal evening occurrence caused by cooler, denser air seeking a lower elevation," the report concluded. "As a result of this general change in wind direction and the increased wind velocities inherent in the initial stages of this situation the behavior of the entire fire was affected."

In other words, there was nothing special to be learned about wind and fire behavior from the Rattlesnake Fire.

A few months later, however, W. R. Krumm, a fire-weather meteorologist based in Missoula, Montana, analyzed the wind data and came to the opposite conclusion: a two-event wind scenario was *necessary* to explain the fire's behavior.

Normal night cooling does not cause winds strong enough to account for what happened on the Rattlesnake Fire, Krumm contended. The cooling effect at night occurs close to the earth's skin, where temperature change is most pronounced. Thus, air drains to lower elevations and canyon bottoms, gathering speed along the way. This means that the downslope wind effect is strongest in the *bottoms* of canyons. As a consequence, fires tend to "creep" downslope at night, rather than explode.

On the Rattlesnake Fire, to the contrary, the wind had been most fierce along the *tops* of ridges, such as Powderhouse Turn. Witnesses attested to this on the night of July 9, and the more careful weather observations on

July 10 and 11 showed the same thing: the highest wind velocities occurred on the ridge tops. And the fire did anything but creep.

"To the author this would suggest that the airmass changed when the fire commenced to burn fiercely shortly after 10 P.M.," Krumm wrote in his analysis of February 1954.

The wind, though, had to be strong enough to turn the fire ninety degrees and send it down into the canyon. The flames chasing Lafferty and the others should have reached the top of Powderhouse Ridge, a scant hundred yards away, in seconds, if all they had to overcome was a normal evening downslope wind. It should have spared the fifteen others heading down the canyon. Instead, the flames did not complete the last hundred yards of the run to Powderhouse Ridge for more than a half hour, until eleven P.M.

For the fire report to be correct, Grindstone Canyon would have had to be filled with air collected from the normal evening cooling process; no lesser amount of air could have produced such a powerful wind at the top of Powderhouse Canyon. But Krumm considered the report's explanation for the air mass illogical; the amount of air required was staggering, far too much to be gathered simply from the normal cooling process allowed for in the fire report. Something else had to explain why the wind had been so fierce, and the answer had to fill Grindstone Canyon to overflowing with rapidly moving air.

Krumm found it. On the afternoon of July 9, a vast trough of low pressure extending from California into Oregon and southern Idaho began to deepen. At the same time, far to the west, an enormous high-pressure ridge was building hundreds of miles offshore over the Pacific Ocean, on a line parallel to the coasts of California, Oregon, Washington, and British Columbia. By seven P.M., the wind-shift line—the trough between the two pressure areas—had moved east over northern California. Winds above Sacramento, Oakland, and other cities, measured at about five thousand feet, were blowing hard from the west and northwest. At the same time, winds close to the ground were relatively calm.

The wind-shift line continued to press eastward, running into the Coast Ranges, just to the west of the Rattlesnake Fire. The winds built up behind the Coast Ranges and sought escape through gaps in the mountains. When the winds poured through the gaps, their velocity was increased by the venturi effect—gases and liquids increase speed when they are constricted. One of the gaps was Mendocino Pass, a jagged opening that marks the head of

Grindstone Canyon. Mendocino Pass is about five thousand feet above sea level, an elevation where the west wind was known to be active.

A virtual river of air poured through Mendocino Pass and filled Grindstone Canyon to the brim. This phenomenon was happening up and down the Coast Ranges: strong winds on July 9 nearly capsized small boats on Stony Gorge Reservoir, south of the Rattlesnake Fire, after passing through a low gap to the south of Mendocino Pass.

Nothing in Grindstone Canyon slowed the wind. Within minutes of 10:15 P.M. on July 9, a great ocean of wind swept down Grindstone Canyon and spilled over the lip of Powderhouse Turn, turning the fire and driving it down Powderhouse Canyon. The normal evening cooling effect already had occurred and had stoked the blaze that had chased Lafferty and the nine missionaries. The movement of fresh wind was so huge that it continued, with lesser force, for the next two days, when it was measured by the fire-weather meteorologists.

That, at least, was Krumm's theory, which ran counter to the official fire report's explanation based solely on the effect of normal evening cooling. Krumm offered his conclusion with some hesitation. "The author believes that this is possible, but the evidence is not strong enough to say positively," he wrote.

The wind that turned the Rattlesnake Fire down the canyon came as a result of a "mild subsidence," the sudden dropping of an air mass at great speed, Krumm concluded; a major subsidence can cause winds of seventy to ninety miles an hour, far stronger than what witnesses reported on the Rattlesnake Fire. The phenomenon of subsidence was well known at the time: dramatic downslope winds called Santa Ana winds occur regularly in southern California, similar chinook winds sweep down the Front Range of the Rocky Mountains, and East winds do the same thing in western Washington and Oregon.

No one, though, expected a major downslope wind after dark in this part of northern California. The fire supervisors, Thomas, Ewing, and Lafferty, had experienced Santa Ana winds. None had translated that experience into preparation for a similar event on the Rattlesnake Fire.

Thomas came closest among the three to addressing the issue afterward.

"We always anticipate and plan on a shift in the wind," he told the Glenn County grand jury. "It's usually a gentle shift. It usually shifts from an up-canyon to a down-canyon at night. We contemplate and plan on it." He offered no explanation why he thought the wind shift on the Rattlesnake Fire was as strong as it was.

Krumm's theory has stood up over time. The first fire-behavior course for firefighters would not be developed until 1959; today, the Rattlesnake Fire has become an object lesson for California firefighters, proof that fires can burn fiercely downslope at night. "Fire behavior was the largest factor in this accident," states a modern teaching manual for CDF firefighters.

The exact cause of strong downslope winds, which are known as sundowners, is not fully understood today, but it most likely involves cooling and heating at ground level combined with a tug-of-war between high- and low-pressure areas in the atmosphere. The ground-level cooling may pull down the upper-level winds under certain conditions, bringing on the sundowners. For firefighters, it is enough to know that they must be prepared for such an event.

For the fifteen who died on the Rattlesnake Fire, it means their example very likely has saved lives and will continue to do so. If they had known that this would be their legacy, some of them might well have chosen a fiery death. They were not a selfish bunch.

"This gentleman has committed a grave crime."

Community outrage against Pattan led to a rash act: District Attorney Larimer tried to indict Pattan for murder. The Rattlesnake Fire and its aftermath caused days of sensational headlines in northern California. The story had bounce, as they say in the news business. Reports of massive loss of life were followed by rumors of arson and then by the confession from the son of a well-regarded Forest Service engineer.

Curiously, the fire did not cause banner headlines nationwide, as usually happens with multiple fatalities in the line of duty. The fatal events took place late on a Friday, and news of the deaths was even later in coming; the story played as a single column tucked to the side of page 3 of the Saturday *Los Angeles Times*. The news arrived even later in eastern time zones. By then, the Saturday run of papers had ended and the Sunday papers were mostly made up; the story appeared for the first time in the *New York Times* on page 28 of its Sunday edition, with a stale Friday dateline.

The religious twist made the story an oddity, if not a pariah, for news organizations; most accounts identified the dead not as fifteen firefighters but as fourteen missionaries and a forest ranger. Four years earlier, in 1949, the Mann Gulch Fire had commanded headlines across the nation when twelve smoke jumpers and a wilderness guard who had been a smoke jumper were killed, the first-ever smoke-jumper fatalities caused by fire. The Rattlesnake Fire, with two more deaths than the Mann Gulch Fire, rated a column in the religion section of *Time* magazine. *Life* magazine ran a news roundup in its next edition that included California fire stories, but it said nothing about the Rattlesnake Fire.

The arson angle, however, received considerable attention. *American Forests* magazine carried a story by Gleeson on the subject. *Official Detective Stories,* a pulp magazine, contained a lurid account in its September 1953 issue that, miraculously, included thoughts and quotations from Ranger Powers. More than a year later, the *Saturday Evening Post* published a credible account of Erhart's investigation as part of a story about California arson detectives.

Less than a month after the fire, a radio show, *Bill Guyman Covers California,* reported a "new angle"—a source had told Guyman that a crew of loggers had refused to go into Powderhouse Canyon before the mission crew was sent there because the location was "a highly dangerous one." Guyman asked his radio listeners why the mission crew had been sent to fight the "dangerous" fire. "This may just be the surface of something that has been covered up," he said.

A Forest Service inquiry confirmed the refusal but concluded that the hazards of steep terrain—and not the danger of the Missionary Spot fire—were the reason the loggers had refused to go into the canyon. The mission crew had been sent to the spot fire long before the loggers' refusal, when it was thought a safe enough assignment.

The Glenn County grand jury heard testimony in the case on July 30. Pattan stood accused of the murder of two of the fifteen victims, the ones who could be identified for legal purposes: Powers, who had been recognized by his badge, metal credit card, and Oklahoma Aggies belt buckle, and Sherman, who had left behind a young widow, Gerry, and not much else—a remnant of gray trousers, another of a blue-and-white-striped shirt, a bronze cowboy belt buckle . . . and a watch.

"Would you describe that wristwatch and band that you found?" Charles Frost, assistant district attorney, asked Howard Sweet, deputy coroner.

"The wristwatch on this body was burned so badly that the watch—you couldn't tell the make, but there was a metal elastic band with the initials R and S in large letters."

Raymond Sherman was the only victim with the initials R.S. The identification of his body from the watchband ended legal interest in his belongings. The watch's glass lens had melted in the heat and picked up bits of shale, making it unreadable. Sherman's things were tucked into an envelope and, when no one claimed them, stored at Forest Service headquarters in Willows, where the watch would keep its secrets for half a century.

Popular sentiment, though, began to swing in Pattan's favor. Murder charges seemed unnecessarily harsh for an act with consequences that had never been intended. On top of that, word had leaked out of Pattan's many misfortunes. "This is the story of Stanford Pattan," Gleeson began a front-page article in the *Willows Journal* a few days after the fire. (Gleeson's byline identified him as "regional editor," a promotion that had followed his big scoop by hours.)

Gleeson portrayed Pattan as a likable but irresponsible mope who had never been in real trouble before in his life. Phrases such as "navy veteran" and "highly respected family" were sprinkled through the text. No questions were raised about his possible innocence or insanity; Pattan had been mentally competent when he'd lit the fire. But Gleeson gave details of the domestic troubles and severe headaches that had deviled him. "Headaches or heartaches, Stanford Philip Pattan, who today sits brooding in his cell at the county jail, must be having his share of both."

The grand jury refused to indict Pattan on the murder charges and instead returned two felony counts of willful burning, one each for the Chrome and Rattlesnake Fires. After a preliminary hearing, the court accepted Pattan's guilty pleas to both counts on August 3, less than a month after the fire. For once, justice was swift. When Pattan was sentenced four days later, however, Judge W. T. Belieu was tougher than expected.

Judge Belieu denied a defense request for probation and sentenced Pattan to maximum terms of one to ten years on each count, to be served consecutively. A serious crime had been committed, the judge said, for which there was no excuse. "This gentleman has committed a grave crime against society and one to which society is entitled to protection. Punishment is not to be made lightly, or little, so that society ceases to have any protection."

Pattan fell into a deep depression. His guards at the jail reported that they were having him paint signs and other things to shake him out of it. He seemed to like painting, they reported.

Pattan tried out religion as well: he mentioned to a newspaper reporter during one of his brief court appearances that he was considering joining New Tribes Mission when he got out of prison, which came as a revelation to that group. "For the first time, I have really read the Bible—both the Old and the New Testament," Pattan told Soto of the *Chico Enterprise-Record,* who was following the story after his timely visit to Fouts Springs before the fire. "I am a baptized Baptist, and before this happened I guess I was about average in religion. If I can, when this is over, I want to do missionary work. Maybe with the New Tribes Mission, or maybe I can rejoin the navy and study for the ministry."

Pattan's hints threw New Tribes Mission a curve. The mission members had been careful to say they were praying for Pattan and bore him no ill will. "We hold no grudge against any man," Hare, the camp director, was quoted as saying. Accepting Pattan as a missionary trainee, however, was another matter. "The Lord might speak to his heart," Joe Knutsen, a mission official, told Soto. "But he will have to get himself squared away before we will take him."

Pattan's jailhouse conversion did not last as long as his prison term, but it had an effect. He was visited in San Quentin by representatives of the mission, including Etherton, the dentist. The missionaries and Pattan remember what happened during the meeting in different ways.

"He came to know the Lord as his Saviour through their faithful witness," Johnston recorded in his history.

Pattan remembers feeling relief when the missionaries said they bore him no ill will. The memory helped him stay out of trouble. He believes in God, he says today, but is no churchgoer.

"They did not die in vain."

The Rattlesnake Fire came as yet another body blow to the Forest Service, whose decades-old war on fire was running a heavy casualty list. Four years

79

later, the toll from this and other multiple-fatality fires would trigger the formation of the famed 1957 Task Force, which produced the Ten Standard Fire Orders in use to this day. The immediate effect of the fire, however, was limited to a formal investigation and report. The chief of the Forest Service in 1953, Richard E. McArdle, charged a board of review to look into all aspects of the Rattlesnake Fire, including possible negligence.

"We can't restore these men to the widows and orphans from whom they have been snatched away," McArdle wrote. "But if ever an obligation was clear this one is—to see, to the extent that it is within our power to do so, that it never happens again."

God as well as the supervisors was to stand in the dock according to McArdle's instructions. "If it was caused by the negligence of any one in the Forest Service, we want to know it," McArdle continued. "If it was an act of God, and by any chance beyond our control, we want to know that."

The board of review was made up entirely of senior Forest Service officials: Edward P. Cliff, assistant chief; Jay H. Price, regional forester; C. Otto Lindh, regional forester; Lawrence K. Mays, assistant regional forester; and H. Dean Cochran, chief of personnel. The situation is little changed today; the Forest Service and Bureau of Land Management, the principal federal agencies for fighting fire, insist on investigating their own fatal accidents, to growing public dismay.

The board blamed no one for the deaths on the Rattlesnake Fire. The board's report does not even discuss whether the supervisors might have been negligent in failing to anticipate the violent wind shift, remarking instead that the wind change appeared to be a normal evening downdraft. It specifically exonerates Lafferty, and by extension Thomas and Ewing, from the charge that they waited too long to warn the mission crew. "There can be no question . . . that Lafferty recognized the threat of danger promptly after the spot fire began to spread rapidly up the hill and acted in accordance with the best judgment he could formulate in the brief moment available for decision."

That "brief moment," though, lasted no less than fifteen minutes. Gleeson reported in his newspaper stories, and others agreed, that fifteen to twenty minutes elapsed between when the spot fires started and when Lafferty took off at a run to warn the mission crew. "The forestry officials gathered around the point where I stood were so concerned at the unexpected change [in fire behavior] that they forgot about the missionaries," Gleeson told the *San Francisco Chronicle,* using more accusatory language for the out-of-town press than he had in his *Willows Journal* story.

The board of review gave some thought to the subject of negligence and initially considered blaming the mission crew for their own deaths. An early version of the report's findings said, "The tragedy may have been avoided had there been another warning lookout posted. An earlier warning would have given sufficient time for escape."

Blaming victims for what happened to them is a dubious business at best, and the final draft of the report takes a milder position: "The decision of Powers and Vote to eat on the Missionary Spot Fire can be interpreted in only one way. What they observed from their vantage point on the Missionary Spot Fire did not appear to present any undue danger to them or their men."

True enough, and merciful to the lost crew in the bargain. History, though, has provided its own lesson: the Rattlesnake Fire has been held up to generations of firefighters as a glaring example of the danger of failing to post lookouts.

A suspicion has abounded for years that the Forest Service deliberately "loses" old fatality reports, just as surgeons are said to bury their mistakes. The Rattlesnake Fire report is no exception. Key portions of the report relating to exact times and distances are missing from the copy kept at the Mendocino National Forest headquarters.

A search of regional archives in San Francisco turned up multiple references to the report, but no complete copy. My inquiry, however, yielded an example of how a report can be lost through simple carelessness. Two days after the Rattlesnake Fire, the Forest Service Northern Region headquarters in Missoula, Montana, mailed the "original" report for the 1949 Mann Gulch Fire to the Mendocino National Forest for use as a reference in the Rattlesnake Fire investigation. By October, officials in Missoula had become worried.

"If this report has served its purpose to you and you still have it, we would appreciate its return," wrote A. E. Spaulding, an assistant regional forester.

Spaulding's letter prompted a paper chase, which ended as these things usually do—with nobody admitting they had seen the Mann Gulch report. "We are not only sorry—but our collective face is red for we cannot locate the Mann Gulch Report," Leon Thomas replied to Spaulding on November 17. "Apparently this original Mann Gulch report has been misfiled or lost."

Years later when another author, my father, Norman Maclean, and his research partner, Laird Robinson, began to pull together the record of the Mann Gulch Fire for what became the book *Young Men and Fire,* they could not at first locate the fire report. "Without the report, we had no concrete foundation," Robinson said. It took a year and a half for them to run down a copy, fortunately tucked away in Forest Service archives.

Likewise, the Rattlesnake Fire report was not lost and gone forever. I interested David R. Weise, a Forest Service fire scientist in California, in the search and—using his computer and a knowledge of fire bureaucracy—he located what proved to be the full report in an archive of old fire documents called Firebase, stored in the Forest Service library at Mare Island on San Pablo Bay, California.

The full report indeed has precise footage for the distances traveled by victims from the Missionary Spot Fire to where their bodies were found. When I found that out, it raised the tempting possibility of a reconstruction of the race with fire.

The twenty-six minutes allowed in the report for the race, from about 10:15 P.M., when Lafferty started out to warn the men, until 10:41 P.M., when stopped watches show that fire overtook the crew, looks dubious at first glance. The ground is rough, but the distances are not that great. It appears, surveying the scene, that men in a hurry should be able to cover the necessary distance in far less than twenty-six minutes.

A reconstruction based on times and distances in the report could settle the question of negligence, I thought. If a rerun came in close to twenty-six minutes, there was no issue. If it was off by as much as fifteen minutes or so, there was. A reconstruction would be helpful in other ways, too. Locating the site of the Missionary Spot Fire should provide a better understanding of what Lafferty, Thomas, and the others had been able to see from Powderhouse Turn. Standing where the spot fire had burned might provide a better understanding of why the mission crew had posted no lookouts.

In any case, hiking the routes taken by survivors and victims would be a chance to walk in their boots, to sweat as they sweated, and to come to a greater appreciation of what they endured—the simple act of staying together, for example, turned out to be a daunting challenge.

Powderhouse Canyon is virtually unchanged today from what it was like in 1953. Despite the effects of another fire in 1988—fires occur in chaparral

Looking down Powderhouse Canyon to the east from High Point today; portions of Alder Springs Road are visible in the center and to the right. Photograph by author

about every thirty years—the canyon is again covered with brush. Alder Springs Road has been bypassed by a new section of paved highway, Route 7, leaving the track along the side of Powderhouse Canyon as rough and pitted as it must have been fifty years ago.

One visible sign of the fire, or what appears to be a sign, is a white wooden cross, taller than a man, at Missionary Rock. The cross is something of a mystery. Anyone familiar with the fire takes it for a memorial, perhaps set by New Tribes Mission. That is not necessarily so; a smaller wooden cross planted deep in one of the canyon's ravines is a memorial to a teenaged couple killed in more recent years when their auto ran off Alder Springs Road.

The white cross has no inscription or tablet to explain itself. It showed up one morning in 1993 and has caused speculation ever since. Who put it up and why?

There is one certain visible sign of the fire, a portion of the bulldozer road used to recover the bodies that goes from just north of Powderhouse Turn to Missionary Rock. Volunteers keep it mostly cleared of brush; photographs taken in 1953, however, show the bulldozer road extending another hundred yards or so beyond Missionary Rock, and that section has disappeared under

David Personen, who fought the Rattlesnake Fire as a teenager and went on to become director of CDF, stands next to the white cross at Missionary Rock a half century later. Photograph by author

chaparral. If that final section could be traced, it ought to be possible, by using the distances in the complete fire report, to fix almost exactly where the bodies were found, and to accurately reconstruct the timing of the race with fire.

The race involved twenty-five men, counting Lafferty. It proved easier than it might sound to collect enough people to take on the many roles. The Rattlesnake Fire stands as the worst disaster for wildland firefighters in the history of northern California. CDF firefighters, because their predecessors helped the Forest Service fight the fire, regard it as their own tragedy. John R. Hawkins, assistant CDF chief in nearby Butte County and a respected teacher of fire safety, had no trouble signing up thirty firefighter volunteers, several of them serious students of the fire, for a reenactment.

We gathered at the foot of Powderhouse Canyon on a mild January day; the lack of summer foliage made it easier to see the ground. The uniformed firefighters arrived in everything from sport-utility vehicles to pumper engines; we drove in a caravan up Alder Springs Road to Oleta Point, where Pattan fired his .22 rifle. Hunters and shooters are today the most common users of the road, which was littered with spent shells. Someone picked up a

.22 shell casing and tried to make a joke—"Hey, Pattan's shells!"—but nobody laughed.

There is a high cutbank at Oleta Point, but 240 feet farther on, at the point of ignition, a little gully with tufts of grass comes down to the road, just right for starting a fire. We divided our forces, and one group went up the little gully to trace the path of the fire. If they followed the fire correctly, they would come out at the point where the fire briefly slopped over the crest of Rattlesnake Ridge.

The rest of us, meanwhile, drove on to Powderhouse Turn and made it our headquarters, just as the firefighters did in 1953. From there, we had no trouble locating the old fire lines. The first one, well marked on old maps, leads straight up from Powderhouse Turn to High Point, on the crest of Rattlesnake Ridge. The climb was short but steep.

The second fire line, along the crest of Rattlesnake Ridge, is now a jeep trail. We paced distances based on the fire report and located the likely spot where the fire slopped over. We waited there for the other group to come up from Alder Springs Road, hoping they would appear at the same spot and confirm our calculations. We waited a long time. When they finally arrived, our location for the slopover proved correct, but they showed up singly or in twos and threes, a herald of difficulties to come. It's easy to lose your bearings on the rocky, brush-covered slopes, which appear to be smooth but are raked with countless deep ravines well hidden by chaparral.

We regrouped at Powderhouse Turn and addressed the day's main problem, the race with fire.

We decided that everyone should follow Lafferty's path from Powderhouse Turn to the likely spot where he first shouted to the mission crew, and then descend downslope to the site of the Missionary Spot Fire. Once there, we would again divide into two groups, one to follow the route of the nine survivors and the other the path taken by the fifteen victims, recording our times for each leg of the journey.

We looked out from Powderhouse Turn onto a bland winterscape, nothing like the dramatic play of lights and shadows on the night of the fire. Lafferty had taken off from here at a dead run along the road to the dynamite shed, then turned up onto a now-overgrown bulldozer line, which had been cut across the slope that day as a firebreak. When he had gone far enough that headlamps winked up at him—the mission crew at supper—he had dropped off the dozer line and down into the chaparral to get close enough to be heard.

We followed his path. It took only a few seconds to reach the overgrown bulldozer line. Dropping off that line into the dense chaparral felt like stepping off the edge of the known world, as it must have felt for Lafferty. The brush closes around you. Vision is reduced to a few feet in every direction except straight up. The brush is rubbery and spongy—but scrapes bare skin. Sometimes you bounce off it and have to back up and find another way through. When you grab the brush for balance, it can break off or pull out at the roots.

It took us an average of a minute and a half to go from Powderhouse Turn to the likely spot where Lafferty began to yell at the mission crew. More seconds passed as the mission crew tried to sort out what Lafferty was saying.

Squiggly contour lines on a map cannot express the intense isolation of the actual location of the Missionary Spot Fire, in a sea of brush on the far side of the first spur ridge down from Powderhouse Turn. From the place where the crew sat down to eat, on the low, down-gulch side of the spot fire, you cannot see either to Powderhouse Turn or to the bottom of the canyon, where a killer fire crackled to life.

The site feels protected, but there are no open paths to safety, no good sight lines. The failure of the crew to post lookouts while they ate was a serious error, later enshrined as a safety lesson in one of the Ten Standard Fire Orders: "Post a lookout when there is possible danger."

At the site of the spot fire someone picked up a rusted lid from a can, possibly a food can, stamped with the numbers 4 51. The can was almost certainly not used by the mission crew, who ate sandwiches and milk, not canned rations. But the numbers 4 51 suggest April 1951, and the lid brought strange looks to people's faces.

The nine survivors had a surprisingly brief scramble ahead of them. They had found different paths up the slope, so we tried several routes. It is not possible to run in the brush, at least not for more than a few steps. Going hard, we took from two to two and a half minutes to cover the ground from the Missionary Spot Fire up to the old bulldozer line. Stous and Etherton, the last survivors to emerge, took substantially more time than the others because Etherton fell down and Stous had to help him along, but most of the survivors likely made their ascent within our times.

It had taken us roughly five minutes to cover the ground from the point where Lafferty began his run to the point where he and the others were safe. Lafferty's run took a minute and a half. Add thirty seconds to a minute for the mission crew to pull itself together. Then add two to two and a half minutes for the survivors' race and you have roughly five minutes.

In most of those first minutes, the fifteen others had no cause for panic. They began to head down the canyon, trusting Lafferty, as the fire ran up the side of the canyon, chasing the nine who would survive. Powers formed the men into a line with himself at the point—the headlamps were seen to move in single file, and later events showed that the ranger was almost certainly first in line.

Everything changed during those first five minutes: the violent wind hit Powderhouse Turn and the fire turned downhill, heading for the fifteen doomed men.

As we left the site of the Missionary Spot Fire and began to follow the route of the fifteen, we instantly discovered that there was no way they could have seen the key developments behind them. At the beginning of their race with fire, the spur ridge blocked their view to the rear. Our first steps put us on a course for the bottom of a draw, from where we would have to start up another spur ridge. The farther we went, the less we could see, to the front as well as the rear. We slid the last yards into the draw's rocky, damp bottom, which is no more than twenty inches wide.

The facing slope is steep, crumbly, and covered with chaparral. We climbed out of the draw, grabbing brush to help ourselves along. The spur ridge behind us continued to block a view in that direction. The fire at this time was becoming an inferno, but it was doing so behind that ridge, invisible to the fifteen men heading down the canyon.

It was not until the fifteen reached the crest of the first spur ridge beyond the Missionary Spot Fire that they could see the monster chasing them. It must have been a terrifying sight. A colossal wave of flame crested the spur ridge to their rear. From this point on, they knew they were in a race for their lives. Someone must have shouted for them to throw away tools, because a pile of shovels and rakes was found within steps of this spot.

We looked around at unbroken chaparral. Every step put us farther from Powderhouse Turn. The canyon stretched ahead, seemingly without end. Alder Springs Road appeared beyond reach.

It had taken us three minutes and forty seconds to go from the Missionary Spot Fire to the crest of the next spur ridge, where the fifteen could see the wave of flame. By then, Lafferty and the nine survivors had begun to trickle in to Powderhouse Turn.

Ahead, we faced another spur ridge, this one with a steeper, rockier slope than the one we had just climbed; this ridge crests at Missionary Rock, where the white cross stands. As we headed for the ridge, we descended a second time into a draw that blocked our vision to the front and rear. The headlamps of the fifteen were seen following this route. More tools were found scattered along the way.

As the fifteen climbed the second spur ridge, the process of natural selection began to assert itself. Two men fell behind. Two others, both fit and strong, split off on their own. Stanley Vote, the foreman who sang and played accordion, headed almost straight up for Powderhouse Ridge. Hitchcock, the farm boy who sang duets with his sister, angled down toward the bottom of Powderhouse Canyon, heading for Alder Springs Road.

There is no pathway to follow. Even with no fire behind us, our group began to break up and head in separate directions. You must keep your eyes on the ground to avoid tripping. You wait in frustration for the man in front to break through the brush, then struggle through yourself while the man behind you waits his turn.

Most of the fifteen had managed to stay with Powers, probably by following their companions' boot heels. As they approached exhaustion, the fire grew more intense. Nearing Missionary Rock, at the crest of this second spur ridge, they again could see the flames coming behind them.

The leading edge of the fire, a shimmering wave of overheated gases, caught the last man in line yards short of the ridge crest, at a distance of 660 feet from the Missionary Spot Fire. The fire swept on and caught a second straggler another 60 feet beyond, still short of Missionary Rock.

The bulk of the crew, eleven now, broke onto the crest of the ridge, struck flatter ground, and briefly accelerated—there is a long gap between the first two bodies and the rest. The eleven almost certainly passed above Missionary Rock, because going below it would mean climbing down and around a sheer rock face.

Directly over the crest of the ridge, the eleven ran into a virtual wall of brush. It's easy to see what held most of them together from this point on:

they were following trail broken by a point man. Two men, though, became separated from the main group, one angling slightly above it and the other slightly below.

Behind them the fire leaped ravines, accelerated on upward slopes, and hurtled through the air on the down-canyon wind.

Every step they took brought them closer to the lip of a ravine broader and steeper than any they had traversed. Their position was hopeless, and they may have known it.

The fire caught the main group of nine in a sea of chaparral at a point "slightly in excess of 1,000 feet from the Missionary Spot Fire," according to the fire report, and a few dozen yards from the precipice leading into the next ravine. The two men who became separated from the others during this final leg of the race were found nearby, at distances respectively of 1,040 feet and 920 feet from the Missionary Spot Fire.

The two men who had broken away earlier, Vote and Hitchcock, made it a long way. Vote struggled almost halfway to the crest of Powderhouse Ridge, where he would have been safe. When the fire caught him, he was 275 feet above the main group, a little more than 300 feet below the crest of Powderhouse Ridge, and 995 feet from the Missionary Spot Fire.

Hitchcock made it the farthest of all, and by a wide margin. He crossed the bottom of Powderhouse Canyon and was less than 300 feet from Alder Springs Road when his legs caught in wild grapevines, his sister Mavis was told afterward. His struggle took him 1,540 feet, more than 500 yards, from the Missionary Spot Fire, half again as far as anyone else.

Rumors and reports, which persist to this day, say the crew dug shallow foxholes at the end and died slow deaths. Hensley, the bulldozer operator who reported that the fingers of one body were broken backward—it was Vote's body—took that as proof of digging. But Vote could have broken his fingers as he clawed his way up the ridge. Or the extreme heat, which can snap the biggest bones in the human body, could have done it.

Gleeson and others reported that some of the crew managed to dig foxholes six to ten inches deep. These reports are frustrating because they are not accompanied by photos and never say where the holes were dug or which men dug them. There is nothing in any official document to support the digging story.

The Forest Service issued a white paper in August 1953 rebutting a lengthy list of rumors, including the reports of foxholes. "All evidence on the ground indicates that [death] was very sudden," the paper says in rebuttal. "Speed and intensity of the fire was such that death was probably instantaneous."

Foxholes and fires were much on people's minds in 1953, which may have helped inspire the digging story. The feature film *Red Skies of Montana,* which is loosely based on the 1949 Mann Gulch Fire, had been released the year before. The movie violates true history in a final scene that portrays firefighters digging foxholes to save themselves, which did not happen in Mann Gulch. That scene, however, echoed the gritty military tactics of the Korean War, then in full swing. The fire historian Stephen Pyne believes the movie scene to be a "clear parable of the Korean War," as well as part of the metaphor of fire as war.

The image of men clawing in the earth in their final seconds, true or not true, stays in the mind.

Our group slowly followed the final yards of the race with fire. Under the chaparral we discovered traces of the uphill edge of the old bulldozer cut, a couple of inches to a foot high, used to recover the bodies. We gave up keeping time for this leg of our journey because we shuffled along, following the edge, but later we figured that the eleven men could have covered the ground in a minute or less. When the edge gave out, we realized we had reached the end of the line.

It was a ghostly moment. The chaparral made it difficult to see people only a few feet away. Everyone except for me was a firefighter and could imagine his own end coming in a lonely spot like this one. No one thought they would have spent their last seconds digging in shale and hardpan. But strange things happen at the extremities of human experience.

One of us speculated on the last thought of the missionaries. They might have taken hope, he said, from the Bible story of the three Jews—Shadrach, Meshach, and Abed-Nego—who were cast into a fiery furnace by King Nebuchadnezzar because they refused to worship a golden calf. "And they walked in the heart of the flames, praising God and blessing the Lord," it says in the Book of Daniel. That story has a happy ending: the Lord, impressed by their faith, intervenes and saves the men.

Whatever the missionaries were thinking, they acted as though they had a message for one another. The nine men found at this place were heaped together—there is no other way to describe it. Perhaps they huddled together to take comfort from a human touch and a common faith. Perhaps Powers, who was found farthest along, in the lead, was stopped by the brush and the others piled around him. They appear in photographs to be straining upward, reaching for the high ground.

There was no protection from the fire. The men almost surely died before the flames arrived, when an advance wave of superheated gas entered their mouths and noses and seared the delicate tissues of the nose, mouth, and esophagus involved in breathing, which ceased to function. Deprived of oxygen, the men quickly fell into unconsciousness and died within seconds.

We stood there thinking our own thoughts until one of our party broke the silence.

"This place is sacred to the memory of those who died here," he said in a conversational manner, though his words echoed the Gettysburg Address and were well considered. "We, by remembering them and learning from their deaths, give meaning to what happened here: that they did not die in vain; that their deaths give the gift of life to others who come after."

No one had anything to add to that. We called it a day and made our way separately back to Powderhouse Turn.

The time had come to pull our data together. We had broken down the race with fire into four distinct legs:

- Leg One: It had taken us one and a half minutes to cover Lafferty's route from Powderhouse Turn to the place where he first yelled at the mission crew. This time matched the accounts of witnesses—Thomas and Gleeson—who said the run took Lafferty no more than a minute or two. Time elapsed: 1 minute, 30 seconds.
- Leg Two: We allowed 30 seconds to a minute for the crew to get up and start moving in response to Lafferty's yells, which seems reasonable, considering the confusion over what Lafferty was saying. Time elapsed: 1 minute.
- Leg Three: It had taken us two to two and a half minutes to cover the route of the nine survivors from the Missionary Spot Fire to the bulldozer line along Powderhouse Ridge. The official report

gives no time estimate for this leg of the race, but survivors say it was no more than a few minutes. Time elapsed: 2 minutes, 30 seconds.

- Leg Four: It had taken us 8 minutes, 15 seconds to cover the route of Powers and the fourteen missionaries from the Missionary Spot Fire to the place where nine of the bodies were found. That breaks down as 7 minutes, 15 seconds for the leg to Missionary Rock and another minute for the final hundred yards. Time elapsed: 8 minutes, 15 seconds.

Added together (not including the third leg, which was simultaneous with the fourth), the total elapsed time for the race with fire, from the time Lafferty started out from Powerhouse Turn until flames caught Powers and the eight missionaries, was 10 minutes, 45 seconds.

Something was way off. Our time was less than half the twenty-six minutes allowed in the official fire report. The difference cannot be dismissed. At least some of the times in the official report had to be flat wrong.

The start time of 10:15 in the official report, being approximate, could be off by five minutes without damage to the report's credibility. The watches stopped at 10:41 may have been off by another five minutes or so. (The report never explains how many watches were found, where they were found, and whether they agreed with each other.) If both these five-minute possibilities were true, the report's time for the race would drop from twenty-six minutes to sixteen minutes, which would bring the official estimate much closer to our elapsed time, rounded off to eleven minutes. But that still leaves a five-minute gap.

Lafferty and the board of review were five minutes short of respectability.

I was due at Mendocino Forest headquarters in Willows the next morning to go over photographs of the fire and other materials with Greg Greenway, a Forest Service archaeologist, who was helping me with my research. We had discovered an archive of photo negatives of the fire, including one of it burning, and Greenway had sent them out to be printed.

As he and I went over the photos, Rich Rushforth, a former Mendocino Hotshot and a forest biologist, overheard us talking about the fire. He darted from the room and returned in minutes with a box of documents and artifacts. I had already looked through the box, but I wanted to see it again. The box contained a torn manila envelope with Raymond Sherman's belongings; I had brought along a plastic bag to keep them from spilling further.

I shook out the contents of the envelope: fragments of trouser and shirt, the cowboy belt buckle, with figures of a bucking horse and rider, and the watch with the initials R.S. on the wristband, which had been used to identify his body. Clearly visible on the back of the watch were the words "water and shock protected"; the watchmaker had failed to anticipate the worst. The crust of shale and glass on the watch face gave it more the appearance of a bracelet than a timepiece.

The more I looked at the watch, the more curious I became. Nobody had checked the time on this watch. What if it reported a time different from the 10:41 the other watches had fixed as the moment of death? What if the five minutes Lafferty and the others needed were under the layer of melted glass and grit on the face of Sherman's watch?

"Greg, would you mind if I tried to scrape this watch face clean?" I said, adding, as much to myself as to him, "I'd be tampering with a historic artifact."

Greenway answered without hesitation. "Go for it. That's why we have this stuff here, to answer questions."

I opened my pocketknife and gingerly poked at the amalgam on the watch face. It was stuck hard. I forced in the knife tip and a big chunk of grit popped off, exposing a portion of the watch face down to bare metal. The numbers were nearly obliterated. Surely the delicate hands could not have survived.

I stuck the knife in again, and out snapped another chunk of grit. What a disappointment! About half the watch face was exposed, but no hands were to be seen.

At this point, I nearly gave up. What I was doing felt like waking the dead. Oddly enough, I drew inspiration at this moment from Chief McArdle, who in 1953 had instructed the board of review on how to treat the relatives of the fifteen victims. "Deal considerately with them and remember the depth of their sorrow," McArdle said in a July 20 letter, directly after the fire. "Imagine yourself, for this purpose, in their position. Nevertheless, within these limits, get the facts."

Be respectful but get the facts. Good advice.

I drew a deep breath and stabbed again with the knife. Another chunk of grit came off, and there, impossibly, was a delicate steel minute hand pointing to the 36 position.

Lafferty had his five minutes.

I yelped. Greenway and Rushforth hurried over, perhaps worried about my mental state, and confirmed the hand's position at 36. I yammered out an explanation of why this was important, how five minutes made all the difference, and their faces lit up, which was a credit to their intelligence and tolerance, because at this point I was too excited to make much sense.

The job was not finished. The hour hand had to be pointing to past 10 to confirm the time.

I was so nervous I bent the minute hand slightly as I tucked the knife point under the last chip of grit and pried upward. The grit popped out, and under it appeared the short hour hand exactly where it needed to be, pointing just past 10. There was no mistake: Sherman's watch had stopped at 10:36.

Sherman had been with the group of nine, so the time on his watch was directly comparable to the time of our modern re-creation of the race with fire. The watches showing 10:41 could have belonged to Vote or Hitchcock, and thus recorded a later time.

With Sherman's watch added to the accounting, the race with fire could fit—barely—within the time estimate of the official report, allowing for variables. The start time of 10:15 could have been off by five minutes or more. The mission crew could have taken more than a minute to pull itself together. The 10:41 time of death could be way off for the group of nine. Sherman's watch itself may have been minutes fast.

Why should everything fit together perfectly? The fire, after all, had fooled everyone. Ewing, the fire boss, made the same mistakes he had made on the Hauser Creek Fire, forgetting a crew and failing to anticipate a wind shift. But when he realized the danger on the Rattlesnake Fire, he put his life at stake and ran toward flames to help the survivors escape.

Thomas, familiar with wind shifts after dark, did not anticipate the strength of the wind shift on this fire. But he was the first to notice the spot fire endangering the mission crew and the first to call for action.

Lafferty forgot about the crew he had placed in harm's way, but the moment he realized the peril he ran to warn them, nearly losing his life in the process.

Gleeson, the newspaperman, could have reminded someone about the missionaries—he had seen them march off to the spot fire.

The mission crew could have done a better job of watching out for themselves.

But no one acted in bad faith or made deliberate, malicious mistakes.

The same could now be said of the board of review. They had not fudged numbers to protect their fellow supervisors—Ewing, Lafferty, and Thomas. Sherman's watch was hard, physical evidence—the kind Erhart, the arson investigator, would have appreciated—that the board had reported the facts as they came to them. The board's report had its deficiencies: it was soft on the men who had failed to post lookouts, anticipate the wind shift, and remember the mission crew. But it was by no means corrupt.

"This tragedy woke up the Forest Service."

Forty years after the fire, a memorial plaque and kiosk were dedicated to the memory of the fifteen firefighters at a site overlooking Grindstone Canyon. The idea for a memorial started with J. W. Allendorf, a Forest Service engine captain, as he fought a 1988 fire in Powderhouse Canyon. Allendorf talked up the idea of a memorial for the Rattlesnake Fire, and it caught on. Federal, state, and county employees as well as private citizens worked hundreds of hours, most of it as volunteers, and contributed thousands of dollars' worth of materials for the project. Unhappily for him, Allendorf was away fighting another fire when the dedication occurred.

The ceremony on May 13, 1993, drew a crowd from across the nation—Arizona, Colorado, Florida, Idaho, Oklahoma, and Oregon, as well as California. New Tribes Mission was officially represented by Johnston, by then chairman emeritus of the group. It was a moist, cool day. The participants, wearing jackets, gathered under a tent at the memorial site, alongside the new road, Route 7, where it would be more accessible to people but three miles west of the site of the fire.

Dan Chisholm, Mendocino National Forest supervisor, told the gathering that the fire community owes a debt of gratitude to the fifteen men whose deaths have cautioned generations of firefighters to beware of contrary winds. As he spoke, the wind fluttered the microphone, underscoring his message.

The deaths made the Forest Service take a hard look at how it manages millions of acres of brushland in California and elsewhere, Chisholm said. The Mendocino National Forest became a pioneer in "presuppression planning," the use of fire and other tools to break up chaparral into more manageable units, and a model for the nation. "You can see some of these units as you look across the canyon," Chisholm said. Behind him, the slopes of Grindstone Canyon bore brown and black scorch marks from prescribed burning.

"Hopefully, there is some solace in the fact that this tragedy woke up the Forest Service and other firefighting agencies," Chisholm said. "Because of this wake-up call, firefighting in chaparral is safer today and the Forest Service is doing a better job of managing its brush."

The first spring after the fire, a pair of young Forest Service men, dismayed by the loss of life, took drip torches and on their own initiative ignited a five-mile swath of brush in Grindstone Canyon—no one was injured. They had been "dabbling gingerly" with deliberately set fire before that, remembered Joe Ely, who helped fight the Rattlesnake Fire and also attended the 1993 memorial.

"There was an undercurrent, which nobody wanted to bring out at the time, that if the Forest Service would do something about these brushlands to keep them safer we might not have had this terrible tragedy," Ely said in an oral history for the Forest Service.

The burning program continued until the 1970s, when it came under legal challenge by environmental groups, who argued that it promoted nonnative grasses. Today, the Forest Service burns 2,000 to 5,000 acres of chaparral each year in the Mendocino National Forest on a rotational basis. Most of the burning is done by helitorch, dropping gobs of flaming gasoline from helicopters.

The memorial dedication turned into a family reunion for relatives of Ranger Powers—about twenty-five of them attended. Robert's brother Don, a retired judge from Oklahoma City, acted as spokesman.

"My brother Bob was a student and a scholar and he was certainly an adventurer," Don Powers said. "He was challenged by God's creation. And most of all he loved people."

Bob was also a bit of a showman, according to his brother. Before leaving for the Pacific, Bob talked the pilot of the B-24 on which he served as navigator into buzzing his hometown of Salinas, Kansas. The giant plane went over the town at an altitude of five hundred feet, an event said to be remembered there to this day.

After the ceremony, some attendees drove down the old road for a look at the fire site. They invited Homer Hancock to join them, but he asked to be excused. Hancock had told his story of vanishing lights many times, but he had seen enough of the Rattlesnake Fire to last a lifetime. He held no bitterness, though. He summed up his feelings about what had happened in a statement for the Forest Service soon after the fire:

"Those of us mission fellows who remain have no ill feelings in our heart because of this, knowing these things rest in the hands of Him who made us and in whom these boys loved."

Some people grumbled that there should be a marker at the actual site of the fire. Sharing this view was Don Will, superintendent of the Mendocino Hotshots, who had helped build the memorial along Route 7. Powderhouse Canyon needed a cross, Will figured, but erecting a Christian symbol on federal land would be a legal nightmare.

Will gathered the Mendocino Hotshots and told them his plan. They found a couple of construction ties and worked on them at night in a trailer. One evening they assembled at a local watering hole, the Timberline Bar and Grill in Stonyford, not far from Powderhouse Canyon, and fortified themselves for the task ahead.

It was no small job to lug a ten-foot-high cross, rock pry bar, posthole digger, and other gear into Powderhouse Canyon in the dark, but the hotshots managed. They donned headlamps, as had the mission crew in 1953.

The hotshots located a crack in Missionary Rock and said a firefighters' prayer. Then everyone put their hands on the pry bar and slammed it down. When the hole was two feet deep, they dropped in a can of snuff, small change, and other pocket items. Then they set the cross, and for years after kept silent about that night.

New Tribes Mission left Fouts Springs a few years after the Rattlesnake Fire. The camp has been run since 1959 as a state youth correctional facility, completing a moral cycle from a shady resort to a place of faith to one promising a chance of redemption. In August 2001 another fire, the Trough Fire, scorched 25,000 acres around the youth camp, a collection of cinderblock buildings that can house 120 young men. Brian Cooley, the youth-camp superintendent, was in his office when he looked out the window and saw a plume of smoke from the fire, which had started from suspicious causes.

The flames blew away to the east, down the mountains. The following afternoon, though, the fire turned on a wind shift and came back uphill toward the youth camp, the reverse of the Rattlesnake Fire and its fatal switch from uphill to downhill.

By the time the fire reached the camp, the perimeter had been cleared of brush, trees, and other inflammables, with three notable exceptions. When the missionaries had left Fouts Springs, their cabins had remained. Over the years missionaries and their families had made return visits, Cooley said, fondly poking around their old living quarters. At the time of the Trough Fire, three mission cabins stood along the edge of the youth camp. The fire turned every one to ash.

New Tribes Mission confounded predictions that it would wither and instead grew from six hundred members in 1953 to about thirty-two hundred today. The current spacious headquarters in Sanford, Florida, is yet another place with a shady past: built as the Forest Lake Hotel in the 1920s, it was a favorite winter haunt of Al Capone.

Sequence of Events

1. Tom Shepard meets at Big Safety Zone around 9 A.M. with Smokey Bear and Dalton Hotshots. Golden Gate 3 arrives and is assigned to burnout operation to dozer line. line to the Big Black, but the wind shifts and once again is wrong. A burn squad is driven by truck back to the Y intersection. Burn operation commences approx. 3 P.M.

2. GG3 head for Y Intersection after 1 P.M. to begin the burn operation, but the wind is blowing the wrong way.

3. GG3 is driven 1.3 miles across the dozer

4. A river of fire heads for the burn squad around 3:40 P.M. In minutes, the burn squad is trapped at this location. At 4 P.M. a call is made for medical evacuation.

Big Safety Zone

To Jiggs Fire Camp

Prevailing winds

Seven miles to Lucky Nugget Subdivision

Y Intersection

Surface winds

Surface winds

Prevailing winds

N

Scale: approx. 1 mile

Detail area

Prevailing winds

FIRE WHIRL COLLAPSES

Safety Zones

Fire front at 3:40 P.M.

Fire front at 3:40 P.M.

THE SADLER FIRE

North Central, Nevada

August 9, 1999

Golden Gate 3 burn squad overrun

Dozer Line

Big Black

Barbed wire fence

2

The Ghost of Storm King

THE SAGEBRUSH AND grasslands of northeastern Nevada seldom see much rain, so the summer of 1999's dry spell would have been nothing extraordinary if the previous winter and spring had not been unusually wet. Grass sprouted rich and thick in the first fine weather, then flourished in the spring rains. As the drought set in, the lush vegetation withered and baked, until by midsummer it needed only a spark to bring it to life—this time as wildfire.

When a dry lightning storm passed over the region on August 5, it ignited a string of fires, the names attached to them reflecting the plainness of the country: the Table Fire, the Horse Fire, and the Pine Fire. The fires burned close to one another—in Nevada, fifty miles doesn't mean much—so among firefighters the blazes were known by a single name, the Sadler Fire. After burning for only a day, the Sadler Fire had blackened 20,000 acres of grass and sagebrush, pinyon pine and juniper trees—no great loss to the eye of a casual observer but a threat to the area's ranchers, who depended on the grasslands for grazing cattle.

Fire-behavior experts predicted that if things went well the Sadler Fire would be under control in three to four days, cover no more than 50,000 acres, and cost about $1.3 million to fight. At worst, they said, it might last a few days longer, cover twice that territory, and cost $1.6 million, an estimate that proved long on hope.

Instead, winds blew, a weather front carrying rain stalled in the far distance, and the Sadler and other fires raged. Over the next days more than four thousand firefighters arrived to battle flames that eventually scorched more than 1.4 million acres across the state. The cost rose into the tens of millions of dollars. A first-year bill for range rehabilitation alone, including four million pounds of seed, carried a price tag of $28 million.

When Tom Shepard arrived to run one section of the Sadler Fire, the conditions stirred the ghost of an earlier tragedy, the 1994 South Canyon Fire on Colorado's Storm King Mountain. Shepard had been superintendent of the Prineville Hotshots when firefighters were caught in the late afternoon using aggressive tactics better suited to the calm of morning.

On Storm King Mountain, Shepard had stationed himself on a ridge top as lookout while half his crew worked far below, in positions decided on by others. Shepard kept in touch with them by radio, but his outpost had a blind spot: in the bottom of a canyon, the very place the fire blew up. Nine Prineville Hotshots joined others in a retreat, but the path to safety was too long, the last yards too steep. Those nine and three smoke jumpers died on that stretch of fire line; two members of a helitack crew were killed on another section of the fire, or fourteen in all.

Shepard escaped the flames but not the emotional undertow that follows real-life tragedy. There was no official censure for Shepard and the other fire supervisors, and he put in another year as superintendent, rebuilding the Prineville Hotshots. But then, when he looked for another crew to boss, he found doors closed against him; nobody wanted to take a chance on the ex-superintendent of the ill-fated Prineville Hotshots.

Shepard found himself playing the unwanted role of a captain who had failed to go down with his ship, a supervisor who had lived while his subordinates had died. He took a job with heavy administrative duties with the Forest Service in Idaho and began spending off hours drinking too much beer.

Shepard has a laid-back manner almost fatherly in its appeal. His own father had been an assistant librarian at the University of Idaho and some of the father's studious outlook rubbed off on the son; Shepard has a willingness to let a decisive moment pass. But in the aftermath of action, he can offer a wealth of ideas about how things could have been done better.

Some of his ideas were good: one day, for example, he decided to quit drinking, just like that. A weekend of sobriety turned into weeks and then into months. Shepard's outlook brightened; after a heart-to-heart talk with a friend, he returned to fire duty, having by this time completed classes—to become a fire-safety officer. At the commencement of the 1999 fire season, Shepard loaded his gear into a green Forest Service pickup and resumed the gypsy life he loved, chasing wildfire across the West.

In early August, with the northern third of Nevada under a pall of smoke, Shepard was assigned to the Sadler Fire and was attached temporarily to a Type I incident-management team, one of only seventeen nationwide that handle wildfires. Members of a Type I team, the most highly rated, must be tightly bonded to perform the demanding work. Most members on this particular Type I team had worked together for years and functioned half by instinct. Shepard was the odd man out, but he had a key post: division supervisor for the place where the fire burned most intensely.

"He likes the heat, he likes the smoke."

The Marin Headlands command a spectacular view of two magnificent achievements of the civilized world, the city of San Francisco and the Golden Gate Bridge. Behind the headlands lies a contrasting wonder of the natural world: more than forty miles of protected ocean shoreline, tens of thousands of acres of parkland, and groves of ancient coastal redwood trees whose foliage creates a world of shadow palaces and deep quiet. John Muir, the great naturalist of a century ago, once called the redwoods "the best tree-lovers' monument that could possibly be found in all the forests of the world." Today, with redwoods, open land, and unspoiled shoreline a fraction of what they were in Muir's day, the Marin Headlands has become an island of the spirit for multitudes.

Rising steeply from the sea to form a natural barrier or fortification, the headlands have also served a military purpose from ancient times. The Spanish erected the first forts here in the seventeenth century. Remnants of America's wars, from weathered rifle pits to rusted nuclear missile installations, are visible.

The headlands presently serve as the Western Region Wildfire Mobilization Center for the National Park Service, where crews gather for assignment during fire season. The mobilization center, which can dispatch crews anywhere in the nation, occupies renovated barracks and offices at old Fort Cronkite, a busy post during World War II.

The lightning burst at the beginning of August in Nevada started 154 fires, making that state the nation's hot spot for wildfire. In its wake, the staff of the mobilization center called up its third crew of the summer, Golden Gate 3, made up of park service firefighters from across California, from giant Yosemite National Park to tiny Lava Beds National Monument to nearby Bay Area parks.

The crew boss for Golden Gate 3, lanky, muscular Tim Horton, looked every inch a firefighter. Horton wore his red hair cropped close, military style, and cultivated a "hotshot look" by wearing his green fire pants cut off at his boot tops. He had been a California hotshot, one of a select few qualified to build fire lines by hand under extreme conditions, and he still had the "hotshot mentality"—alert, aggressive, always looking for the main chance. "He likes the heat, he likes the smoke," an admirer said. "He gives 150 percent all the time."

Horton longed to be a hotshot superintendent, one of the most coveted jobs in firefighting. He was obsessed with his career, talking endlessly about it to a point many found disturbing. At the age of twenty-nine, he had already spent two and a half seasons as a hotshot and six more years working on engine and helicopter crews, serving as crew boss on more than a dozen fires.

Horton, though, was in one sense what old-timers call a "fire virgin," one untempered by disaster. Although this was hardly his first fire, he had never been in charge when things went bad and people got burned. He preached fire safety, but the message a lot of people heard was more about job advancement for Horton.

A few years earlier, Horton had won a plum appointment to the National Wildland Firefighter Academy at Fort Hunter-Liggett, near King City, California. The posting included pay and benefits and guaranteed long-term employment to graduates, an end to the fire world's curse of seasonal employment. After four days, however, Horton had quit the academy to take what looked to him like a better opportunity, a job with the National Park Service—leaving academy officials with an empty bunk and a bitter memory of Tim Horton. When summoned as crew boss for Golden Gate 3, Horton was working as boss on the fuels crew at Sequoia and Kings Canyon National Parks, mostly conducting prescribed burns.

Horton's number two, Alex Naar, was a thirty-five-year-old law-enforcement ranger permanently stationed at the Marin Headlands who worked on fire crews during the summer. Like Horton, he was sturdy but not muscle-bound, well suited to the demands of fighting wildland fires for physical endurance as well as strength. Naar, like Horton, was intense, driven, and self-confident to the point of taking himself too seriously. He was also a stickler for rules, a trait reinforced by his job as a lawman.

Naar had a broad background in fire and emergency medicine. He had graduated from the National Fire Academy in Emmitsburg, Maryland, completing a course in urban, or structural, fire, not wildland fire, and then had served as a lieutenant on a municipal fire department in Massachusetts before heading west. A "crew-boss trainee," Naar was being trained by Horton to become a crew boss himself.

The pairing of Naar and Horton spelled trouble. Each man had strengths that might have compensated for weaknesses in the other, and they both made good-faith efforts to forge a partnership. Given time, they might have worked things out. But they had hours, not weeks or months, before they would be flat on the ground, side by side, with flames closing over them.

Trouble started that first day at the Marin Headlands. After the last of the firefighters had trickled into Fort Cronkite and stowed their gear, Horton called everyone together, introduced himself and Naar, and began to go over personnel qualifications.

Golden Gate 3 numbered twenty-one, including Horton and Naar—mostly young and eager firefighters on the lookout for adventure and tuition money, plus a few older hands happy to get away from home for a few weeks and pick up overtime. They were a Type II crew, the grunts of firefighting—qualified to handle chores ranging from mop-ups to the simpler burning operations, but less capable than Type I crews, the hotshots, smoke jumpers, and helicopter crews trained to take on fire at its most dangerous. Thirteen of Golden Gate 3's members worked on fire crews at national parks; the other eight held other park jobs. Five had never fought a wildfire before.

Most had never met any of the others, let alone worked or trained together. They attended different colleges and universities, or worked at parks far from each other, or were kicking around in fire work before taking up a lifetime career—a grab bag of backgrounds, occupations, and aspirations. They had one thing in common: all had passed the basic physical test for federal firefighters, a timed hike while wearing a pack. The minimum requirement is to cover three miles in forty-five minutes or less while carrying forty-five pounds, no running allowed. The point of the test is to measure physical strength as well as endurance. But even that common denominator was misleading: one crew member, Lydia Mingo, was in such poor physical condition that she could not keep up with the others, a failing that would change the way fire crews were put together in the future.

The rest were fit enough, and several had years of fire experience. Keren Christensen, twenty-three, had been recruited while doing volunteer work at a fire station on her eighteenth birthday. She was climbing over a fire truck when a fire marshal spotted her and asked if she would like to become a real firefighter. Christensen, who had been active in high school sports, was about to graduate and was looking for a physical outlet. A firefighter's badge sounded like a ticket to adventure. She filled out an application and got the call that summer.

Christensen's lifetime ambition had been to work with animals, perhaps become a veterinarian, but instead she'd embraced the comradeship and hard work of fighting fire. She had a buoyant, friendly personality, an open-heartedness that made her welcome wherever she went. After four summers in fire work she was training to become a squad boss, the equivalent of a corporal, in charge of a portion of a crew of twenty. She had been stationed at Yosemite National Park when summoned to the mobilization center.

For David "Ty" Deaton, fighting fire was part of a personal quest to help others. "If you personally help someone out, you see the rewards right away," said Deaton, who had joined the Marine Corps in pursuit of his goal and had served fourteen months on the island of Okinawa. The marines, however, had not been a fulfilling experience. Deaton turned to firefighting and graduated from the Butte College Fire Academy in Chico, California. When summoned to the mobilization center, he had been on a fire-engine crew in Sequoia and Kings Canyon National Parks, where, coincidentally, Horton was a crew boss. On the Sadler Fire, Deaton would come to discover that dreams demand a high price: to help save someone else, he would have to risk his own life.

Derek Hyde was the "brain" of the group, well-spoken and even-tempered, a graduate of the University of California with a degree in aerospace engineering. His clean-cut looks and solid, powerful build made him a poster boy for wildland fire; this would be his fourth season fighting fire. Hyde would go on to become a computer analyst for the prestigious National Academy of Sciences in Washington, D.C.

Peter Giampaoli led a gypsy life—a little of this, a little of that. He was trying to squeak through his first fire season without expensive fire boots, the kind made of heavy leather and with their soles screwed on, not glued. Before the Sadler Fire was over, he would wish he had the best boots money could buy.

Horton made certain everyone could be away for a full-duty tour of twenty-one days, no days off. They would march in single file like a hotshot crew, he said. If he called a meeting for 9:00 A.M., they would show up on time to the minute, like a hotshot crew. They would establish a regular tool order so that chain saws and hand tools would be in the proper place in line to begin work.

No one had ever been injured on one of his crews, Horton said. Safety came first, always. If someone felt uncomfortable—if they had no lookouts or escape routes, for example—they should speak up. "This stuff is dangerous; I don't want anyone hurt," Horton said.

He and Naar would function as equal partners, he added, a word from Naar being as good as from him. This was a generous but risky gesture; shared responsibility seldom works in an authoritarian system like firefighting.

Horton then used a phrase that would ring in memory. "It's all about money," he said, repeating it several times.

Some thought the remark motivational. Horton, after all, would make out their time sheets; now they could hope for a generous hand with overtime. "Ninety percent of the crew got a big old grin out of it," recalled one firefighter.

"It was said jokingly," Horton himself said later, in his own defense. "I mean, why do people take fire assignments anyway?"

Others, Naar in particular, did not share in the merriment. When Horton turned the meeting over to Naar, Naar began by saying, "It's all about *safety*."

No one missed the tension. "They each had their set ways," one firefighter remembered later. "You saw the difference and it was understood."

One crew member, Angela Hawk, slipped in late to the briefing from sorting equipment. As she hovered at the edge of the group, she picked up what she believed was a pungent and familiar odor: alcohol. For Hawk there could be no mistake—she had been a bartender before becoming a firefighter.

Seated apart from the group was the crew's bus driver, Ellis. "He was an old guy who loved fire, but he had bad knees and couldn't do it anymore," one firefighter said.

The pungent odor came straight from Ellis.

As the meeting broke up, Hawk reported her suspicions to Horton and Naar. That's great, they thought. They had just told everyone to abstain from alcohol, even beer. Now they might have a drunken bus driver on their hands.

Horton and Naar confronted Ellis together. Have you been drinking? they asked. Ellis, surprised and indignant, responded no, he certainly had not. He had been minding his own business and smoking his pipe.

Naar, ever the lawman, reminded Ellis that drinking alcohol violated a host of rules covering the operation of a motor vehicle for the federal government. He could be in serious trouble. Now, once again, had he been drinking?

Absolutely not, said Ellis.

The smell, they concluded, was Ellis's pipe tobacco; it certainly had a pungent odor. Ellis did not appear drunk; his denials were coherent. Horton and Naar decided to let the issue go. "You can only do so much," Horton said later. "Who they send to drive is who they send to drive."

With Ellis at the wheel, Golden Gate 3 climbed aboard the bus and headed to town for dinner. The bus was small, old, and rickety. As Hawk passed the No Smoking sign at the front, she thought that if the odor truly came from Ellis's pipe, he had broken the no-smoking rule. But she figured she had used up her quota of complaints.

"There is an intimidation factor," Hawk said later. "These crews are predominantly male. Most of the guys won't question things. They take someone's word at face value. And I didn't want to become *not part of the crew*."

As the bus followed the winding road out of the headlands, a heavy fog swept in from San Francisco Bay. The fog rolled over the roadway and Ellis had trouble making out turns. A one-lane tunnel marked the exit from the headlands, and as Ellis headed into it a warning glowed dimly at the tunnel entrance. The bus lumbered into the tunnel anyway, its engine noise echoing off the walls. Everyone held their breath until it cleared the far end, without incident.

When Golden Gate 3 awoke in the barracks the next morning, fog covered the hills and shoreline. Invisible seabirds uttered cries out of the mist. The crew had no fire assignment yet, and the day stretched emptily ahead. They spent the morning putting their tools in order, but by afternoon they had run out of work and grown restless.

Horton decided that a hike up the headlands would help them blow off steam while it would give him a chance to size up his crew's physical capabilities. Golden Gate 3 set out twenty-one strong in full gear, heavy boots (except for Giampaoli), and packs, carrying one hand tool apiece.

The headlands rise steeply in a half bowl behind Fort Cronkite, which faces the bay. The hike to the crest is mild enough to be popular with tourists, but Mingo had trouble keeping pace. She stopped to huff and puff while others passed by with a word of encouragement. Mingo was short and strong, capable of handling a chain saw with ease, but she had no wind. "We were trying to get some teamwork going, so I helped her up one hill," said Deaton, always mindful of others. "But her attitude was kind of 'I don't care.'"

Horton radioed back to Christensen, who was bringing up the rear, and told her to stay with Mingo. "Lydia was frustrated and disappointed," said Christensen. "But what made me mad—what made everybody mad—was she was a *smoker*. I had to stay behind to help someone who smoked cigarettes. A bunch of us said, 'You need to stop that if you're going to be in fire.' After that, I didn't really talk to her."

The crew reached the crest of the headlands and played tourist while taking a breather. A World War II firing pit was nearby. The pit had been ringed with bags of dry cement; the burlap sacking had worn away, leaving behind hardened cement with crisscross markings from the burlap, giving it the look of a war memorial.

Golden Gate 3 turned for home, heading off the trail, into brush that happened to be laced with poison oak. As they worked their way down, a radio call came from the mobilization center. Golden Gate 3 had an assignment: Nevada, the nation's hotspot. They were to report within twenty-four hours to fire camp near Elko, six hundred miles away.

When they got back to the mobilization center, Horton and Naar both complained to their superiors about Mingo's lack of physical conditioning, but were told nothing could be done. Mingo had passed the pack test. Dropping her would set off alarms about discrimination; this was, after all, California.

The higher-ups might have taken a more rigorous stand. Lack of conditioning and inability to adapt to heat can have fatal results, and a crew member's supervisors can be held responsible. Later that month, a Santa Barbara city firefighter, Stephen Masto, was hiking alone to join a crew on his first wildland fire near Lake Cachuma, northwest of the city, when he collapsed from heat stroke. Masto, twenty-eight, was said to be in good physical condition, but he was overstressed by the twenty-one pounds of clothing and fourteen-pound backpack. He died before help arrived. An investigation team concluded that flawed safety procedures had "failed to protect Stephen Masto from the hazard of heat stress."

By the time Golden Gate 3 pulled their gear together, it was about five P.M. on Friday, August 6. Naar suggested waiting for the heavy preweekend traffic to clear, but Horton was in no mood for delay. Load up and go, he ordered.

The bus seated twenty, so someone on the crew of twenty-one had to find another way to Nevada—doubling up on a seat on an overnight drive was no option. Naar and another firefighter took a separate car, but they quickly became separated from the bus. When Naar radioed Horton that he was stopping for gasoline, expecting the bus to follow, Horton either missed the call or ignored it and kept going.

"Alex went freelancing out in front of us," Horton said. "I know how to stay together. I tried and tried to get him on the radio."

Naar said that he, too, tried to reestablish contact, even phoning the mobilization center to see if Horton had checked in. Naar stopped for the night at a motel, as he and Horton had agreed, but Horton pressed on. Horton did not seem overly concerned about losing contact, according to several firefighters with him on the bus. They remember Horton saying, "Naar needs us more than we need him" and making a slighting reference to Naar being a law-enforcement ranger, not a full-time firefighter. Horton said he has no memory of uttering those remarks, but word of them got back to Naar and further soured the relationship.

The firefighters dozed fitfully as the bus followed Interstate 80 across northern California, over the Sierra Nevadas and down into the Great Basin, the arid plain broken by mountain ranges stretching from the Sierras across Nevada and Utah into western Colorado. Darkness brought cold to the desert. The bus's heater failed. Hawk snuggled up to her seatmate, a man she had met only the day before, and slept badly. Ellis looked too tired to be driving at night, she thought, but again she kept her own counsel.

"We talked about stopping, but Tim wanted to get there, work a shift, and then sleep," said Hyde, who was seated directly behind Horton. "We told Tim numerous times that the bus driver looked tired."

Horton did not order Ellis to keep going, Hyde said, but asked him questions such as Are you okay? Do you want to keep driving? Ellis replied that he could handle it, though later he complained to Naar that he had felt pressured to go on.

The bus pulled into the fire command post near Elko in time for breakfast the next morning, hours ahead of schedule. The prospect of hot food and a rest lifted everyone's spirits. Horton went to report for duty. He had a gift for snagging good fire assignments; over the next several days, he would obtain one demanding job after another for Golden Gate 3. Their first assignment, however, was no glamour post: the crew was assigned to mop up a swath of burned sagebrush and grass, a good match for their qualifications. They climbed back aboard the bus and headed out to meet the fire.

"Where are your anchor points? Your safety zones?"

Northern Nevada is a place of soul-wrenching emptiness and echoing silences, of barren mountains separated by flat basins stretching beyond sight. The mountains rise without preamble, stark and abrupt, from the beds of vanished, ancient seas. A scattering of clouds and an occasional gliding hawk or eagle seem all but lost in the vast reaches of sky.

The events of the Sadler Fire, from its ignition by lightning to its convergence with Golden Gate 3, were dictated by ancient geologic events; the region's present-day topography began to form about seventeen million years ago. According to geologic theory, two plates of the earth's crust in what is now the western United States began to tear away from each other along a north-south line extending from Canada to Mexico. As the plates pulled apart, enormous chunks of rock tilted upward and became mountain ranges. In the slow time of geologic change, shallow inland seas formed between the mountain ranges, then filled with silt as the mountains eroded. The seas gradually dried up and left behind raised, flattish basins.

Today, only the tops of the mountains remain visible, the lower parts having been covered by silt. This accounts for the steepness of the mountains and for the high altitude of the basins, which are four thousand to five thousand feet above sea level.

Within this broad area, known prosaically as Basin and Range, there is a geologic singularity, the Great Basin: no water escapes from it except by evaporation. The Great Basin is immense, 200,000 miles square, or a fifth of the West. Shaped like a ragged heart, the basin extends from southeastern Oregon south across almost all of Nevada and a little bit into Mexico, and from California east of the Sierras into western Utah. All waters within the Great Basin proceed inward; rivers rise, flow, and then disappear into "sinks" or marshy wetlands. Some sinks have become historic landmarks—the Carson and Humboldt Sinks were favorite resting places for pioneer wagon trains.

Water cannot escape the Great Basin by going underground; it rises again as hot springs, propelled to the surface after heating by the earth's magma. Such springs are surprisingly frequent in this otherwise parched land. It is said that from any point in the region, surface water can usually be found within a five-mile radius, though many have died of thirst looking for it. If you want shade in Nevada, it is also said, carry your own.

The bleak landscape provides a spectacular opportunity for wildfire. Brush fires look easy to handle early in the morning; fuels are short and you are tall, as veterans say. Rookies wonder why the fire hasn't been hooked. A few hours later, with flames ripping across the landscape, propelled by powerful, erratic winds, it's another story. Firefighters, their mouths dry as cotton, ask if the wind blows *all* the time.

Range fires can cover miles in minutes. A flame front races along on what appears to be a predictable course, then with a wind shift veers off like a destructive, willful child, sometimes slamming into a mountain. The wind can blow harder at night, too.

Hot ground and tricky winds create dust devils. Add fire to a dust devil and it transforms into a fire whirl, an awe-inspiring sight. A fire whirl can cross a field in seconds, jump roads and gulches, incinerate livestock, and ultimately collapse in a heap of sparks, as though dying of laughter at its own antic behavior.

The ancient seabed is not uniformly flat, and this gives firefighters their chance. The shorelines of the vanished seas remain as shelflike formations or low hills descending step by step into the basins. Erosion has cut breaks into the hills, little draws and canyons that twist, turn, and lead nowhere. These formations can trap a fire—or a fire crew, as Golden Gate 3 was about to find out. The low hills provide a line of defense, but a treacherous one.

As the bus carrying Golden Gate 3 headed for the mop-up assignment, smoke appeared on every horizon, as though they were in a sea of fire. The crew found its assigned spot and began grubbing in ash for live embers. Horton went to scrounge a better assignment, and by the time the crew finished lunch he had found it: they were off to conduct a burnout on a flank of the fire.

The crew eagerly piled back onto the bus, but when Ellis hit the starter, nothing happened. It took twenty minutes to fix a faulty switch, not the last time the bus would fail.

A couple of fire engines and a water tender had shown up in the meantime, headed for the same place as Golden Gate 3. The vehicles formed a convoy, led by the bus. A helicopter scouted ahead, its pilot relaying directions to the ground. Terrain always looks flatter from the air, however, and the convoy began to wander.

"Is this the road?" Horton would say, and then second-guess himself. "No, no, I think I see it." They missed a turn and came to a halt; a column of smoke appeared in the middle distance, on track for the convoy.

"There was black smoke coming right at us," said Hawk. "If we'd stayed there, we'd have been burned over."

People yelled at Ellis to get the bus moving, but there was no room to turn around. Ellis started to back up and nearly rammed the water tanker. By the time matters were sorted out, the bus was at the rear of the convoy. The procession got under way again but immediately took another wrong turn, following tire ruts up one of the no-account gulches. The convoy made it up the gulch to a plateau, but the bus could go no farther.

The crew piled out and there, below the plateau in the direction from which they had come, rose a column of smoke. For Horton, it looked like opportunity calling. If they lit a backfire, he thought, they had a chance of stopping the fire right there. Taking a fire head-on, though, was an aggressive move even with the best crews.

Horton radioed the helicopter pilot and asked if he could see the convoy and whether their present location was a safe place to anchor a fire line, a barrier dug or scraped to mineral soil. The pilot, however, wasn't prepared to make that sort of judgment.

"I told the crew I was going to take a look," Horton said. "I didn't personally feel they were in that bad a position. I asked them twice, if not more often, 'Do you feel comfortable with this?'"

Horton disappeared over a rise.

"Tim jumped out and ran up a hill, and then we saw this big ol' smoke," Christensen said. "We felt sure it wasn't going to come down on us. But we also felt sure it would cut us off to the rear."

As the crew watched, a nugget of flame appeared in the mouth of the gulch, the one the convoy had driven up. There was nothing to stop the fire from coming up the gulch after them. They were trapped; several firefighters took out fusees to burn a safety zone.

"People were running around, we couldn't get Tim on the radio," said Christensen. "Nobody was screaming, but there was intensity, high energy."

The nugget of flame churned at the mouth of the gulch, then unexpectedly sped away, leaving behind scorched earth and a shaken Golden Gate 3. At this moment, with everything in confusion, the door of a white Chevy Suburban, which had joined the convoy minutes before, opened. Out stepped Alex Naar.

Naar lost not a moment in asserting himself—with Horton absent, Naar was technically crew boss. He ordered Golden Gate 3 to form a search party to go looking for Horton.

No one moved. Why divide the crew further by sending out a search party? someone asked. Naar himself had been absent for nearly twenty-four hours, and nobody had gone searching for him.

After Naar's chase car had become separated from the bus, Naar had driven to Winnemucca, in north-central Nevada, where he'd stopped for a few hours of sleep. Winnemucca, a garishly lighted casino town, looked like a Hollywood set for a wildfire movie. Uniformed firefighters roamed the streets. Motel parking lots were filled with fire vehicles: the heavies, big red or yellow engines; smaller brush buggies with coils of narrow hose; sport-utility vehicles painted green and tan; the occasional ambulance.

The next morning, Naar arrived at the fire camp near Elko too late to catch Golden Gate 3. Naar, though, turned out to have a knack for scrounging transportation similar to Horton's for digging up fire assignments. He discovered that the supervisor of the division where Golden Gate 3 was working was without a vehicle, so he volunteered to drive one there—the Chevy Suburban—thus securing a ride for himself.

Unable to put together a search party, Naar decided to report Horton's missing status. Horton was unaccounted for and fire had swept his last known position, Naar reported by radio. He asked that a helicopter commence a search. "It was fairly dramatic for the crew," Naar remembers, with a note of satisfaction.

"Alex was trying to play catch-up, trying to control a volatile situation," said Hawk. "We had an agitated crew, a missing crew boss, fires spotting all over the place and blowing out everywhere. You could see several people getting pretty scared."

The search effort may have been high drama for some, but for Horton it felt like comic opera; the crew boss never considered himself in real trouble. When the fire had begun to boil near him, Horton had stepped into the black—onto charred ground—and watched in safety as flames passed by. He had tried to contact Golden Gate 3 and the division supervisor by radio, but he'd never gotten through.

He had no trouble *hearing* radio communications, however, especially as the helicopter pilot who was searching for him informed everyone within broadcast range that Horton had walked away from his crew and gotten lost.

"I was safe in the black and people wouldn't shut up on the radio," Horton said later with exasperation. "The helicopter pilot jumped in and I could hear him saying excitedly, 'Get those vehicles out of the way!'

"I wanted to say, 'I'm fine; I can see the bus; I'm walking back toward the bus.' I guess I got a little belligerent with the pilot."

The pilot, in actions described in excited detail over the radio, spotted Horton, swooped down, and picked him up.

"That wasn't a very good spot you were in," the pilot remarked, trying to be casual.

"It looked fine to me," Horton replied with heat.

Tempers did not improve when the helicopter deposited Horton on the plateau in front of Golden Gate 3.

Naar greeted him with "You left me and then you abandoned the crew!"

"Hey, we left messages all over for you," Horton shot back. "And I was fine; I didn't need that helicopter."

Horton and Naar retired behind the bus to continue the quarrel out of the crew's sight. Horton directed his anger into less dangerous territory, complaining to Naar that the division supervisor's plan for fighting the fire was no good. He, Horton, had a better one.

"He was really pissed off at the division supe," said Naar. "He felt an opportunity had been lost, a moment where there was a chance to do a burnout and stop the fire from blowing out."

Both men calmed down.

"Let's not lose it here," Naar said.

They rejoined the crew, and Horton made a little speech.

"I did not abandon you," Horton said. "I was looking out for your safety. But maybe I was jumping two steps ahead, maybe I didn't let the whole crew know enough about what I was doing." In the future, Horton said, he would seek less risky assignments. Safety, he said, mattered more than anything else.

His remarks quieted but failed to unite the crew. Some thought Horton had done a good job of scouting the fire and looking out for their safety; others felt he had abandoned them.

They divided, too, over Naar's performance. Some admired the way Naar had tried to calm a volatile situation; others felt he was trying to win over the crew from Horton. Either way, the clash between Horton and Naar set a pattern. Before the fire was over, Horton and Naar again would split up, Horton would win an assignment putting Golden Gate 3 in front of a fire, and the two leaders would join up in a moment of crisis.

The bus managed to lumber to the division assembly point, where Horton, smarting from embarrassment, hunted down Kelly Martin, the division supervisor. Martin was the source of his trouble, he figured, and he told her

Golden Gate 3 prepares its first burnout late on August 7; the landscape is typically flat and spacious for northern Nevada. Courtesy Derek Hyde

so. She had sent Golden Gate 3 up the wrong road. She had failed to seize the opportunity to stomp the main fire with a head-on attack. And his helicopter "rescue" had been totally unnecessary and humiliating.

Martin listened without sympathy.

"He was a bit short with me," Martin said later. "He couldn't believe people had gone looking for him, he was angry about that. But he had kind of abandoned his crew. You could hear the panic in everyone's voice on the radio because they couldn't find the boss.

"So I told him, 'We couldn't contact you, Tim . . . and we had to move your crew.'

"He wanted to do a burn at the head of the fire. He said at one point, 'I have a lot of experienced people on my crew.' So I asked him, 'Where are your anchor points? Where are your safety zones?' He didn't have any."

It later struck Martin that the incident was a dress rehearsal for what was ahead.

"That's one lesson I learned," Martin said. "'Never accept a crew boss's estimate of a crew's experience until you've seen them in action yourself." Martin tried to caution others about Horton's rash behavior, but her team was relieved before the warning could be passed on.

Golden Gate 3 puts fire to the ground the evening of August 7, burning out from a road to create a fire break. The crew was working well together at this point. "This was a good day," Keren Christensen remarked later. Courtesy Dan Bowmen

The Horton-Martin spat came to an end when Naar intervened. He pulled Martin aside and told her, "Look, we've got a crew. What do you want us to do?"

Martin assigned Golden Gate 3 to conduct a burnout in a relatively safe spot on the flank of the fire. Heavy engines and a hotshot crew would stand by in case of trouble.

By the time Golden Gate 3 found the place, evening was at hand. The wind had quieted down, and the temperature was slipping off the day's highs, which had been mild enough, around eighty. In a conciliatory gesture, Horton put Naar in charge of crew assignments.

The crew was to light a backfire along a dirt road and let it burn toward the main fire. They dipped torches to the ground and a swath of fire crackled to life; as the flames rose, the crew's mood lifted. Smoke that had filled the sky with menace during the day disappeared in the gloaming. Scattered fires on distant hills, invisible in daylight, popped out like evening stars; pinpoints of firelight merged into starry constellations, died out, and were born again in flashes as new fires started up, as though the history of the heavens was being played out on the night sky in seconds instead of eons.

The strains of a long day gave way to a kind of peace. Golden Gate 3 had been without real sleep for thirty-six hours, but soon they would be fed and in their tents. They had endured the bus, with its faulty heater, balky engine, rattles, and shakes. They had escaped a golden nugget of fire. Their captains, Horton and Naar, were at last working in tandem after a day of separations and quarrels. They belonged to something bigger than themselves, a campaign fire with hundreds of people, scores of vehicles, and a fleet of aircraft. And they were in company with visible energy on the loose, wildfire. For the first time, Golden Gate 3 felt like a crew.

"We've done some burning. We'll take care of it."

Golden Gate 3 were camped at a staging area at Jiggs, a dip in the land about twenty-five miles south of Elko on the opposite, or east, side of the fire from the main camp. The dip accommodated a one-room school, a Grange Hall, a volunteer fire station, and a combined saloon and grocery. The crew, wakened at dawn's first light by an overeager supervisor who shook their tents, stumbled toward the Grange building, which served as a mess hall.

There, Tom Shepard sat by himself finishing breakfast. Both he and the Golden Gate crew had arrived in Nevada on Saturday, two days earlier. A division supervisor, Shepard was assigned to a section already blackened by fire. He had spent the previous day riding with an engine crew in search of smoke and finding only one lone flare-up.

After the deaths on Storm King Mountain, Shepard had attended a string of funerals, asking himself each time, What would this person want us to do? How best should we remember him or her? After the funerals, Shepard had gone home to Prineville and brooded, until one day a friend took him out for a round of golf and a heart-to-heart talk. The time had come for him to return to the fire line, the friend said, as much for the sake of the fire community as for his own mental health. Storm King had shattered everyone's confidence.

Shepard reported for duty within days, joining seven Prineville Hotshots temporarily attached to the Redmond Hotshots. Their first assignment was a mop-up.

"It was the hardest thing I've ever done," Shepard said. "I was scared shitless." A press photographer caught up with the crew; Shepard remembers the man peering at him "as though he was trying to look into my soul . . . but I never let him in."

Later, during a backwoods fire, Shepard stepped off a helicopter to a surprise welcome hug. The hugger, facing retirement that fall, recalled the scene in a posting on a firefighter Web site: "Just one more time, I would like to be in that same meadow hugging Tom Shepard and feeling like I drained off some of the pain."

The outpouring of sympathy was not universal. Some firefighters thought Shepard had played too passive a role under conditions that screamed danger. "If you see Tom Shepard on a fire, go the other way," one critic said, albeit in private.

But the public show of support had a good effect. "Most of us found answers, probably none the same ones," Shepard said. "Some of those answers generated new questions. So here I go again, looking for answers. For me, the place to find those answers is the fire line." On Monday, August 9, he found himself in charge of a hot division on one of the biggest fires in Nevada history. As challenges go, the Sadler Fire would be hard to match.

Before Shepard finished breakfast, Dan Huter, an old-school firefighter, aggressive, knowledgeable, and sure of himself, strode into the Grange Hall and announced that the morning briefing was about to begin. The Sadler Fire had been divided into several divisions; Huter was in charge of this section. His manner that morning seemed hurried to Shepard.

"Okay, let's go," Huter called out.

Hold on, Shepard thought, there's folks outside who should hear this. Some people had finished eating and left the mess hall, and others were just showing up. The session was under way in a moment, however.

Huter began the briefing with the weather forecast. Expect another hot, dry, and windy day, he said. Temperatures would be in the mid- to high eighties, five to ten degrees higher than the day before. The humidity would drop to the single digits. The upper atmosphere was unstable, meaning fickle winds. Those details amounted, literally, to a red flag for firefighters, the certainty that extreme fire weather was on its way. Huter, though, made no mention of a red-flag warning, the formal alert for those conditions. One had been issued the night before, but a communications glitch had kept Huter from knowing about it.

At 9:00 P.M. the previous night, Chris Maier, a National Weather Service meteorologist, had issued a fire-weather forecast for the region with a red-flag warning. Maier had picked up signs of an approaching storm front with increasing turbulence. "Dust devils and fire whirls will occur again," Maier had predicted. Those conditions warranted the red flag, but the decision to post the warning was not Maier's to make—it lay with his superiors in Reno.

Maier, though, had to meet a 6:00 P.M. deadline for handing in his evening forecast. He submitted the forecast on time but minus the red-flag label, and it was issued an hour later, at 7:00 P.M.

"We had to go to press without the headline," Maier said.

It took two hours, until 8:00 P.M., before the red-flag warning was approved. Maier then updated his forecast and telephoned the warning to fire camps. The updated forecast, issued at 9:00 P.M., went by fax to the Sadler Fire incident-command post, the main one set up on the west side of the fire, not the camp at Jiggs. The 9:00 P.M. forecast never caught up with Huter.

"There was a communication breakdown," Maier said, adding ruefully, "and communications is the most important part of forecasting."

When interviewed a year after the fire, Huter said he was surprised to learn there had been a red flag. Nevertheless, the details of the forecasts at 6:00 P.M. and 9:00 P.M. were identical. If there was any doubt what the weather conditions implied, an accompanying fire-behavior analysis, high-lighted in boldface type, said, *"Extreme weather conditions exist for high rates of spread today. Expect hotspots along all sections of the fire perimeter."*

The rest of Huter's morning briefing was . . . brief. Huter put a few copies of the day's agenda, the incident-action plan, or IAP, on a table, but not enough to go around—a copy machine at the main fire camp had broken down. More copies might not have helped, since the document had nothing to say about a plan to fight the fire.

The key to every IAP is a section marked "control operations," which sets out the strategy for the day. Under that heading, the plan distributed by Huter said, "Will be announced at briefing."

The Sadler Fire investigation report cites the plan for creating confusion.

"The IAP was incomplete, contained a number of errors, and was not distributed to all of the crews and overhead," the fire report said. "People on the line that day reported persistent confusion over division locations and designations, resource numbers, and assignments."

Huter says he scouted the fire the night before and found a place to pinch it off with a bulldozer line. He acknowledged, though, that he never formally wrote down his plan.

Another odd thing happened at the briefing, though accounts of when and exactly what transpired vary considerably. At some point, perhaps as early as the morning briefing, Horton publicly claimed that his crew had conducted several burnouts. Huter then supposedly called Horton's unit "my Golden Gate 3 hotshots." Huter scoffs at the notion that he ever put Golden Gate 3 in the same class with hotshots. "*Never* were they called hotshots," Huter says.

Horton, however, remembers being taken aback by the promotion.

" 'Sir, we're not hotshots, we're a Type II crew,' " Horton remembers saying. "I thought I got the message across. There's a huge difference between prescribed fire, which we had done, and wildfire. I told [Huter] we were not an organized-burn crew. I should have made him repeat back to me, We're not hotshots. Maybe that was one of my mistakes."

It is not clear where, to whom, and under what circumstances Horton made his claims concerning Golden Gate 3's qualifications. But it is certain that his superiors—Huter and Shepard in particular—feel that he oversold the capabilities of his crew.

Though Huter's morning briefing was skimpy, Shepard had formed a favorable impression of Huter a month earlier, when he'd seen him in action on the Railroad Fire in Utah. Shepard was in training as a safety officer on the fire when a report came through of an engine crew overcome by fumes. The engine crew had been working near an old mine when a puff of red, evil-smelling smoke went up from a mound of tailings. The crew, dizzy and nauseated, jumped in their engine and started to drive off.

Huter, the division supervisor, arrived and ordered the engine crew to pull over and wait for medical assistance. He also instructed Shepard, who was standing by, to summon a hazardous-materials specialist; the fumes turned out to be sulfur, sickening but not fatal.

Shepard had admired the way Huter had put firefighter safety first and defused a potentially dangerous situation—nauseated, anxious people driving a fire engine. Huter's behavior looked especially good, Shepard thought, in contrast to that of two other supervisors who had shown up at the accident scene, toothpicks stuck in their mouths. In Shepard's opinion, they'd made fools of themselves by "horsing around" and telling "inappropriate jokes." Shepard would have reason to remember the two, Skip Hurt and Buzz Vanskike, operations chiefs for the incident-management team.

If Huter's briefing on the Sadler Fire was unclear, so was the general situation. The fire had become a threat to a cluster of homes to the north, the Lucky Nugget subdivision. Ranchers and other locals were pressing for a quick knockout because the fire was burning their grass and threatening their ranch buildings. Several ranchers dug their own firebreaks to protect their property; others camped out on the range to battle the fires. Many of them complained, then and later, that their efforts were not supported by federal firefighters.

Tom Tomera had watched a section of the fire near his Stonehouse Ranch, south of Elko, blow up into a cloud of smoke "like biblical times." The fire burned out 18,000 acres of grass in eighteen minutes. "We timed that one," Tomera said later. "It was like nothing you've ever seen. It barbecued the cattle, a horrible sight." Tomera runs about eighteen hundred head of cattle on 70,000 acres of private land and an additional 70,000 acres of leased public land.

"The feds drug their knuckles for a week or so and let that fire get going. About five-thirty in the afternoons, when the winds hit, they'd jump in their trucks and go to dinner. We lived like wildcats out there, moving from ranch to ranch, staying out in the hills. That's the only time you can fight those fires, at night."

Tomera and other ranchers met several times with federal fire supervisors, but went away angry. "They wouldn't integrate us into their meetings. We didn't know what was going on."

The federal government was not popular in Elko County, a center of the Sagebrush Rebellion, a broadly based antigovernment movement in the West. Gloria Flora, supervisor of the Humboldt-Toiyabe National Forest, in Nevada, resigned in November 1999, claiming she feared for the physical safety of federal workers as a consequence of clashes with local people. "Fed bashing is a sport here in Nevada," she said in an open letter to employees.

A flash point was the *Elko Daily Free Press*, which "fueled anti-federal attitudes," the Forest Service claimed in a community-relations study made after the fire. The Elko newspaper attacked individual employees as well as the Forest Service, and failed to print stories about federal projects of benefit to the community, the study said. On the occasion of the Sadler Fire, the newspaper opined, under the heading "Barbed Wire," "In a typical governmental response, fire crews showed up in Elko a couple of days too late to be much help with the range fires that began Aug. 4, but just in time to claim the credit."

The newspaper has since changed hands, but at the time of the Sadler Fire public pressure was a "contributing factor" to the push to control the fire quickly, according to the Sadler Fire investigation report.

The federal firefighters, meanwhile, had problems among themselves. On the day of Huter's briefing, the Sadler Fire was being passed from a Type II incident-management team to the more capable Type I team, a normal procedure when fires grow complex. The handoff, though, was rushed. The old team usually sticks around for twenty-four hours to ensure continuity, but not this time.

The Type II incident-commander, Paul Hefner, said he had called for the Type I team himself. "People were tired, the overhead was stretched thin, we didn't have the resources," Hefner said. But he remembers feeling pushed aside by the fresh team, and others remember him complaining about it at the time.

The new team, however, had complaints of its own. Ed Storey, its commander, said later that Hefner's team left without providing adequate information about the fire. No one from the departing Type II incident command team, for example, attended Huter's morning briefing at Jiggs.

"We did not inherit anything of significance from the previous team," Storey said. "We didn't even have good intelligence on the fire, where the fire line might be, how far the fire had advanced. We were flying blind on how to attack it."

The Type I incident command team had an enviable safety record—no time lost to accidents during seven years of operations—but had been involved in an incident the year before over questionable claims for hours worked and travel expenses while fighting fires in Florida. They were exonerated, but a bad feeling lingered on. Storey was a new addition to the team; he was considered a competent firefighter but mild-mannered to a fault. "Ed doesn't like to hear bad news," a team member remarked later.

Huter's morning briefing broke up quickly, and crews began to form up at once. Golden Gate 3's leaders went off in different directions. Giampaoli's cheap boots were falling apart, and Horton told Naar to accompany him to Elko to have them repaired. Horton told the rest of the crew to hustle aboard the bus to move out before the hotshot crews, the Smokey Bear and Dalton crews, who were heading for the same rally point, were ready.

"Let's not let them beat us to the fire," Horton said.

"Tim got into his hotshot mode and was pushing us," Hawk remembers. "He wanted to look good in front of the hotshots. I wasn't uncomfortable with that; I wanted fire. What I did *not* agree to was [the later] violation of safety rules."

The bus headed through dry rolling hills dotted with sagebrush and pinyon pines. Dust filled the bus so thickly that firefighters had to tie bandannas over their faces to keep from choking. Horton passed around a note: Keep heads up for a wind shift!

The bus labored up one especially steep rise, its tires slipping in the dust, and died. "Oh, God, not again," someone yelled, but by then the crew was too cranky for bus jokes. The crew piled out of the bus, picked up their gear, and began to slog toward the rally point nearly a mile away, a broad, open spot called the Big Safety Zone, on the east side of the fire.

By the time they arrived, a sizable force had gathered: bulldozers, fire engines, water tenders—and the Smokey Bear and Dalton Hotshots. Horton had lost his first race of the day. Shepard was there, too, talking with the Smokey Bear and Dalton superintendents.

According to the fire-investigation report, in the course of the morning the superintendents refused Shepard's order to conduct a burnout in front of the advancing fire. The hotshots were "reluctant" to do the job until they'd secured the eastern flank of the fire, the report says. The report commended the hotshots for recognizing "the hazard inherent in backfiring" and insisting on securing the flank first.

Shepard says there was no refusal. He agreed with the hotshot superintendents that the east flank had to be secured first. At no time, he says, did they refuse a direct order from him.

A refusal is no small thing in the quasi-military culture of wildland fire-fighters. Every supervisor has the right to turn down an assignment considered too risky, but crews have been relieved or called "chicken" for just saying no. After the South Canyon Fire, however, where overly aggressive actions contributed to the fourteen deaths, the "just say no" response became common practice among crews.

What happened between Shepard and the hotshots was more complex than the description in the fire report. After leaving the Jiggs fire camp, Shepard took a wrong turn on his way to the Big Safety Zone and drove south toward the advancing fire front. He wound through the hills until he came upon a finger of fire in an area called Crane Springs. The flames were low, scattered, and sparse, but if they livened up, they could flank the Big Safety Zone.

"There was no immediate danger, no deep flame front," Shepard said later.

He reversed and drove to the Big Safety Zone, where he met the superintendents, Rich Dolphin of the Smokey Bear and Neil Metcalf of the Dalton Hotshots. Dolphin and Metcalf had seen the smoke from Crane Springs for themselves and realized the flanking potential.

Shepard raised the subject of the hotshots conducting a burnout to the north along Huter's bulldozer line, which was under construction. Shepard says "ordered" is too strong a word for what he did at this point, and Dolphin and Metcalf agree. "I told the two supes somebody needs to scout the flank to the south and I couldn't be two places at once," Shepard remembered.

"They both volunteered, and thinking two heads are better than one, I left it at that."

Dolphin and Metcalf remember taking more of the initiative themselves. "There was no firm plan in place at that time, except to check things out, come back, and meet again," Metcalf said later.

"Everybody was fine with us scouting," Dolphin said.

It was just past 9:30 A.M. when the hotshot superintendents set off to reconnoiter, leaving their crews behind. Shepard headed in the opposite direction to check on the bulldozer line.

As Shepard drove along, the country began to change. The trees thinned out. The hills became a series of ledges, reminders of the ancient shoreline of the post–mountain building geologic era.

The dozer line, which was Huter's idea for stopping the fire, was being constructed at the point where the ledges gave way to a flat basin, dotted with sparse sagebrush and grass. A dozer line by itself would not stop the Sadler Fire: flames in Nevada that summer were jumping dozer lines six blades wide. But a crew could walk along the line and light backfires, which would burn out fuel in the path of the main fire. If the plan worked, the main fire and backfires would burn into each other in a spinning pyre of flame and die out.

It was not an unreasonable plan. The point was to keep the fire from spreading into the basin, where it would threaten scattered ranch buildings, grasslands, and housing, including the Lucky Nugget subdivision seven miles to the north. The objective to "keep fire south of Lucky Nugget subdivision" was noted as early as the previous day in the Type II team's action plan, though that plan said nothing about how the objective was to be carried out. Hefner, the Type II incident commander, says there was talk on his team about stopping the fire with a bulldozer line, but he remembers no specifics.

When Shepard reached the dozer line, it was not yet completed. He drove the length of the line, about a mile and a third, and encountered two bulldozers widening it and pushing out rectangular safety zones every quarter mile or so. The safety zones looked too small to Shepard, and he left orders to enlarge them.

The dozer line ended at a large previously burned area, which came to be called the Big Black. Shepard figured that if he staged a crew in the Big Black, he could begin the backfire operation the moment the dozer line was finished. The exposed east flank of the fire would be secured by the road there, as long as the weather stayed calm.

"It was a simple procedure," Shepard remembers. The burn crew could take a safety zone with them as they walked the dozer line—the very fire they would be lighting. If the burners moved slowly, the backfire would follow at their heels. If anything went wrong, they could step into the good black created by their backfire.

At this hour "a kindergarten class could have handled the burnout," Shepard said later. A fire always looks its best in the morning, when temperature and humidity are low, winds generally calm, and crews fresh. "That was my plan, take it easy, maintain control, do the burnout in strips," Shepard said.

It was about 10:30 A.M. by the time Shepard returned to the Big Safety Zone, intending to assign one hotshot crew to the burnout and the other to securing the east flank. Shepard would take charge of the burnout, and Mike Head, a division supervisor who had shown up looking for an assignment, could oversee the flanking operation.

Shepard approached the Smokey Bear and Dalton Hotshots, who were waiting for their superintendents to return from scouting. The following episode, which was characterized in the fire-investigation report as a refusal, turned into a professional and personal catastrophe for Shepard.

Shepard told the foremen of the Smokey Bear and Dalton Hotshots that he needed a crew to conduct the burnout. "I talked to the two foremen and the first words out of their mouths were, 'Well, we don't like to do anything without our supes.' And I thought, Boy, what's the deal with this? As a hotshot supe myself I trusted my foreman to make decisions. I was available on the radio for consultation.

"I told them, 'You got radios. Call them up and let them know what my plan is. You decide which one of you is coming along, doesn't matter to me. I just want a hotshot crew.'"

The order did not sit well with John Kennedy, foreman of the Smokey Bear Hotshots. "I expressed my feeling that I was uncomfortable initiating a tactic such as the burning operation without the information that was being obtained by the two crew superintendents," Kennedy remembers. "The same misgivings were voiced by the overhead on the Dalton crew. I stated that we should continue to wait for the crew supers to return with the results of the reconnaissance."

"What about safety zones?" one of the foremen asked Shepard.

Shepard said the zones were under construction. "You got a three-blade-wide dozer line, safety zones every quarter of a mile, and we're improving them to make them large enough to accommodate crews," he said.

The foremen would not budge.

Shepard felt more than a little put out. Here he was, a former hotshot superintendent, now a division supervisor, being stonewalled by a couple of hotshot foremen. But he had few alternatives. He offered to go back to the dozer line and check for a second time on the safety zones, jumped in his pickup, and left.

Minutes later, the two superintendents, Dolphin and Metcalf, returned to the Big Safety Zone, worried by what they had seen—an active, running fire threatening the east flank.

With Shepard gone, it fell to Head, the spare division supervisor, to brief the superintendents.

"This is where things get funny," Dolphin said later. "There was no big argument. We were asked to initiate burning to the north [along the dozer line]. I said, 'No, we're going to go back down and do this.' I got my crew and took off. If that's considered a refusal, I refused."

Metcalf agrees.

"A person can read it as if we refused an assignment," Metcalf said later. "But nobody really refused anything. I thought Shepard was out of the picture, gone to another division."

The fire-investigation report, though, reads as though the superintendents, not the foremen, refused to conduct the burnout.

"About 11 A.M. the hotshot superintendents returned from their reconnaissance to the south," the report says. "When Shepard asked them to burn the dozer line across the head of the fire, they refused to accept the assignment until the east flank to the south was secured."

Bob Lee, leader of the fire-investigation team and the BLM's fire-management officer for New Mexico, says the hotshot superintendents repeatedly told investigators that they'd refused the burnout assignment. "Rich Dolphin said he told Shepard, 'No way, we're not going to do that,'" Lee remembers. "We asked him if he was sure, and he said yes."

Conflicting accounts aside, several things happened for certain. Shepard tried to get a hotshot crew to conduct the burnout. Two hotshot superintendents and their foremen turned him down. The hotshots just said no, whether it was loud and clear and whether or not it was to Shepard's face.

One intriguing question is what would have happened if a hotshot crew had conducted the burnout that morning, while weather conditions were calm. The hotshots might well have brought it off. But their east flank would have been exposed, contrary to standard fire procedures—it took forty hotshots until afternoon to secure that flank. In the judgment of the hotshots, seconded by Lee's investigation team, the risk was too great.

While all this was happening, Golden Gate 3 hung out at the Big Safety Zone, alternately bored and excited. They could hear the fire, several lines of hills away, rumble with the sound of a distant stampede. Even from that distance, the fire put on quite a show.

The smoke formed a rainbow above the fire: black smoke shot through with orange-yellow flames formed the lowest arc, billowing gray smoke the next, and a layer of wispy white smoke the topmost ring. Several firefighters snapped photos.

"You look at those pictures now and think, 'They put us in front of *that* fire?' " one said later.

Huter, meanwhile, showed up at the Big Safety Zone looking for a crew to carry out his plan for a burnout along the dozer line. With the hotshots at work on the east flank, Huter approached Golden Gate 3.

As Huter remembers it, he asked Horton, "Do you guys want to do it?" and Horton replied, "Yeah, yeah, we can do it. We've done some burning. We'll take care of it."

If Horton had been honest about Golden Gate 3's lack of experience, Huter said later, he would have gotten a couple of hotshots to handle the burnout. "We've done burns three times worse with hotshot crews," he says.

Horton remembers the episode differently.

"I told him we had been burning the past several days, but I tried to say we were not like an organized burn module. We weren't hotshots."

Huter radioed Shepard that Golden Gate 3 was on its way to the dozer line. He also ordered a helicopter aloft to scout during the burnout and dispatched a strike team of fire engines in support. Huter's orders covered the bases, Shepard thought, but it sounded as though Huter was running the burnout operation.

"My first thought was, Jeez, is this Dan's place to be directing the resources on my division?" Shepard said. "I didn't raise a stink about it at the time because I'm a fairly easygoing person, I can go with the flow. At this point the flow looked all right."

Shepard thought conditions for the burnout at that time, about eleven A.M., were "perfect." The fire was a good mile and a half to the south of the dozer line. There was hardly any wind. There were plenty of fire engines and bulldozers standing by in support. "At the time I felt that even an inexperienced crew could handle the assignment with the proper supervision," he said later.

Golden Gate 3 hangs out at the Big Safety Zone the morning of August 9, the day of the entrapment. The Sadler Fire is visible in the background. After several hours of waiting, they went by truck from here to the dozer line for the burnout. Courtesy Derek Hyde

The morning, though, was slipping away. A string of minor screwups, none fatal in itself, had caused one delay after another—the clumsy communication of the overall plan, the dozer line not being finished, the trouble over assigning a burn squad. No one person was responsible for what happened. Rather, there was a series of mistakes and misjudgments on the part of many people, each error attaching itself to the next in an unbroken chain, and by doing so giving a perverse legitimacy to the whole process of making mistakes. As the errors mounted up, the sum became greater than its parts.

"There was no way to recall the burn."

"Gather up," Horton called out, and the electricity in his voice gave it away. After hours of watching a fire in the hills, Golden Gate 3 was going to fight it. Horton told the crew to throw their gear into a waiting truck; half of them would make up a first load, and the others would have to wait.

"I remember this feeling of leaving a safety zone, and there, running parallel to us on the left, is this huge fire," said Hyde, the science whiz. "There was oohing and aahing, but I don't remember anybody being scared."

Hawk, the ex-bartender, thought they were leaving because fire threatened the Big Safety Zone. She clambered aboard the truck with the gear, remembering the lesson to always stay within hand's reach of tools and fire shelter.

As the trucks started off, another vehicle approached from the opposite direction. What followed was a scene from every grade-B war movie: in the back of the approaching vehicle sat a group of firefighters, hollow-eyed and dust-covered from having spent the night on the fire. The fresh troops stared at the slack-jawed vets. Hawk could almost hear a narrator's voice intone, *Don't turn your head; that's what you're going to look like in a few days.*

The truck dropped the crew off at the Y intersection, where the road met the dozer line about two miles north of the Big Safety Zone. When the full crew had assembled at the intersection, it was decided to have them march the full length of the dozer line to the Big Black, so the wind would be blowing the right direction for the burnout. They needed the wind in their faces, to stop the fire they would light from racing ahead of them and possibly swinging around and endangering them. They began to slog through the ankle-deep dust of the dozer line, with the wind at their backs. Once they reached the Big Black, they could turn, face the wind, and commence the burnout.

The terrain was gentle and even Mingo, the smoker, had no trouble keeping up.

Christensen, the firehouse recruit, had begun to wonder about safety zones when she saw the first one. Cool, she thought. "It was a small safety zone, but the bells didn't say, 'It's small.' The bells said, 'Okay, that's one.'"

As they approached the Big Black, Christensen checked her watch. It was 2:00 P.M.; the morning was long gone. She took out a humidity gauge, swung it through the air, and checked the result. Something was wrong.

"I couldn't get a constant reading," Christensen said. She walked into the brush and tried again, but the gauge gave different readings each time she swung it; all were low, in the vicinity of a skin-cracking 13 percent.

Maybe I'm swinging the thing wrong, she thought, but how hard is it to swing a humidity gauge? She asked another firefighter to try, and he had the same problem.

"It didn't settle right, but no major bells went off," she said. Mixed humidity readings, though, are one sign of rapidly changing conditions.

The fire, more than a mile to the south, appeared calm. Acting on Huter's orders, an aerial observer, Ken Bailey, had boarded a helicopter at about 1:30 P.M. to scout the area. Bailey reported seeing no intense flames, no fast-burning runs. But he had to cut short his scouting mission because a tight flight helmet was giving him a screaming headache.

"It looked like the green light," Shepard remembers. "We had missed my personal deadline to finish the burnout in the morning, but conditions hadn't changed yet."

Everything was in place: Shepard, Huter, and Golden Gate 3 were at the Big Black. Fire engines stood by at both ends of the dozer line. Horton had picked three of his more experienced hands to join him on the burn squad: Christensen, Deaton, and Hyde. The other fifteen would remain in the Big Black.

"Horton appeared to me to know what he was doing," Shepard remembers. "This looked like a pretty simple assignment for him."

Huter handed over the operation to Shepard.

"Okay, it's your baby," Huter said.

"Let's do it," Shepard replied.

The burn squad lit drip torches, which drooled flaming blobs of gasoline mixed with oil. At that moment the sky darkened to the south, over the fire, and the wind freshened. A heavy smoke column arose, flattened, then rose again, an unmistakable sign of gusting winds.

"We missed it! We missed the time window!" Deaton told Christensen.

Shepard had seen enough; he ordered the burn squad to snuff the torches.

Smoke rose in gray, cloudlike billows, but there was no plume to signal that the fire had exploded. A day's work had been directed toward this moment: nobody wanted to give up this close to the finish.

Huter, Shepard, and Horton held a hurried conference. The fire was moving slowly, but if left unchecked it would jump the dozer line and spread into the basin. There was a contingency plan to construct a fire line around the Lucky Nugget subdivision to protect it, but thousands of acres of rangeland could be lost.

As they talked, the wind settled back down. But instead of blowing in their faces, it had shifted direction and blew at their backs, the wrong direction for a burnout.

"Okay, we can't do it from here," Shepard said.

Horton had an idea: Why not go back to the Y intersection and burn out from there?

Well, why not? Horton's idea could save the day.

"If we didn't attempt a burnout, the fire would get away," Shepard later wrote in his log. What he remembers saying at the time was: "Sounds good, let's go do that"—a remark he would come to regret.

"What I *should* have said was 'Let's go *look* at that,'" he remarked with the wisdom of hindsight.

Horton has his own regrets.

"Straight up, at no time did I demand that we do the burnout," Horton said later. "The crew was involved. I told them, 'If you don't want to do this, speak up.' They had plenty of opportunity to open their mouths. I would have honored that—I always have." A year earlier, on a small fire in Idaho, Horton had ordered a helicopter crew into a safety zone after a single complaint about the potential danger of a burst of fire.

"On the Sadler Fire, I *should* have said. 'I feel comfortable but I'm not getting feedback' and stopped it," Horton said. "I don't have forty eyes, I can't see everything. Nobody did."

It was now nearly three P.M.; the red-flag warning had cited the afternoon, with its winds and dryness, as the time to expect extreme fire behavior. But Horton's idea sounded too good to pass up. Shepard, hoping to speed matters, put the burn squad in the back of his pickup to drive them to the Y intersection, a violation of safety rules, which forbid letting firefighters ride in the open back of a truck.

"Here I was, a safety officer, division supe, and ex–hotshot supe, and I'm carrying people in the back of my truck," Shepard later said ruefully. "Probably not the smartest thing to do. But I wanted to get that crew over there as soon as I could."

The Golden Gate 3 crew members left behind in the Big Black watched nervously as their comrades disappeared in Shepard's pickup. The Big Black did not appear to them directly linked to the dozer line—they saw what looked to them like an unburned strip of ground fifty feet wide lay between the two. If the burn squad had to run from the dozer line into the Big Black, they could be cut off. Inside the Big Black, much of the sagebrush was only lightly charred and could reignite. On top of that, a barbed-wire fence ran through the Big Black and could hamper a retreat.

A better name than Big Black, Golden Gate 3 decided, would be "*Unclear Black.*"

Shepard drove along the dozer line "as safe as I could," feeling guilty about having passengers in the back. A more pressing safety issue presented itself directly. Christensen, riding in the cab with Shepard, remembers Shepard remarking, as they passed one of the safety zones, "I told the dozer to make those bigger; I'll have to get them out here to do that."

"I was thinking, Why not do it now? But I never said anything," Christensen said.

As the pickup neared the Y intersection, two men appeared ahead and Shepard braked to a stop. The men, Bob Hawkins, a field observer, and Joe Reyes, a division supervisor, told Shepard that Huter had sent them to look for an assignment.

Here we go again, Shepard thought, Huter making assignments without telling me. Shepard had a job for the pair, however. He quickly briefed them on the burnout plan and asked if they would keep an eye on the burn squad when it went past them. Reyes could stay where he was; Hawkins could post himself on a nearby hummock.

"The crew boss [Horton] was anxious to get started, so they drove on ahead," Hawkins told fire investigators later. "I remember Joe and I commenting on how young the crew looked."

Shepard was pulling into the Y intersection when he heard Horton say, "Okay, as soon as we get there, jump out, light your torches, and let's go!" For Shepard, this became the crucial moment, the point at which he lost responsibility for what followed.

"That was the whole thing right there," Shepard said later.

Shepard's claim for diminished responsibility, however, depends on Horton having done exactly what he describes: ordering the burn squad to begin firing immediately and without checking further with Shepard.

Christensen, sitting next to Shepard, says she could not hear anyone's voice from the back of the truck. "I don't know how Shepard could have heard Tim say anything," she said later.

The answer to that may be simple enough: Shepard says his window was rolled down and Christensen's was rolled up.

Horton has a muddled recollection of the episode. He remembers telling Shepard that he was going to light a test burn, not the burnout itself. If it was a test, it was a short one, that quickly became the real thing. He also has a vague recollection, which he himself doubts, of telling Shepard, "You're my lookout, right?"

The two others in the back of the pickup, Hyde and Deaton, say Horton had grown frustrated by the delays. When Shepard stopped to talk to Reyes and Hawkins, Horton became agitated, as noted by Reyes and Hawkins.

"Tim's attitude was, Who are these guys?" Hyde recalls. "Tim wanted to go."

As the pickup neared the Y intersection, Horton began to tug on work gloves, which rang an alarm bell for Deaton: Horton never wore gloves; he liked to work barehanded. Pulling on gloves meant raised stakes. Next he'll be pulling down the heat shroud from inside his helmet, Deaton thought. He tried to make a joke of it: "If you pull down your shroud, Tim, I'm going to get nervous."

Horton told him the situation was not that extreme, but he admitted to feeling "an urgency."

"Yeah, me too," Deaton replied.

Did Horton or did he not tell Deaton and Hyde to hit the ground running?

"Yep, that was when we got there," Hyde said.

Deaton remembers Horton's instructions almost word for word the way Shepard does: "When you get out of the pickup, I want those torches lit and ready to go."

Horton and the others moved fast—Christensen had to bolt from the cab to catch up.

Shepard watched the squad deploy—"just shaking my head," he said. Then he sensed something very wrong: once again, the wind had shifted 180 degrees—*it was blowing from the east, at the firefighters' backs, the wrong direction.* It was going to push the fire ahead of the burn squad, exactly the situation they had twice crossed the length of the dozer line to avoid.

"We're putting fire on the ground!" Horton announced over the radio. The burnout flared smartly; in moments orange flames rose forty feet high.

Shepard, too far away to be heard by voice, yelled into his radio, "Don't get ahead of your support!" Engine No. 3636, assigned to the burn squad, was just pulling out of the Y intersection, following them.

Once fire touched the ground, Shepard thought, it was over. "There was no way to recall the burn," he said later. "All I saw was Tim Horton, head to the ground, torch in his left hand, humping up the hill on the Cat line."

Shepard stood next to his pickup like a man adrift. Five years earlier he had watched nine Prineville Hotshots step off a ridge on Storm King Mountain, heading to a fire line out of sight below him. Shepard had arrived late on the mountain, and no one had asked him, the Prineville superintendent, for an opinion about the assignment; he had not offered one. He had taken up a lookout position on the ridge and stayed in touch with the hotshots by radio. A few hours later, minutes after four P.M., Jon Kelso, a Prineville squad boss, had called him: "Tom, there's a spot across the draw."

"Abandon the line, get out," Shepard had replied, but by then it was too late.

On the Sadler Fire, Shepard watched the burn squad disappear over a rise.

"At this point I knew a mistake had been made," Shepard said later. "The big mistake was Tim Horton not checking conditions and not confirming with me that he should go ahead and light. Once it was lit, we were committed."

Shepard took a flare pistol out of his truck; if he shot a flare, he reckoned, it might create enough heat to suck flames back toward him, away from the burn squad. Shepard fired several flares. Hawkins came down from his lookout post after the burn squad passed him and joined Shepard. Hawkins had never seen a flare gun fired before. Shepard showed him how to do it, and Hawkins fired a round. The flares sputtered out to no effect.

"Help me, I'm burning!"

A dollop of fire from a drip torch turned sagebrush and grass into a furious blaze. Everyone on the burn squad—Horton, Christensen, Hyde, and Deaton—started out with a torch or fusee. "It went perfect, it was beautiful," Horton said later—except that one torch was more than enough, and after a minute the others left the firing to Horton.

Horton bowed and bent, skipped and ran as he dripped liquid fire onto the ground; the burn squad broke into a jog to keep up. Everyone slowed momentarily to let Engine No. 3636 catch up, which it did at 3:05 P.M., according to the log of Todd McDivitt, the engine captain.

The backfire sent heat pulsing over the dozer line. Horton hollered to McDivitt to have someone toss fusees into the fire to draw it back from the burn squad, the same tactic Shepard had tried without success. Three crewmen jumped off the engine.

The wind shifted again, now blowing from the direction of the main fire, to the south. "Smoke was very thick and started to roll over the dozer line," McDivitt's log records at 3:12 P.M. The engine became a ghost ship for the burn squad, visible through the smoke only by the flash of its emergency lights.

Three minutes later, at 3:15 P.M. by McDivitt's log, the backfire jumped over the dozer line.

"Spot over the line! Spot over the line!" McDivitt barked into his radio. "Stop the burning!"

McDivitt's crew turned from firing flares to battling the spot fire. Smoke boiled upward; Huter, standing near the Big Black, called into his radio at around this time, "Everybody get back and into safety zones!"

Not a single soul on the burn squad remembers hearing Huter's or McDivitt's warnings. The squad was using its own radio frequency, not the main work channel on which the calls were made. Horton says he monitored the main work channel, but it was filled with routine radio chatter. There was a safety zone a quarter mile ahead, but the squad kept right on burning, and had a pretty good time doing it.

A minute or two before the warnings, Horton had passed off the drip torch to let the others have a chance with it. "Trade off when your arm gets tired," Horton told Deaton, who quickly fell under the spell of the fiery wand. The torch spilled flaming goo onto the ground, producing darts of fire, which transformed into bonfires bright as the sun. A landscape of fire came to life under Deaton's touch. When someone asked if his arm was tired, he said, No way.

The immediate danger passed as the engine crew brought the spot fire under control.

The wind flapped at the backfire; one minute the burn squad had to jog to stay ahead of it, the next they had to stop and wait for it to catch up. Christensen had just begun her turn with the drip torch when she came upon a big juniper tree, on the same side of the dozer line as the main fire. If the juniper caught fire, she figured, it would send embers showering across the dozer line. She began to circle the juniper with the torch to create a fire break; the rest of the squad stopped to watch.

"Everybody was glowing by then," Christensen said. "It was so much fun."

As Christensen finished the ring, a truck appeared out of nowhere. Once again, at a moment of crisis, the irrepressible Naar made a dramatic reappearance by jumping out of a vehicle.

"Hey, nice timing," Christensen sang out.

Naar and Giampaoli had driven to the Jiggs fire camp after the emergency boot repair in Elko and had heard about the breakdown of the crew bus. If a hill had been too steep for the bus, they figured, they would never make it in the sedan they were driving. Naar, however, located a tow truck headed out to the bus and, with his flair for improvised transportation, hitched a ride for himself and Giampaoli.

After a few miles, they saw heavy smoke rising from the fire.

"I told Peter, and I have lived to regret the words, 'Look, if it's not safe we're not going in,'" Naar remembers. "'We can sit in camp and watch it from there.'"

The tow truck took them as far as the stalled bus; from there, Naar raised Horton on the radio. Naar remembers Horton saying, "Great! You're here. We're starting to burn. We can use you." Those remarks sound too welcoming, considering the relationship between the two, and Giampaoli has a different memory. "Alex tried to contact Horton, but it was unclear to me that Tim was aware of our intent to join the crew," Giampaoli said later.

Naar managed to find another ride, this time aboard a State of Nevada truck driven by a man who gave his name as Harley, a firefighter coming off an all-night shift. Halfway to the Y intersection, they saw the Smokey Bear and Dalton Hotshots conducting a burnout from the road, securing the east flank of the fire. Flames from the burnout lapped across the track. Harley gunned the truck engine and headed off-road. "If he'd slowed down, we wouldn't have made it," Naar said later.

When they reached the Y intersection, everything there seemed "fairly relaxed" to Naar. The intersection was clear of smoke. None of the crews or supervisors seemed agitated. Naar talked Harley into driving him and Giampaoli on to the dozer line; in minutes, they saw the burn squad standing in a circle around a juniper tree.

Afterward, everyone asked, Why did Naar and Giampaoli not go on to the Big Black, where the majority of Golden Gate 3 was stationed? It was the natural assignment for Naar, taking charge of the crew left at the Big Black. The burn squad was down to using a single drip torch and did not need more hands.

Fire, though, is a captivating mistress. Naar yanked on his fire gear in such haste that he tore off his wristwatch, jamming it into a pocket instead of taking the time to strap it back on. He turned to thank Harley, but the off-duty firefighter had seen his chance and fled.

Naar remembers a warm welcome from Horton: "Tim said he was glad to see us," Naar said later.

Horton remembers the encounter differently.

"At the time I honestly believed that we could pull this off, everything was still going fine," Horton said later. "And here were two more bodies, one that I didn't really want. Wow. Okay. At the time, I dealt with it."

The hour was late, past three-thirty. The main fire drew closer. The wind blew every which way or not at all.

As the burn squad, now numbering six, resumed firing, a gigantic fire whirl erected to its rear in the direction of the main fire, a spinning mass of fire and dust shaped like a tornado—narrow at the base and gaping open at the top. The fire whirl danced and bent like a mad genie, nodding maniacally toward the dozer line. And it roared out a mighty bellow that shook the air.

"Stop! Stop!" Horton shouted. "Watch that! Watch that!"

What Horton meant was watch out, but the burn squad took him too literally and stopped to watch the show.

"It was a beautiful fire whirl," Deaton said later in a voice of wonder. "It was as big around as a car, maybe bigger. It was twenty feet tall, or taller. And the sound was like standing next to a freight train."

"It was louder than a freight train," added Naar. "Way louder."

Christensen, concentrating on her drip torch, heard someone shout, "Watch this!"

"I looked up and there's this . . . *wall* coming at us," she said later. "I'd never seen anything like it. It was monstrous. I stood there shocked."

The likely cause of the fire whirl was the burn squad itself; fire scientists later theorized that the squad's backfire collided with the main fire to create the whirl, which then sucked up everything in its path—sticks, tumbleweed, branches, and flame. The heavy top of the whirl leaned tipsily over the dozer line. As its narrow base followed, skittering across the line, it picked up white dust, which spiraled upward into the fiery whirl.

Striped like a candy cane! thought Hyde, watching from yards away.

As the whirl passed over the dozer line, it shut off the burn squad's view of Engine No. 3636. But, alarmingly, they could *hear* the vehicle: a pulsing *beep, beep, beep* from the backup signal told them that the engine crew had no choice but to retreat, leaving the squad alone.

The episode of the fire whirl proceeded in shutter stops for the watchers, one memorable frame after another. The weight of the dust bent the fire whirl to the ground on the opposite side of the dozer line. When the whirl touched ground, it burst like a bomb, scattering embers into the brush. A half dozen tiny new fires popped to life.

Hyde and Deaton took a few steps forward, intending to beat out the flames, but the little fires joined together and spread with mercurial swiftness.

Naar radioed for help.

"Golden Gate," he said to identify himself, trying to keep his voice level. "We've got six spots. We need air support. Air support would be helpful."

No one answered.

In the moments it took Naar to call, the six spot fires merged into three and then into a single wavering pool of flame. Naar had seen this happen before, in a training exercise when a pool of gasoline had been ignited. With their retreat cut off, the expanding pool of flames could flank and entrap them.

"Come on, let's keep burning, get the torches back up!" someone shouted.

"I was thinking, Let's get a buffer," said Christensen, who began to run and dip her torch at the same time.

In a flash the temperature around her soared and moisture was sucked out of the air. "My left side was starting to feel the heat—it went from ninety degrees to a hundred and thirty degrees in a moment. I was gasping. All I could think was: Burn, get a buffer, oh God, keep going."

Deaton was right behind Christensen with another torch. The dozer line dipped into a gulch, which made running easier but cut off their view. They knew their retreat was blocked and that they were being chased by two prongs of fire: the backfire along their left flank and the pool of fire on their right flank.

"Then we saw ahead, coming over a rise, the main fire," Hyde said later.

The trap was complete.

The main fire had paused at the crest of a ridge a half mile south of the dozer line, as fires will do at ridge tops before shifting to a downhill run. On the slope ahead, the juniper trees thinned out and the hills gave way to a series of open, grassy ledges. Among the ledges was the dozer line, and along it scurried a handful of human forms, no more relevant to the progress of the fire than pebbles. Beyond that lay the flat immensity of the basin.

The flame front on the crest was narrow, only a few hundred yards wide. But if it swept the dozer line unchecked, there would be no stopping it for miles and miles.

The fire gained body as it paused. The fresh south wind coming up behind it had increased in velocity as it funneled between surrounding mountain ranges; in a venturi effect, it gained power from compression. When the south wind hit the crest of the ridge, a "river of fire" spilled down the slope, in the words of Dan Huter, an experienced observer.

The flames cascaded from ledge to ledge. Juniper trees turned into geysers of fire. Swaths of grass burst into flame in a finger snap. At a distance of about sixty-five yards from the dozer line, the river of fire collided with the backfire, which probably created the fire whirl.

Flames, following behind the fire whirl, poured into a narrow gulch that pointed straight for the dozer line—the same gulch the burn squad ran into after seeing the fire whirl. The narrow gulch gave the flames a booster shot of energy, again from the venturi effect.

A line of flame twenty feet high and higher bore down on the burn squad. Smoke covered the sun. The roar of the fire swept the squad in a thunderous wave, and primitive terror struck at last.

Deaton asked what to do with the drip torches.

"Forget it—get rid of those things," Horton shouted, and began yelling at everyone to run.

Christensen tried to stub out her drip torch with her gloved hand, but the flaming mess would not snuff out. "I was sweating and couldn't breathe," she said. Three times she grabbed at the flaming wick before Horton screamed, "Drop it! Drop everything and run!" And still she held the torch, running now, but holding both the torch and a shovel-like tool. Everyone ran, each in a world where only legs and luck counted, blessed, miraculous luck—and maybe prayer too, if there was time for it.

Giampaoli, leading the pack, saw a hellish vision to his left: an unbroken wave of fire more than three times his height erupting black smoke. He ran parallel to the wave and so, as in a nightmare, he could not gain a step on it. Then ahead he saw what appeared to be a clearing, a safety zone, on the right side of the dozer line, away from the main fire. He yelled the news to the others and plunged on. He started up the far side of the gulch and slowed on the rise. His boots slid in the dust but held together. Hot, dry air tortured his lungs.

"I don't remember much about what I was thinking, except to continue running," Giampaoli recalled. "I did not want to burn. I remember a fast, rushing wind, incredible noise . . . fear and panic."

He felt a slap on the left side of his face and a terrible stinging.

"I ran into the safety zone, out from under the smoke, into sunshine." He did not stop running until he reached the side of the safety zone, as far from flames as he could get. He had kept his drip torch, not wanting to leave it burning in front of the others. He took out his fire shelter and, holding it folded like a brick, moved to where he could look back for everyone else.

Hyde, coughing and with his pack half unbuckled, tumbled into the clearing behind Giampaoli. Hyde's lungs screamed for air; he felt as though he had just climbed through a fire on Mount Everest. Hyde had started to race the fire at the first blast of hot air, shedding gear along the way: first the fusees from one hand and then, when someone yelled, "Drop your tools! Drop your tools!," the shovel from the other hand, regretting having done so when he realized he could have used the shovel as a heat shield. With both hands free, he undid the waistband of his pack.

At that moment he saw the blurry outline of the safety zone and raced toward it, his pack hanging half off. He tumbled into the zone and fell to his knees.

Where's everyone else? he thought. Where is everybody?

Deaton had watched Christensen struggle with her drip torch and had joined the chorus yelling, "Drop it! Drop it!" When Christensen finally let the torch go, Deaton began to run, checking for her over his shoulder. Christensen fell behind, and Deaton lost sight of her in the smoke.

"I was getting scared," Deaton said. "Keren was in good shape, but she was shorter and ran slower than everybody else. I yelled, 'Keren, run!'"

Deaton came to a halt and peered into the smoke. Horton and Naar, steps behind him, veered off the dozer line as though shoved by an invisible hand, and then the same wave of heat swept Deaton. He began to pull off his pack, grappling with the straps, but succeeding only in knocking off his hard hat.

As Deaton dived for the hat, Naar somehow accidentally gave it a kick. The hat was worth his life, Deaton thought. He had to cover his head. Almost sobbing, Deaton slid to his knees, grabbed the hat, and jammed it back on his head. Squatting in the grass, he wrestled off his pack and pulled out his fire shelter.

"I saw the grass turn to fire," he said. "It was too late for the shelter."

Deaton tried to slow his breathing. Don't inhale the hot gas when it comes, he told himself. Hot gas kills. He lay down in the grass, covered his face with his arms, and waited.

From the moment they began to run, Horton and Naar matched each other stride for stride, a working pair at last. They were a two-man chorus shouting, "Go! Go! Run! Run!" until everyone got the message. They brought up the rear of the squad to sweep the line, making sure everyone was accounted for.

When Don Mackey had swept the line on Storm King Mountain five years earlier, it had cost him his life. Mackey had been the smoke jumper in charge when the fire blew up, the man responsible for the section of fire line where the nine Prineville Hotshots and a group of smoke jumpers were working. Mackey directed one bunch of smoke jumpers to safety, then turned back to check on everyone else—nine hotshots and three smoke jumpers. One smoke jumper escaped; Mackey died with the others.

Naar was able to slip out of his pack with no trouble. In preparation for such a moment, he kept essentials—fire shelter, water bottle, and fusees—on a separate web belt. He held on to his shovel for a heat shield.

The wind tore at his hard hat, and he pulled down the chin strap with the guilty thought that it should have been in place long before. The heat pressed on him, but he tried to stay in the dozer line—the grass was a pool of unburned gasoline, as far as he was concerned. Christensen, a step or two ahead of him, swerved into the grass.

"Right there, I wrote her off," Naar said. "To me, she was gone. I'm not a martyr, and this was triage."

Naar heard Horton a step away praying out loud. He's gone, too, Naar thought.

Naar felt a searing pain in his chest: one moment he had been gulping in huge breaths, the next moment nothing but dry heat. His lungs recoiled. He would be dead in seconds if he stayed upright. Naar dived headfirst into the unburned grass.

Horton, running flat out next to Naar, figured it had to be the weather that had betrayed him. He had known the afternoon winds would be strong; he had known the fire was building up. The burnout, though, had proceeded beautifully. He and his crew had been at the head of a major fire, conducting the day's biggest operation, the crucial burnout. He had picked people who could handle the job. There would be more plum assignments to come.

Then out of nowhere a gigantic fire whirl had appeared, followed by a wall of flame, and suddenly it was the worst moment of his life. It had to be a dirty trick of the weather, not something he had done himself.

God would not betray him like this. It had to be the wind.

"Oh God," he cried out, "don't let me die today." He had not lived long enough. He had a wife and children. Oh God, take care of them, he thought. Lord, don't let me die!

Things began to happen at speeds Horton had only heard about. Low grass transformed into tall flames. A wave of airless heat struck him a blow. He felt a stinging pain on his neck and dived headfirst into the grass, landing next to Naar. When he opened his eyes everything around him—the ground, his gloved hands, the exposed skin of his wrist, and his yellow fire shirt—shimmered an incandescent white, except for one dark, round patch under his head, as though an atomic bomb had gone off and all that remained was a nuclear shadow.

"I was the shadow," Horton said. "I thought that was me burning up. I thought, I'm not going to make it, and yelled out loud, 'God, I don't want to die today.' I'll never forget the white, not ever—it was bright, clean white."

Christensen shrieked from a few feet away, "Help me, I'm burning!" Standing up to help her would be suicidal, Horton knew, and he stayed on the ground.

Christensen had forced herself to stub out the drip torch before she threw it away. "I knew we were in trouble, but I didn't want that torch to explode in front of everyone," she said later. She began to run. A scant ten feet of unburned grass remained between the advancing wall of flame and the dozer line. A blast of heat reached ahead of the advancing flames and scorched her face.

"The burning on my face wouldn't stop," she said. "The fire was on us."

The heat sent her stumbling into the grass and sagebrush. She took a quick glance over her shoulder and saw fingers of flame following her.

"The tops of the flames were way over my head, trying to claw me, pull me back into the fire." Oh God, she thought, I don't want to be here. Not with all this *fuel*. Where is everybody else?

She had never felt so alone. Then she took a breath of dense, heavy smoke. The fire was closing around her in a fist.

She grabbed her radio—her last link to the outside world—and yelled "Help me!," but she had not yet depressed the transmission button. Then, thinking she had released the button and was in her own private world, she cried out from the deepest part of herself, "Mommy, help me! I'm burning!"

Her call, which was one radio transmission heard clearly this day, stunned the rest of Golden Gate 3 at the Big Black. Though the quotation was blacked out of testimony in official reports, it became widely known and a source of embarrassment for Christensen. No one knows for certain what they will say or do when faced with death. But Christensen's words echo the cries of untold thousands who have faced imminent death in wars and natural and human disasters, probably dating back to the origins of the human race, and there is no shame in it.

Christensen stumbled on, fumbling her fire shelter out of her pack. Just ahead lay a patch of ground free of sagebrush and juniper, a place to shelter. She had nothing with which to burn a larger safety zone—she had used up her fusees—and no time for that anyway. Desperation growing, she tore off her pack and threw it away.

As she staggered toward the open ground, she wrestled with gloved hands to grip the tab on the plastic case of her fire shelter. Her hands shook uncontrollably as adrenaline drained blood from them, sending it to her heart and lungs. The faces of people she loved swirled into her mind's eye.

I will never see my boyfriend, Casey, again, she thought. He is going to be so mad. My mother and father, never again.

She made herself stop and take a deep breath. She gripped the tab on the fire shelter with all her might and gave it a yank. As the shelter spilled out, the wind caught the material and slammed it into her face and chest, blinding her.

She forced herself to think. She turned and faced the wind and fire to keep the shelter against her body. She peeled the shelter off herself and stepped into its straps. Crouching with the shelter over her back, she took a final glance around.

Her last thought was: Oh God.

In that moment the sky turned blue. The wind dropped to nothing. The smoke lifted, and the fire's terrible roar died out. Flames straightened, shortened, and burned quietly.

The six members of Golden Gate 3's burn squad rose Lazarus-like from the ground, not trusting the last-second reprieve. Deaton looked up to find himself only a few yards from the comforting outline of the safety zone, already occupied by Hyde and Giampaoli. But where was Christensen, he thought? She had been a step behind him; she had to be close by. He looked back the way he had come.

The Sadler Fire seen from the Big Black as it trapped six members of Golden Gate 3.
Courtesy Dan Bowmen

A BLM firefighter tries to raise Golden Gate 3's burn squad on the radio from the edge of the Big Black during the entrapment. Courtesy Don Bowmen

Deaton and Christensen saw each other at about the same moment and locked eyes. Christensen rose to her feet and tucked her fire shelter under her arm: she had fought hard for that shelter and was not going to give it up lightly.

"I'm here, are you okay?" Deaton called to her, as they stumbled toward each other.

"Her shelter was unfolded," Deaton said. "Her face was red. She probably looked like me—scared." They helped each other to the safety zone.

Horton and Naar got to their feet and joined the others in the safety zone. The entrapment was over; they had escaped the flames.

The Sadler Fire report does not explain why the fire turned away at this crucial moment except to say that nothing unnatural happened. The report puts it this way: "The investigators had no reason to believe that any unforecasted fire event occurred," which means the episode can be explained without citing supernatural or divine intervention, abundant invocations of these forces before and during the episode notwithstanding.

Any number of "natural" scenarios cover the facts. Perhaps the three arms of fire—the main fire, the burnout started by Golden Gate 3, and the spot fires started by the fire whirl—briefly canceled one another out. It could have happened that way, fire scientists said later. Perhaps a lull occurred as the wind shifted onto another tack, which it had done many times that afternoon. Fire behavior is made up of many variables, and science can explain and predict only so much.

Whatever happened, firefighters came to call the escape a little miracle. Some, like Horton, believe the hand of a merciful Providence intervened to give nature a nudge. Others think Lady Luck deserves the credit. Still others were left bewildered. In any case, for once the natural world seemed to give a damn about what happened to the people in it.

"If Horton had waited . . . "

The worst was over for Golden Gate 3, but trouble had just begun for Shepard. The picture of his fate emerged as from a developing negative, drawing him back to a past he had no desire to revisit and forward into a

A firefighter, kneeling in sage next to the Big Black, holds his head in despair as the entrapment occurs. Courtesy Don Bowmen

149

clouded future. Again and again, Shepard would return in his mind to the scene of Horton jumping out of his pickup, as though it held the key to personal redemption. He had to make people understand: the entrapment was *Horton's* fault, not his.

"I couldn't believe that anybody would pull a stunt like that," he said later. "Horton started lighting with no consideration whatsoever and oblivious to the fire's environmental conditions and without getting approval from me." Again: "Horton displayed his stupidity by commencing ignition without authorization, and with the wind at his back." And the kicker: "If Horton had waited . . . for my go-ahead, I guarantee we would not have attempted that burnout." And more in that vein.

After Horton and the burn squad took off, Shepard had handled other business—shooting the flares, problems with fuel for the bulldozers—until he felt "overwhelmed," he later told investigators, though he regretted the remark and tried to recant it.

"I think I may have told the investigation team I was overwhelmed by the sheer number of resources, but this was a poor choice of words," he said. "I was up to my ears with developing a plan, getting the lay of the land, scouting the fire, observing fire behavior and weather, and generally getting the big picture . . . and trying to figure out why the division had so many division supervisors. But I was not overwhelmed."

The burn squad had been out of sight for several minutes when someone called by radio for a bulldozer—the backfire had spotted over the dozer line. There was a bulldozer available, but it was low on fuel. Shepard asked how urgently it was needed; urgently enough, came the laconic reply. Shepard dispatched the machine and minutes later, when it showed up, the tardy fuel truck. He felt no alarm at this point—spot fires happen all the time. Then he heard an airplane overhead and radio chatter among air personnel about a spot fire of about seven acres, which quickly expanded to twenty acres.

Shepard felt a stab of anxiety. A spot fire growing that fast meant trouble; he needed to see it for himself. He jumped in his pickup.

By the time Shepard arrived at the spot fire, it was under attack by the bulldozer, the crew from Engine No. 3636, a helicopter, and air tankers. Shepard drove on through billowing smoke until he topped a rise where the smoke cleared and he could see to the Big Black. The burn squad was nowhere in sight.

Huter, though, was standing a couple of hundred yards ahead, in the dozer line. Shepard pulled up next to him. A couple of crew members had been "singed or burned a little," Huter told him. The news jolted Shepard.

"It was kind of unnerving, but the way he was telling me was casual, no cause for alarm," Shepard remembers. "He said he'd given them his truck and they were in the Big Black."

Huter, seeing the fire build up, had driven onto the dozer line and had watched with growing disgust as the burn squad worked its way toward him. They pecked along like chickens with their heads in the dirt, he thought. They needed to be heads up, right now.

Huter's repeated radio warnings received no response. The fire report cited this communications failure, and poor communications in general, as a major contributing factor to the entrapment: Huter's warnings came early enough to have saved the day.

Huter made his calls on the main tactical or work channel, which the fire report said was "grossly overloaded." The situation is common on big fires: one or two radio channels are not sufficient to handle communications about everything from Porta-Johns to entrapments. As a consequence, crews often use their own "private" frequencies to talk among themselves, while monitoring the main channel.

In this case, the problem may have been complicated by a switch in frequencies that was never passed on to Huter. Memories are confused on this point, but Shepard recalls instructing Horton, while in the Big Black, to use the main tactical frequency during the burnout. After leaving the Big Black, according to Shepard, Horton asked to switch to Golden Gate 3's private frequency. Shepard agreed, but has no memory of relaying the change to Huter. Horton says he scanned the main channel, but his attention was engaged doing the burnout single-handedly.

One thing is certain: nobody reacted to Huter's timely warning.

Communications problems were widespread. The fire report says Shepard and Huter failed to stay in touch with each other during the burnout. Further, the two operations chiefs, Vanskike and Hurt, were "unaware of the backfire plan or its initiation," a grave charge. Huter says Vanskike and Hurt called him on the radio several times to ask how things were going, but even so, they were absent from the scene of the biggest operation of the day. Vanskike and Hurt later said they were engaged in helping a less experienced

151

supervisor run another section of the fire, and knew and trusted Huter to do his job.

The lack of involvement by Vanskike and Hurt amounted to the worst single mistake on the Sadler Fire, according to Bob Lee, the fire-investigation leader. "That's why there are two of them, so one can be in the field and the other can deal with administration," Lee said later. "They were off together somewhere in a pickup."

Huter gave up on the radio and began to yell and wave his arms. The burn squad, with fire at its heels, broke into a run as a river of fire poured down.

"The blast of fire burned behind them on their shoulder and smoke went over them," Huter said later. "I lost them for maybe thirty seconds."

Huter started forward when the smoke cleared.

"I could see one girl, or I should say person, reaching for a fire shelter. A few others were meandering around. With screaming, waving, yelling, I finally got their attention and told them to get up here. They started *walking*. I was really upset and I said, 'No, *run*. And they came chugging up the line.

"They were all pretty excited. One girl was coughing, wheezing, it could have been from the heat, from being out of shape, from running. There were no apparent burns to anyone that were life threatening."

The entrapment never would have happened, Huter thought, if the burn squad had been as good as Horton had advertised. The burnout, in Huter's opinion, should have been a cakewalk.

Horton should have kept his head up and acted as the burn squad's eyes and ears, and not been poking along with a drip torch. The squad should have moved smartly—what had possessed them to stop and watch the fire whirl? Somebody should have heard him yelling. If the burn squad had kept running and not dived into the dirt, everyone would have made it without a blister, an opinion not widely shared.

Huter would finish off the burnout himself. He should have done it that way in the first place, he thought bitterly. The operation was already half a success; it had stopped most of the fire from crossing the dozer line.

Shepard felt assured by Huter's manner. The wind had turned gentle and the fire had quieted down.. A couple of minor burns were not the end of everything. But as Shepard drove on to the Big Black, he confronted an unsettling sight.

There in the Big Black was a bunch of firefighters—the fifteen members of Golden Gate 3 who had been left behind—wildly swinging shovels and Pulaskis. That's odd, Shepard thought, maybe they're clearing a landing spot for a helicopter. He got out of the pickup and walked over.

"What are you guys up to?" he said.

"We're improving our safety zone," one replied.

Doing *what*? thought Shepard. The Big Black, about a hundred acres in size, looked slicker than a greased frying pan to Shepard. "There was absolutely no possibility of a reburn," Shepard says.

He moved on, looking for an engine to support Huter as he finished the burnout. He found one idling, but when he tried to make the assignment he met his second rebuff of the day.

"This engine captain looks up the line where Dan is and says, 'I don't think I like that idea,'" Shepard remembers. "I was surprised. Dan was making progress. Here's a heavy engine with five hundred gallons of water. I'm thinking, What's going on here? I've got this feeling now that something bad has happened."

Engine Captain Ken Smihula logged an encounter with Shepard about this time, but said nothing about declining an assignment. "The ignition crew arrived back. I asked them how is it going and one crew member showed me an empty fire shelter case and said that's how it's going. . . . Meet with division [Shepard] and explain to him that the crew needs to get out of the area."

Smihula, who noted in his log that he moved his engine nearer to the fire line after talking to Shepard, declined to comment further when contacted.

Nearly everyone in the Big Black seemed spooked. They had witnessed the entrapment—some had taken photographs as it happened. The stranded members of Golden Gate 3 had thought that their friends had been killed and they were next.

After the burn squad departed in Shepard's pickup, the rest of Golden Gate 3 tried to relax, slipping off their packs and listening to radio chatter. The mix of boredom and anxiety made them edgy; someone scratched "Nowhere Nev" in the dirt.

"I kept watching the ridge in front of me, but it was hilly and we did not have a good vantage point," Hawk said later, remembering the peak of the confusion. "I couldn't see the burners, but I could see a smoke column, pretty serious smoke, building up."

Waves of heat shimmered on the ridge top to the south. "Maybe it was my overactive imagination," Hawk said, "but it was like fingers of fire waving at you, then dropping back down." The heat waves became a line of flames, which poured off the ridge, heading for the burn squad.

The crew in the Big Black began screaming into their radios and heard in response Christensen's cry, "Mommy, help me! I'm burning!"

The waiting crew, in their words, "freaked out."

"I thought she was dead," Hawk remembers. Someone else had a momentary flashback to the death of a sister. The squad bosses hustled everyone into a line and began herding them toward the center of the Big Black, but they bunched up at the barbed-wire fence, as they had feared might happen. In her mind's eye Hawk saw the crew tangle in the wire as flames closed over them.

"Everybody stay back! Everybody stay in line!" Hawk screamed.

The crew snipped the barbed wire and poured through the gap. Several members started up chain saws and began to hack at the sagebrush, but within minutes every saw had thrown its chain. Someone overswung with a shovel and its handle broke; a tool flew out of someone else's hands.

An engine crew, meanwhile, watched this display in amusement, "kicking back on chairs with hands crossed," as one member of Golden Gate 3 recalled.

Golden Gate 3 felt abandoned. The Big Black was no safety zone; it was a bad joke, and they were a laughingstock. No one understood what they were going through—the loss of their friends, the threat they faced.

The crew's concerns about the Big Black—the gap, the barbed wire, the burnable sagebrush—could be verified a year later. The gap was still visible, the fence remained in place, scorch marks on the sagebrush could be rubbed off with a fingernail. For Golden Gate 3, these were deeply disturbing conditions.

A host of experienced firefighters, however, say the Big Black was a more than adequate safety zone. This group includes not only Shepard and Huter, who are interested parties, but the fire-investigation team, other firefighters present during the entrapment, and even Horton, who later called the Big Black "bombproof," though sober judgment was not his strong suit.

Golden Gate 3 acted in an overanxious manner, but at least the crew took steps to improve their situation and make the Big Black safer. Two years later four firefighters would be killed on the Thirtymile Fire in Washington State because, among many other things, there was too little preparation before trouble arrived. It takes no psychologist to point out that it probably wasn't the condition of the Big Black that spooked Golden Gate 3 so much as hearing Christensen's scream and thinking their friends had burned to death. The real question is why a relatively inexperienced crew was put in that position in the first place.

The Sadler Fire, after trapping the burn squad, swept north into the basin. Flames lost their intensity in the sparse sagebrush and juniper, and the fire became easy pickings for bulldozers, helicopters, and air tankers.

The burn squad, meanwhile, straggled into the Big Black by truck and on foot. They huddled in twos and threes, jittery and shaken. Their faces were ashen, their eyes glazed. Deaton, trying to break the tension, remarked to Horton, "That was close, huh?"

"Yeah, Ty, that was close," Horton replied with heavy sarcasm. Horton walked off by himself, sat on the ground, and let his face sink into his hands.

Shepard went from bunch to bunch, asking how everyone was doing. "Okay," most said, their appearances to the contrary. When Horton's turn came, he replied, "I'm just worried about keeping my job"—a remark he would repeat many times.

"Hey, you don't need to worry about your job, you didn't do anything wrong," Shepard said, hating himself later for the lie.

Christensen and Giampaoli sat together in the cab of Huter's pickup. Christensen, hooked up to an oxygen cylinder, had red blotches on her face and neck. Giampaoli's forehead was scarlet. Their burns had not yet blistered. When Shepard looked in on them, they seemed to be holding up mentally, even laughing together.

Despite the apparent good spirits, Shepard recognized the unmistakable signs of post-trauma stress. These folks needed a formal critical-incident stress debriefing, Shepard thought, and this time around he would see that the job was done properly.

The day after the South Canyon Fire, there had been a semipublic counseling session that wound up being a model of how not to conduct a psychological debriefing. A psychiatrist hired for the occasion appeared to know nothing about fire in general or the South Canyon Fire in particular. The survivors wanted a coherent account of what had happened to them. Instead, the psychiatrist delivered a lecture, using flip charts, on the stages of the grieving process, from anger to resolution. The surviving members of the Prineville Hotshots led a walkout; they later had a professionally supervised debriefing session, where they talked among themselves about the fire and its aftermath, to their relief.

Shepard had attended both sessions and knew he had the experience to make a difference now for Golden Gate 3. When Shepard saw Huter come into the Big Black after completing the burnout, he told him the crew needed an immediate stress debriefing.

Huter was skeptical.

"You think so?" he asked.

"Yes," said Shepard, "they have that classic glazed look in their eyes."

Huter, whatever he thought of the idea, went about ordering a counseling session. He also summoned a helicopter to transport Christensen and Giampaoli to a hospital and assigned a spare division supervisor, Steve Nemore, to escort the rest of Golden Gate 3 to Elko and settle them in a motel.

When the helicopter arrived and Christensen and Giampaoli went aloft, they saw for the first time the extent of the fire, which spread in every direction. The memory of their brush with death came rushing back—air sucked from their lungs, the sting of being burned, the thunder of flames. The frantic thought struck that the same thing was about to happen to the people below in the Big Black. Christensen and Giampaoli alone could see the threat. Only they could warn the others in time. They had to save those people!

They tried to get the helicopter pilot's attention, but he flew on wordlessly, and they collapsed in helplessness.

After their escape, they had staggered, coughing and hacking, toward Huter, who offered them his truck, gave them a bag of emergency medical gear, and told Naar to take care of them. When they reached the Big Black, Naar had popped cold packs and applied them to their burns, and had set up an oxygen cylinder for Christensen.

But then Naar and Horton had turned on each other again, in front of everybody.

Naar saw Horton sitting off by himself moaning, "What did I do wrong? What did I do wrong?" No one was more willing than Naar to answer.

"Tim wasn't doing *anything* a crew boss should do," Naar said later. At the time, though, Naar tried to reassure Horton: "Tim, we did everything we could. The lookout [Huter] let us down."

Horton struggled to regain control of himself . . . and the crew. He wanted to brief everyone, regroup, and get ready for another assignment.

"Tim, it's over, we're *done*," Naar said.

"I'm the crew boss, I'm in charge," Horton said.

"I don't care," Naar shot back. "We're done. It's over."

The two were "in each other's face, going back and forth," Hawk recounted. "Alex kept rehashing all the things Tim had done wrong. Tim kept saying he was the crew boss and he had done what he felt was right. I thought they were going to start swinging."

Horton has little memory of the episode. "Alex says I was out of it, and to be perfectly honest, I might have been. I thought I had adequate lookouts; I didn't. Afterward I apologized to everyone who helped me make crew boss. I didn't mean to make them look bad. But I did."

Shepard, meanwhile, had turned his attention back to the fire, which had spread a mile or so beyond the dozer line. Two air tankers dropped retardant on it. Bulldozers cut fire lines along both flanks, aiming to pinch off the fire at its head. As Shepard drove his pickup along one flank, he figured the fire would be under control in a few hours.

Word of the Naar-Horton quarrel, meanwhile, spread quickly, as bad news will. When Shepard stopped to help a truck driver with a mechanical problem, a helicopter swooped down and landed nearby, kicking up a cloud of dust. Out stepped the operations chief, Skip Hurt.

Hurt told Shepard about the Naar-Horton altercation and asked him to go back, find them, and try to straighten things out.

"Is it really our business to be getting into an internal, crew thing?" Shepard asked.

"In this case, yes," Hurt replied.

There's something wrong here, Shepard thought. Type I operations chiefs do not fly around in helicopters settling crew disputes. But if that's what Hurt wants, Shepard thought, that's what he'll get.

It was past six P.M. before Shepard caught up with Golden Gate 3, who had retired to the Jiggs fire camp. Horton and Naar stood apart from the rest of the crew in animated discussion. Shepard approached them.

"Hey, ops sent me over. There seems to be some kind of conflict between you guys," Shepard said.

"Yeah, there's a conflict," Naar said with heat.

Horton rolled his eyes.

"Why didn't you listen to me?" Naar spat at Horton. "Why didn't you slow down when I asked you to?"

"You didn't have to yell at me," Horton said.

The exchange added to a growing picture for Shepard of an inexperienced crew run ragged by Horton, forced to march and fight fire like hotshots, and divided by squabbling between its supervisors. Golden Gate 3 soon would face a critical-incident stress debriefing, traumatic in itself.

"I felt sympathy for them," Shepard said. "I've been a crew boss many times. Crew members want to know everything they possibly can, and I was always one to supply the information.

"All of a sudden I felt this urge to talk to the whole crew."

Shepard, unsure what he was going to say, gathered Golden Gate 3 around him. The setting was made for a speech. The group was off by itself in a meadow with a setting sun for a backdrop. The sky was full of the colors of fire, flame-scarlet rays of setting sun and smoke-gray clouds.

Shepard began by introducing himself: he was Tom Shepard, their division supervisor. But he had a closer bond with them than that. As Shepard spoke, he began to unbutton his yellow fire shirt. That morning, by chance, he had put on a Prineville Hotshot memorial T-shirt, one emblazoned with nine stars for the nine lost hotshots.

"Here's my shirt," he told Golden Gate 3. "You've got to know I've been real close myself."

Then he told them the story of the botched psychological-counseling session after the South Canyon Fire and included a funny anecdote about the psychiatrist—"that brainless doctor"—they tried to stick with a huge bar bill for "liquid counseling." He described what a good debriefing session was like: a quiet sharing of memories, thoughts, and emotions among those who had been there.

"Hopefully you'll make the best of it," he said.

When he finished, several firefighters stepped forward and shook his hand. "They seemed pleased, proud to meet with me. It was a real nice gesture."

Looking along the flank of the Sadler Fire after it crossed the dozer line, which is visible on the lower right. Courtesy Keren Christensen

Not everyone felt so inclined.

"He discredited the [debriefing] process we were about to go through," complained Hawk. "The psychologist did no good for him, so he went out and got drunk. I thought it was really inappropriate. I almost wanted to scream out, 'You almost lost six other people today!'"

It would be dramatically satisfying, and an act of mercy, to let nightfall ring down a curtain on the ambiguities and misunderstandings, missed cues and mistakes, quarrels and aggrieved feelings that are the stuff of the Sadler Fire. But this is no theatrical production, these are not actors, and a series of fitful aftershocks remained to be played out before this day could limp to its conclusion.

Christensen and Giampaoli transferred from the helicopter to an ambulance for the last leg of the ride to Elko General Hospital. "And then we got the giggles," Christensen said. "We would laugh about the stupidest things, feeling all the emotions in a minute."

At the hospital they were draped with nasal cannulas for oxygen and intravenous tubes. Christensen was also given an antiallergy shot, to help her labored breathing and suppress a case of poison oak contracted on the training hike back in California.

The rest of Golden Gate 3 decided to visit them and drove by bus from Jiggs to the hospital. Naar remembers hearing over the fire radio en route that the accident site had been flagged and there was no need for an overnight watch, which struck him as cavalier.

Many on Golden Gate 3, and others who fought the Sadler Fire, believe to this day that the dozer line was widened and safety zones added after the entrapment, to make this line look safer than it was. No one, though, has proved this charge.

Medics at the hospital checked the new arrivals and decided to keep Naar—who appeared overwrought, perhaps as a result of smoke inhalation—overnight for observation. Christensen and Giampaoli had already been admitted. It was past eleven P.M. before the rest of Golden Gate 3 left the hospital. Lights dimmed and the place quieted down. Monitors continued to pulse; a faraway telephone rang.

Naar took a shower and fell into an exhausted slumber. In the dead of night, he awakened to the shriek of an alarm, followed by the sounds of a medical crisis: rushing footsteps, shouts, the rattle of a metal tray. His first, disoriented thought was of Christensen and Giampaoli. The emergency, though, turned out to be an elderly woman in cardiac arrest.

Meanwhile, Steve Nemore, the spare division supervisor, had escorted Horton, Deaton, and Hyde, the remainder of the burn squad, to find something to eat. They drove to the Stockman's Casino and Hotel, which has a twenty-four-hour restaurant. Even at midnight, rows of glassy-eyed, chain-smoking patrons stuffed quarters into slot machines. Lights glittered off mirrors, making the place overbright. The firefighters slid their dirty, rumpled forms into a booth with shiny red plush seats.

Horton kept repeating, as though in a trance, "I really screwed up; I'm going to lose my job." Nemore tried to talk him out of it, but he might as well have tried to separate the gamblers from their slot machines.

Shepard rounded up the rest of the crew and accompanied them to the Thunderbird Motel, opposite the Stockman's. He would do his best for them, he thought—get them a place to wash, eat, and sleep, and then check on a stress debriefing. He left them sorting keys at the motel desk and headed for the BLM office at the other end of town.

There, he submitted a formal request for a critical-incident stress debriefing, then made a telephone call to the Sadler Fire command post. He left a message there saying he would be in town the next day taking care of Golden Gate 3, and not on his division at the fire.

He was driving back to the motel when his cell phone rang and an angry Jeff Luff, the management team's planning chief, asked him what he thought he was doing. Shepard had active fire on his division; he had better show up to fight it.

Shepard, taken aback, said he had been *assigned* to care for Golden Gate 3. He had been *told* to smooth over the Horton-Naar quarrel. He was needed in town.

Luff interrupted, "We'll handle it," and the connection went dead.

Shepard was not without sympathizers. Hurt, the operations chief who had ordered him to straighten out the Naar-Horton mess, telephoned minutes later and took a more diplomatic approach. Shepard's expertise would be appreciated on the fire the next morning, he said.

Shepard had parked at the motel by then, and as the conversation continued, a sleepless member of Golden Gate 3 came up to his pickup and peered in the windshield. Getting no response, the firefighter wandered away like a lost soul.

"I felt pretty bad about that," Shepard said later. "I was feeling pretty low."

Shepard went to his room and took a shower; by the time he flopped onto the bed it was past one o'clock. He was drifting off when the phone rang: it was the incident commander, Ed Storey.

Storey was "congenial," Shepard remembers. But he was also insistent. The entrapment was likely to trigger a full-scale investigation, Storey said, an estimate that proved correct. Fire investigators would need to talk to Shepard at the scene. He had to go back to the fire.

"We did a lot of soul-searching."

For most of the twentieth century, the Sadler Fire would have slipped into the past without a ripple. No one was killed or seriously injured. The decision by the hotshots to decline an assignment fell short of a full-blown refusal, instances of which have occurred in the past to little notice. If history was a guide, Shepard would not have been drawn further into a web of personal tragedy, because for most of the twentieth century the entrapment would not have been investigated, let alone resulted in disciplinary action against top fire supervisors.

The fire was put out without further incident. Three days after the entrapment, a sudden desert storm wreaked havoc at the main Sadler Fire camp, upending tents, blowing over Porta-Johns, and making a shambles of mess tents. The accompanying rain drowned the fire, which the federal government had spent $1.8 million trying to extinguish.

The Sadler Fire, however, became the talk of the fire season. An Associated Press story that fall began with this provocative sentence: "An inexperienced government fire crew and its supervisors broke practically every rule in the book and were nearly burned alive during a Nevada range fire last summer before a shift in the wind saved them."

Word of Shepard's role quickly spread through the fire community: the man who had lost a crew on Storm King Mountain had nearly lost another on a burnout operation that had been refused by two hotshot crews. "I was a crew member on the incident," began an anonymous entry on an Internet posting site for firefighters. "You just had to be on that park service crew to see what went down. Leadership is not made. It is an inherint [*sic*] quality. Until the Park Service gets away from its assinine [*sic*] position that a Ranger is a born leader of men (When all know that the person is an idiot) and the Forest Service quits putting hot shits in charge, these problems of safety will not go away. I have been to Nevada twice and been entrapped twice and both were B.L.M. shows with lots of ex-shots and jumpers in the overhead. BLM stands for Basically Lousy Management." The entry was signed "Done In."

There was contrary opinion, to be sure.

"This is in response to DONE IN'S comments about the Sadler Fire and BLM management in Nevada. I have fought fire for the BLM in Nevada since 1995 and I think that you need to take a look at yourself before you start placing the blame on other people for what is your ultimate responsibility, YOUR SAFETY. . . . You have to keep in mind that when the order was sent it was made with the assumption that whoever filled the order would have the experience and qualifications necessary. . . . If local management knew they were getting a crew thrown together from Golden Gate Park with minimal or zero experience they would have never been allowed on the fire." The writer was "NVFIREFIGHTER (6 years in NV and not one entrapment)."

The Sadler Fire made history on a number of fronts. First, the fire-investigation report cited seven members of the management team and Horton for poor performance, which triggered a review of their professional qualifications. Next, an oversight group disbanded Storey's Type I incident-management team for incompetence in fighting fire, a first.

Then the Occupational Safety and Health Administration (OSHA) cited the Sadler Fire operation as being unsafe, its first such finding since the 1994 South Canyon Fire. Later, the National Park Service revamped the way it puts crews together, including a closer check on physical conditioning thanks to Lydia Mingo, who had faltered on the training hike. In a spontaneous reaction from the fire community, the Sadler Fire became a lesson in "just say no."

Why all the fuss? What had changed so much by the end of the twentieth century to justify a furor of this magnitude over a couple of minor burns that caused no lasting damage? Those who lost their professional reputations over the affair continue to ask that question.

The morning after the entrapment, Shepard drove back to the main fire camp with a sick feeling. There was no active fire on his division, as he had suspected, but there was an abundance of supervisors—he quickly ran into two spare division supervisors, either one of whom could have handled the division. He could have stayed with Golden Gate 3.

By chance, a four-member Fire and Aviation Safety Team, called a FAST team, was in Nevada this day looking into the general fire situation. When a report came in of a "smoke-inhalation incident" on the Sadler Fire, the team was assigned to look into it.

The word *cover-up* is probably too strong, but the FAST team discovered that it had been many hours before word of the entrapment reached people who should have heard about it right away, including higher-ups responsible for the fire itself. It took six hours, for example, for a report to reach the BLM office in Elko, and about as long to reach the Sadler Fire's radio-dispatch operation.

Lee, who was a member of the FAST team, wrote in his field notes, "1st dispatch heard about it was when emergency room called . . . team didn't call dispatch when incident occurred."

Lee and Stan Palmer, another investigator, caught up with Shepard late that day. "Tom, we're wondering if there's enough meat here to do an investigation," Palmer asked, according to Shepard's recollection.

"Yes, there's some lessons to be learned. You should get the word out, and maybe it will help folks down the road," Shepard remembers saying.

When Huter was contacted by the FAST team, he said, to the contrary, that he did not believe the circumstances serious enough to justify a full-scale investigation. Dee Sessions, the fire's safety officer, agreed. In a statement he submitted later, Sessions argued that the incident did not qualify as an "entrapment."

"A FAST team decided to treat it as entrapment, with which I disagree," Sessions said. "According to the standards for fire operations, an entrapment is 'a situation where personnel are unexpectedly caught in a fire behavior–related threatening position where planned escape routes or safety zones are absent, inadequate, or have been compromised.' This was not the case. The crew reached a pre-built, adequate safety zone, and to emphasize this, 14 out of a 20-person crew had already been placed in a safety zone ahead of the crew in the black." (Actually, it was fifteen people out of twenty-one; he may not have been counting Horton, the crew's leader.)

Sessions said that when he visited the injured crew members in the hospital most "seemed in good spirits yet scared a little." Naar, he said, seemed "mad and upset."

By evening, the FAST team had learned enough to recommend that their inquiry be expanded into a full-scale fire investigation. As a result, the FAST team converted to a Serious Accident Investigation Team, and Lee transferred over as its head. For the next several weeks the investigators struggled not only to gather facts but to confront the dilemma of how to treat supervisors who made errors, Shepard in particular. The South Canyon Fire Investigation had left the victims to take much of the blame for their own deaths, but subsequent inquiry disclosed that a host of management errors over many days contributed mightily to the disaster. For instance, the fire wasn't fought for the first three days, air tankers that could have extinguished it were not used, and the command structure was inadequate. Nevertheless, two of the managers most responsible for those errors were rewarded with pay raises and a congratulatory memo, signed by one of them. After that, it became more difficult to overlook the role of managers in causing accidents.

Shepard, though, was a special case. Everyone had sympathy for him, but he had undeniably played a central role in the entrapment.

"We did a lot of soul-searching," Tom Boatner, one of the investigators and the BLM's fire-management officer for Montana, said later. "We talk about firefighter safety, but do we really mean it?"

The fire-investigation report concludes that the Sadler Fire was a management fiasco from start to finish. The National Park Service assembled Golden Gate 3 in a haphazard manner. The transition from a Type II to Type I incident-management team was rushed. The day of the entrapment began badly with an inadequate briefing by Huter.

The plan to set a backfire "from the head of a 170,000 acre fire in the afternoon during red flag warning and extreme fire behavior conditions" invited trouble. None of the top field supervisors—Shepard, Huter, Vanskike, or Hurt—gave adequate attention to the burnout operation.

Horton made one mistake after another, the report said. He told Shepard and Huter that his crew had "lots of burning experience," then left fifteen of them behind because of their "lack of experience and training and low fitness level." He became overly involved in the burnout and "did not provide for the safety of his crew, had no communication with lookouts, and was unaware of the location of the main fire until just before the entrapment."

Everyone on the fire was too "mission oriented," willing to do anything to stop the fire.

Immediately after the entrapment, Sessions, the safety officer, "overlooked the extent of the injuries, did a cursory follow-up at the hospital, and did not instigate an investigation." Further, Sessions "downplayed the incident in his report and to the investigation team."

Huter, who was not qualified to serve as an operations branch director, acted without sufficient care for the welfare of the firefighters, the report said. Huter placed the crew in harm's way, then failed to monitor their situation. After the entrapment he handed over responsibility for their well-being to Naar, one of the victims.

Air support was next to nonexistent while the burnout operation was under way. Confusion reigned about "division locations, division assignments and chain of command." Communications were a mess. Safety zones along the bulldozer line were spaced too far apart. Even the vinyl pack for Christensen's fire shelter had failed to function properly.

The Ten Standard Fire Orders were violated and thirteen of eighteen Situations That Shout Watch Out were triggered.

The report also tossed a couple of bouquets. It commended the Dalton and Smokey Bear Hotshots for turning down the burnout assignment. The hotshots, the report said, "provided for safety first by securing the eastern flank [of the fire] south of the Big Safety Zone." And Shepard was praised for his attention to Golden Gate 3 after the entrapment. "Shepard made a substantial effort to assist and comfort the [Golden Gate 3] crew," the report said. "He met with the crew in town that night to give what help he could." By contrast, when Shepard was ordered to report to the fire the next morning, it displayed "a lack of concern" by Storey and others.

Shepard did not escape censure, by any means. Shepard "was a critical player in this scenario," Tom Boatner wrote in an e-mail to other investigators. "He was one of only 3 or 4 people in a position to do things right and he didn't."

Several of those disciplined later accused Boatner of being a "hatchet man." Boatner acknowledged that he had a tendency to "take a hard line" but said the entrapment was a grave matter. "I've been looking for some kind of 1990s 'You're magic, don't ever change, every way of doing this is beautiful and valid' kind of response," Boatner wrote in one e-mail. "But I'm past that.

"No firefighting resource in the country is given more responsibility for the lives of others and the expenditure of millions of dollars than a National Interagency Type I team. At the same time, there is no organized procedure for reviewing the ongoing performance of these teams. . . . The only reason we know this team's performance was sub-par is because they almost killed some people.

"We've been flapping our lips long and hard about our commitment to putting firefighter safety first every time, no excuses. If we mean it (and I believe we do), then our recommendations should send a loud and unequivocal message: Disband this Type I team for failure to provide adequate fire line supervision and for failure to put firefighter safety first."

In the end, the investigators cited Shepard; Storey, the incident commander; Vanskike and Hurt, the operations chiefs; Huter, the branch director; Luff, the planning section chief; Sessions, the safety officer; and Horton, the crew boss. The investigators forwarded the fire report to the Great Basin Coordination Group, an interagency committee charged with putting together and overseeing Type I and II incident-management teams in the Great Basin region. The coordination group summoned the six named regular members of Storey's team plus Shepard to the National Interagency Fire Center in Boise, Idaho, in late September. Horton, who was not a member of the incident-management team, was not included. The seven were given a copy of the report just before their hearing—accounts vary from forty-five minutes to "four or five hours" before, but in any case, they had little time to digest it.

"It was a railroad job," Storey said later. "They did not want us to take issue with anything the investigation team said. They said, 'What do you have to say for yourselves? Our time is short.' I've never seen a more closed body of people in my life. That was probably the angriest I have ever been."

The seven tried to make a case, but the coordination group was not in a listening mood.

Storey held up a letter from Kelly Martin documenting her clash with Horton the day before the entrapment, when he left his crew behind. For Storey, the letter proved a recent history of irresponsible behavior by Horton.

"They wouldn't listen to that, they said it had no bearing," Storey said.

Huter started to diagram on a blackboard how things had happened and explain the safety precautions taken, but he says he was cut off. "We got crucified on a pretty small situation."

Matters reached a climax when Hurt, flanked by Vanskike, began to speak. Hurt told the coordination group members that they were picking on the team because of its previous brush with scandal over overtime and other issues in Florida. When someone told him to move on, Hurt replied, "No, you got to let me speak my piece."

Voices rose.

"We don't have to hear it," someone said. Shepard remembers Hurt becoming "a little bit belligerent, a little bit arrogant, a lot defensive."

Shepard and others reconstruct Hurt's remarks like this: "You've got to let me speak my piece. We trust Dan Huter. We know Dan Huter's qualifications, we know what he can do. We trust Tom Shepard, we know what he can do. We didn't worry about that branch, that's why we weren't there. We were more worried with another branch with a new branch director."

A member of the coordination group, Sheldon Wimmer, the BLM fire-management officer for Utah, then asked, "What would you do differently if the same thing happened again?"

"We would do the same thing tomorrow," Hurt replied, according to everyone's account.

That ended the discussion. The fate of the incident-management team was sealed.

"We'd have done anything to keep that team together," Wimmer said later. "But when you have guys who lean back in their chairs with toothpicks in their mouths and say, 'There isn't anything we would have done differently,' then *you* lean over and say, '*Yes, there is.*'"

Shepard made so many mistakes he did not qualify as a special case, Wimmer added. "We quit putting people in the back of pickup trucks with drip torches twenty-five years ago," Wimmer said. "Shepard says they hit the ground running and took off—*and he let them go.* That's not responsible."

The coordination group formally dissolved Storey's Type I incident-management team at the end of September. No one was fired; the coordination group does not have such power. But it endorsed the recommendation of the fire investigators that federal and state agencies review the qualifications of those cited. In effect, the agencies were asked to demote their employees one notch in fire grade—not pay grade. Everyone could be reinstated at their former level of fire qualification if they submitted to reevaluation and retraining. The recommendation, though, was intended to have a chilling effect on any reinstatement efforts.

Lee said he was "pleasantly surprised" to learn of the ruling.

Storey and the others were incensed at what they regarded as unfair treatment. Five of them—Huter, Hurt, Vanskike, Luff, and Sessions, but not Storey or Shepard—joined in a formal appeal, which challenged the findings, the five were Forest Service employees. The appeal was denied.

Storey returned to his job as a forester with the State of Utah, which supported his claim that he was wrongly judged and did not demote him. Embittered nevertheless, he decided never to fight fire again. He took a regularly scheduled retirement two years later, in August 2001.

"They treat criminals in this country better than they treated us," Storey said when interviewed after retirement at his home near Monroe, Utah. "They had a whole range of other options. They could have sent a team out with us the next time to make sure we were following all the rules and regs."

Sessions submitted to retraining and returned to duty as a safety officer. Huter initially would not budge. "It's like giving in if you go back," he said when interviewed two years later at the Council Ranger District in west-central Idaho. But he returned to the fire line as a division supervisor in 2002.

Horton started to reclaim his Park Service job the next summer, but he found himself under a cloud.

"We planned to sit down with Tim and review what happened, but he was welcome to come back," said a Park Service supervisor. "As the old-timers say, Tim hadn't got religion yet." At last report, Horton had taken a job in construction.

That fall, after the fire, six members of Golden Gate 3—Naar, Hawk, Giampaoli, and three others—got together at the Marin Headlands for a postmortem. The session lasted six and a half hours and was summarized in an eleven-page document, a mix of quibbles and factual corrections, self-serving arguments and on-the-money remarks, the sort of thing that gets said in an off-the-record bitch session but seldom sees the light of day. Only in this case, the summary was passed on to higher-ups.

Some of the comments are thoughtful but smack of overreaching—for example, a plea for fire-investigation teams to be expanded to include outside experts. Some of the comments strain credulity—a charge that the official report is "not accurate" when it claims Horton and Naar did not work well together. "They were working well together up to the time of the accident," the summary says, citing Naar as a source.

The document also raises a very serious charge, that a bulldozer tampered with the scene of the entrapment. Members of Golden Gate 3 visited the site a few days after the entrapment and observed a bulldozer working in the area behind flagging placed to secure the scene. When challenged, the bulldozer operator "left without answering." The safety zones appeared to some to be larger and more numerous than they were the day of the entrapment.

The bulldozer incident came about this way.

When the fire investigation began, Golden Gate 3 insisted on stress counseling before being interviewed. The fire investigators agreed, and the crew had a private session with a professional. "It was worthwhile," Hawk said.

Hawk and the rest of the crew, though, regarded the investigators as generally "confrontational" and unsympathetic. At one point, Naar and Lee exchanged heated words in a parking lot. Naar complained that the investigators were pushing the crew around; Lee found Naar "arrogant and full of himself."

The investigators wanted to interview the crew in groups; the crew insisted on individual interviews. The investigators did not use tape recorders; several crew members purchased tape recorders for the sessions.

Before leaving Nevada, several members of Golden Gate 3 wanted to return to the scene of the entrapment for a last look. Christensen and Horton went first, on Thursday, August 12, three days after the entrapment. As they headed out of Elko, accompanied by several investigators, they passed a tattoo parlor, and Christensen had an impish urge.

"Tim, stop the car!" she cried out. "'I'm going to get a tattoo. I'm going to get *Elko Nevada* tattooed right across my ass! Pull over, Tim."

A flustered investigator remarked, "'You know, you should think about that before you do it."

Christensen smirked. Horton drove on.

When more crew members went back to the scene the next day, Friday, August 13, they saw a bulldozer in one of the safety zones shoving back the dirt berm. Someone asked the operator what he was doing, but he mumbled and drove off. The crew was later told the bulldozer had been engaged in normal rehabilitation work, but Hawk, Naar, and others remain suspicious to this day that the dozer line was widened and the safety zones enlarged to make it appear that the situation had been safer than it was.

There is no question that a bulldozer was at the fire line the day of the second visit: the crew took photographs of it and they all tell the same story. But there is substantial evidence to support the view that the bulldozer was indeed engaged in rehabilitation work.

The site had been formally released for rehabilitation the day before the bulldozer was seen. Orders for the Sadler Fire day shift for Thursday, August 12, begin, "Put all berms back into dozer line. Spread cat piles back into the dozer line, as long as they don't contain burning materials. If cat pile was pushed into the black spread it out in the black. If it's not possible to push the cat pile into the dozer line just spread it out."

The incoherent response of the bulldozer operator can be explained as the reaction of a man who felt challenged and out of his depth. Lastly, the fire report criticizes the spacing of the safety zones as inadequate, an unlikely tack if there was a broad conspiracy to "improve" the safety zones by enlarging them.

Golden Gate 3 flew home later that Friday.

Keren Christensen looks at the remains of her pack at the site of the entrapment on August 13, four days after the entrapment. Courtesy Derek Hyde

For days afterward, Christensen had trouble catching her breath, as though the wind had been knocked out of her. She could not cross a parking lot without stopping. She returned to work at Yosemite National Park, but the first time she encountered flames again, she felt shock and terror.

"It's an odd feeling to love something so much you hate it," she said. "You think, 'You didn't get me. You're not going to make me stop.'"

Christensen stayed with fire work and became a popular speaker before audiences of rookie firefighters, telling the story of her close call. "It's just like I am reliving it all over again," Christensen says. "I get so excited by doing it that I sleep the whole next day." Rookies turn silent as she speaks, and afterward many take a pledge to practice diligently with their fire shelters before they go out on the line.

Christensen has relevant prior experience as a public speaker. When she was a rookie herself, she was asked to read to the class from the South Canyon Fire Investigation.

"When I got to the part about the fourteen who were killed I just stopped," she said. "Then to find out later that Tom Shepard was *the* Tom Shepard—I felt like I had been thrown back to 1994.

171

The burn squad, minus Tim Horton, at the site of the entrapment four days later. From left to right: Peter Giampaoli, Alex Naar, Keren Christensen, Ty Deaton, Derek Hyde. Courtesy Derek Hyde

"I didn't want that to happen to anyone else. If one person had spoken up, things would have been different," she said, referring both to the South Canyon Fire and the Sadler Fire.

Shepard, meanwhile, went his lonely way.

Shepard had walked out of the meeting with the Great Basin Coordination Group thinking he had defended himself well. When his turn came, he held up the fire report and said, "This isn't the story. It's flawed, it's full of inaccuracies." So he was unbelieving when notified of the group's decision to disband the team. He was going to lose his rank as a division supervisor, which felt odd because at the moment he got the news he was coordinating a training course for division supervisors. He was allowed to finish that project.

Shepard knew he could have done some things better—insist that a hotshot crew conduct the burnout, for instance. But why, when he had told the investigators about Horton jumping out of the truck and starting the burnout, was there no word of that incident in the fire report?

Over the next several months Shepard composed his own, twenty-five-page account of the fire. "'I would appreciate an opportunity to set the record straight," it begins. He disputed many factual matters, such as the assertion that the Smokey Bear and Dalton Hotshots refused an assignment from him. Predictably, Horton's name appears many times. "It is not anyone's fault but Horton. . . . Once Horton began lighting from the Y Safety Zone, there was no turning back."

Shepard continued to fight fires; in an ironic twist, when he lost his rank as division supervisor he reverted to his next-highest fire qualification, as safety officer. But he never again wanted responsibility for a crew. That part of his life was over. "I could care less if I'm a division supe," he said during one of many interviews for this book. "This was too close for me; I do not need this to happen again."

He wanted to walk out proud, though. He wanted the satisfaction of having his qualifications as a division supervisor restored before he quit for good. He sent the twenty-five-page document up the chain of command, and after a series of rebuffs came a final reponse.

"We are in a new era when actions and mistakes of this nature will not be tolerated," Jack Blackwell, a regional forester and Shepard's superior, replied on November 21, 2001. The disbanding of the incident-management team and the recommended demotions were "precedent setting," Blackwell said, and he was glad of it. The fire report gave "more than adequate" support for the disciplinary actions. While Golden Gate 3 was "partially responsible" for what had happened, the greater burden fell on Storey's incident-management team, Shepard included.

"Individuals and teams will be held accountable for their actions. Our actions will demonstrate a zero tolerance for accidents and deviations from safety standards," Blackwell said.

Appeal denied.

That was the end of a long road for Shepard. After receiving Blackwell's letter, he made plans for retirement.

The Sadler Fire signaled new rules of accountability. No longer were top fire managers exempt from public censure; no longer was being absent from the scene of trouble an excuse; no longer were the mistakes of firefighters on the line good cover for errors by supervisors.

Golden Gate 3 came within seconds of death because of overreaching pride and indifference to the power of fire. But this time no one paid the ultimate price.

3

The Last Survivor

Memo to Press, August 6 [1949] 9:15 A.M.
The first serious accident in many years occurred to smoke jumpers
employed for the Forest Service in this Region late Friday afternoon. At
the present time, due to lack of communications and precipitous country
our information is very incomplete.

Helena, Montana

AGE HAD BENT him, but he stood taller and looked sturdier than most
in the crowd. His eyes were sharp and bright, his cheeks ruddy. His most
prominent feature was a head of shining white hair. When he walked to the
podium on the lawn of the state capitol in Helena, Montana, the crowd went
silent.

Bob Sallee was a living legend, the last survivor of the Mann Gulch Fire,
which happened fifty years to the day before this anniversary gathering held
August 5, 1999. In the intervening years, images of Mann Gulch had become
historic icons of firefighting. Jumpers parachuting into a wilderness. Sallee
and his best friend, Walter Rumsey, racing to safety up the side of the gulch.
The foreman, Wagner "Wag" Dodge, lighting an escape fire in the path of
the main fire and surviving in its ashes. The rest of the crew—twelve smoke
jumpers and a wilderness guard who had been a jumper—lost forever.

Mann Gulch carried the promise that never again would smoke jumpers
die as they had that day, in the flames of a blowup. And for forty-five years,
the promise held true.

It was a young world back then. The smoke jumpers had been in existence

175

for only a decade, and firefighting was a simple, adventurous affair—get to every fire quickly, the standing orders said, and have it under control by ten A.M. the next morning. An occasional fire threatened ranch buildings and cabins, but there were no expansive subdivisions in the woods, no wildland-urban interface to defend.

Some things, though, do not change. The day of the fire the thermometer reached a record ninety-seven degrees in Helena; it surely topped that in the narrow confines of the gulch, about twenty-five miles to the north. On the anniversary day fifty years later, it was hot and dry, a perfect day for fire. A lightning burst in northern Nevada on this day ignited the Sadler Fire, which a few days later overran and nearly killed six firefighters.

The anniversary crowd in Helena was smallish by urban standards—about 250—but the participants' concentration was intense. In brief, moving remarks Sallee acknowledged that the Mann Gulch Fire had kept a hold on the fire community for half a century. But the time had come, he said, to put the fire to rest.

"I know how much pain Mann Gulch has caused over the years," he said. But fifty years is a long time, he added; the millennium was approaching. "Maybe it's time to let go."

The Mann Gulch Fire did not stop burning when the last ember died out. To the contrary, it burned like Old Testament sin into generations of family, friends, and others touched by the thirteen deaths. Those who live on after tragedy fires have a hard role to play. They find themselves forever at a distance from the final moments of those they loved and lost. They try to bridge the gap with secondhand dope—official reports, news accounts, hearsay. A survivor's tale provides an authentic, living link to what happened, and Sallee was the last person who could say, "I was there, in the fire, that day."

Sallee had been two weeks shy of eighteen years old when he parachuted into Mann Gulch, his first-ever fire jump. As he floated down, he felt little except relief at escaping a lurching aircraft and a rush of adrenaline at the prospect of what lay ahead. In the aftermath, youth and mental toughness helped Sallee put disaster behind him. He went on to a successful career in the timber industry, raised a family, and for many years did not look back.

Decades later, though, he felt the pull of the gulch. A series of events—a return visit to Mann Gulch, an earlier memorial get-together, the deaths of

Rumsey and Dodge—cast him in a star role for the fire community as the last living survivor.

A tough, bluff man, Sallee had no desire to relive ancient trouble. When he first spoke publicly about the fire, after a forty-year silence, he sounded like the boyish lad of seventeen whose grand adventure had gone wrong. Under the influence of revived memories, though, his attitude began to change. By renewing old ties, he learned the depth of the fire's effect on loved ones of those who had not been able to walk away as he had. And he came to appreciate the importance of his memories to others.

Sallee had been a self-assured youngster. He stood well over six feet tall and, around the time of the fire, weighed 186 pounds, six pounds above the limit for smoke jumpers. None of it was fat. "I believe I could walk off and leave any man in the entire smoke-jumper crew that year," Sallee claimed years later.

The Forest Service had accepted Sallee's fib about being eighteen with a wink and a nod. The cream of America's able-bodied men had returned from World War II and flooded the nation's colleges and universities, thanks to the G.I. Bill, leaving the woods desperate for good help. A former supervisor penned these admiring words on his application: "This is a good boy from the standpoint of being industrious, dependable and woodsmanship. If the age factor is O.K. he should make out all right. He is a rugged, big fellow and a splendid hiker."

Sallee was a match for Mann Gulch, a funnel-shaped crevice cut deep in the rugged mountains of what is now the Gates of the Mountains Wilderness, named for a canyon of the Missouri River that Lewis and Clark described as their entry point into the Rocky Mountains. The gulch can be reached by foot trails from more scenic canyons nearby, but most of the trickle of visitors approach by boat along the Missouri River, which crosses the mouth of the gulch. There are no roads for many miles. Mann Gulch today is a place of memories and mountain goats, white crosses and rattlesnakes, blackened snags and a grassy, amphitheater-like expanse at the wide head of the gulch where tragedy once played out.

The Mann Gulch Fire was first spotted in late morning on August 5, 1949, on the point of a ridge overlooking the river and the mouth of the gulch. The C-47 carrying Sallee and fourteen other jumpers arrived over the gulch at midafternoon. By then, the fire had disappeared from its point of origin and migrated more than a mile along the ridge top, up from the river. The smoke jumpers landed in the head of the gulch, a half mile below visible fire.

They gathered gear as Dodge climbed the ridge to scout. He returned in minutes with William Harrison, once a smoke jumper himself and now a wilderness guard assigned to neighboring Meriwether Gulch, a scenic wonder and the only piece of ground worth saving from fire for miles around— today, Mann Gulch would be allowed to burn. Harrison had fought the blaze alone since morning.

Dodge muttered something about the fire being a "death trap" and ordered the crew to begin hiking down the gulch toward the river, more than a mile away. Dodge, meanwhile, stayed in the makeshift camp to gulp some food, thinking he was about to work all night. Without Dodge to push them, the crew ambled along.

Rumsey later described the fire at this point as "a very interesting spectacle"; some of the men took photographs. Sallee and Rumsey carried unwieldy two-man saws, dangerous to others, which exempted them from carrying packs and put them at the end of the line, which helped save their lives.

When Dodge caught up to the crew, he took the lead and quickened the pace. Something about the fire had spooked the foreman, though he offered the crew no explanation; Dodge was a man of long silences. He also had a touch of the poet and may have used silence to cover his sensitivity.

Nights are sultry and it seems
Each night he's wakened from his dreams
By raindrops on the window panes
The thunder and the lightning chains.
                                    —Wag Dodge, "The Lookout," Noxon High School

Halfway to the river, Dodge crested a rise, turned, and came rushing back toward the crew. Ahead, a seething ball of flame roared straight up the gulch. As Dodge passed Sallee and Rumsey, he told them to throw away the two-man saws "before somebody gets hurt." As everyone turned in retreat, Sallee and Rumsey found themselves at the head of the line, behind Dodge, and unencumbered by packs or tools.

Mann Gulch in 1949. Courtesy U.S. Forest Service

"That was our advantage," Sallee would say later.

Flames, which boiled in the crowns of Douglas fir and Ponderosa pines, catapulted forward on heavy winds partly of the fire's own making—a classic crown fire. The fire was right behind the men as they emerged from the timber onto a broad, grassy slope, the amphitheater-like expanse. The flames dropped from the crowns of trees into dry grass and began to close the gap with the men.

At this point, to the astonishment of his crew and future generations, Dodge halted and took out a book of matches. Lighting his escape fire, a separate fire in the path of the main one, he called on his crew to join him in its ashes.

"Did Dodge appear excited at this particular point?" a Forest Service interrogator asked Sallee afterward.

"No," Sallee said.

"Now I'll ask the reverse question: did he appear cool?"

"I'd say, yes."

Cool but insane, was Sallee's true opinion. He thought Dodge had gone "nuts," a view apparently shared by others.

"I heard someone comment with these words, 'To hell with this, I am getting out of here!' and for all my hollering, I could not direct anyone into the burned area," Dodge later told Forest Service interrogators.

Sallee, Rumsey, and another jumper, Eldon Diettert, headed for the ridge top on a course parallel to Dodge's escape fire, which was running straight uphill at a ninety-degree angle to the advancing main fire. They pounded through unburned grass on the upgulch side of Dodge's fire, so that Dodge's fire acted as a buffer for them to the main fire. Long afterward, Sallee would recall two thoughts from those frenzied moments: "Please God, I'm not ready to die" and "That bastard Dodge is trying to burn me to death."

As the trio neared the top of the ridge they found their way blocked by a wall of rimrock. One smoke-filled crevice beckoned, but there was no way to tell whether it led to safety or a dead end. Sallee and Rumsey made for it. Diettert left them, apparently searching for a better crossing spot, and was never seen alive again.

Rumsey tumbled into a heap in the crevice and Sallee came up behind him, giving him a wordless look that started him out the far side of the crevice. Sallee was about to follow when he took a last look back and saw below the stuff of nightmares.

A black scorch mark shaped like an arrow pointed from the crevice to Dodge's fire, marking the path of the escape fire. Dodge stood at the point of the arrow mouthing silent shouts as four or five jumpers hesitated nearby. The air trembled. Dodge waved at the men, urging them to join him in the ashes of his fire. Two pine trees stood as exclamation points behind Dodge. The main fire, a battle line of smoke shot through with darts of scarlet-orange flame, thundered down on the group.

Sallee took a mental snapshot, turned, and followed Rumsey out of the gulch.

Dodge survived by lying in the ashes of his fire. As the main fire passed, it picked him up and shook him like a dog with a bone. After the flames had passed, Dodge climbed to the ridge top and made a ghostly appearance in front of Sallee and Rumsey, who had found shelter in a rock slide on the opposite side of the ridge. Dodge was grimed but unhurt. The three of them then found Bill Hellman, Dodge's second in command, and Joe Sylvia, both terribly burned. Hellman and Sylvia died of their injuries the next day.

Sallee was warned from the outset to be careful about how he told his story because careers were on the line. A Forest Service investigator, A. J. "Bert" Cramer, cautioned Sallee that being underage could get him in "big trouble" if he said the wrong thing. When Henry J. Thol Sr. brought suit against the Forest Service for the wrongful death of his son, one of the victims, Cramer had Sallee and Rumsey sign statements exonerating the Forest Service from any wrongdoing; the statements were almost certainly written at least in part by Cramer.

Sallee remained a smoke jumper for one more summer, making four subsequent fire jumps, before he quit. Dodge and Rumsey tried to carry on as smoke jumpers, but neither could bring himself to leap from an airplane again. We are left to imagine the emotional cost to Dodge, who suited up and went aloft three times, failing to jump each time, and to Rumsey, who tried twice.

Sallee went on to earn a business degree, and over the next quarter century rose to chief of manufacturing for the Inland Empire Paper Company near Spokane, Washington. Then one day in the 1970s, history came knocking in the person of my father, Norman Maclean, who was writing *Young Men and Fire,* an account of the Mann Gulch Fire. My father convinced Sallee and Rumsey to return to Mann Gulch to revive old memories and see if anything new could be learned.

That became the first of many return trips to the gulch by Sallee, who over time became the last living survivor: Dodge died in 1955 of Hodgkin's disease, and Rumsey, who spent his career with the federal Soil and Conservation Service, was killed in 1980 in an airplane accident in Nebraska while on a business trip.

Sallee gave his first public talk about the fire in May 1991 at the dedication of a memorial to wildland firefighters at the smoke-jumper base in Missoula, Montana, the starting point for the ill-fated flight to Mann Gulch. On this occasion, Sallee said little about the Mann Gulch disaster—he had not known the other jumpers well, he said, except for Rumsey. Instead, he described in cheerful, boyish terms what it had been like to jump out of an airplane for the first time. There is no better way to overcome fear, Sallee said, than to take that first leap into space.

"When you are a boy you go through a series of steps to overcome fear," Sallee said. "In the beginning you are afraid of everything. One by one you overcome these anxieties until you decide to put the question of courage aside forever. And there is no better way than jumping out of an airplane to convince yourself and show the world that you are not afraid."

The posthumous publication a year later, in 1992, of *Young Men and Fire* added a sense of tragedy to the events of Mann Gulch. The book portrayed the fire as part of an ageless convergence of proud youth, the smoke jumpers, and the flames of passion, represented by the fire.

The book also flatly contracted Sallee's memory of his last look back. The escape fire and rock cleft were hundreds of yards farther down the gulch than Sallee remembered, the book argued. It cited as evidence Rumsey's memory, which put those places closer to the Missouri River, and the discovery by my father of a wooden locator post for the escape fire, which had fallen down and become hidden by bushes. The book also implied that Sallee had changed his story under pressure from Cramer, the Forest Service investigator.

After the book came out, I thought that, as a common courtesy, Sallee deserved an opportunity to have his say with someone who had been close to the author. While staying at my family cabin in Montana, I telephoned him and made a lunch date in Spokane, a half day's drive away.

There is a particular excitement in meeting someone out of a book because you have already met them in your imagination. You hope for them to be bigger than life, but capable of the common touch. Sallee was no disappointment. He has a gracious, almost courtly manner, a striking physical appearance, and a sharp mind.

Over lunch, Sallee said that the account of the fire in *Young Men and Fire* had not shaken his memory of the location of Dodge's fire and the cleft in the rimrock. Rumsey had thought they were farther down the gulch, but Rumsey had fallen into the crevice in a crumpled heap and never looked back. As for the wooden marker, snow and ice could have moved it down the gulch.

"Movable markers," Sallee said with a dark look.

The implication that he had changed his story to please the Forest Service, however, brought fire to his eye. Sallee asked to see the supporting documents—two statements attributed to him, one taken directly after the fire in 1949 and the one taken by Cramer two summers later, in 1951. I promised to mail him the documents, and we agreed to meet again, if possible, after he had read them.

Two years passed before we met for another lunch in Spokane, but we picked up the conversation with hardly a break.

"Somebody has done some rewriting," Sallee said. "The first statement is an eighteen-year-old kid up there with eighteen-year-old answers.* And the second, there's a very substantial difference in the answers and the language that was used.

"I doubt very much if I developed that much in that length of time."

The key paragraph is in Sallee's 1951 statement. Henry J. Thol Sr., who sued the Forest Service over the death of his son, was a retired Forest Service ranger with an intimate knowledge of fighting fire. The elder Thol alleged, among other things, that Dodge's fire had kept Henry Thol Jr. and the other smoke jumpers from racing to the ridge top, contributing to, if not causing, their deaths. The location of Dodge's escape fire became a central issue in the case.

In response to the suit, Cramer took Sallee and Rumsey back to the gulch for another look. The statement attributed to Sallee afterward goes to great lengths to support the Forest Service position that Dodge's fire had nothing to do with the deaths. The statement sounds formal and argumentative, far different from the "yes sir, no sir" tone of Sallee's statement directly after the fire.

"Judging by what I saw I am positive that the fire Dodge set had nothing whatever to do with burning the boys," reads the later statement, which was witnessed by Cramer and dated December 12, 1951, months after the trip into the gulch with Cramer. "I also feel just as positive that the group of boys which I could see near Dodge, just before I went over the ridge, understood that Dodge wanted them to join him inside the burned out area but for some reason elected not to do so. I feel certain that it was the fire that I had noticed in the gulch bottom and ahead of us which swept up the slope and caught the boys."

Today a statement as obviously doctored as this one would be ridiculed in the media and torn to shreds in court. How could Sallee make such judgments?

---

*Sallee had turned eighteen by the time the first statement was taken.

He had no way of knowing what his fellow jumpers "understood" about Dodge's escape fire—none had survived. The 1951 statement says Sallee thought Dodge was creating a safety zone, which if true would help the Forest Service defend itself against Thol's charges.

But that is not true, Sallee says today. At the time he thought Dodge had created a buffer to the main fire, not a safety zone, and that is why he raced up along the edge of the escape fire. Sallee makes that point in his 1949 statement: there, he says he thought the foreman wanted the crew to "follow his fire up along side [to the ridge top], and maybe his fire would slow the other fire down."

The likeliest explanation is that Cramer wrote, at minimum, those portions of Sallee's statement that explicitly exonerate the Forest Service. Perhaps he acted under pressure from superiors, perhaps not. Thol's lawsuit against the Forest Service was dismissed.

Cramer, who served as a smoke-jumper foreman for a time, retired from the Forest Service with a reputation as a good, tough man in the woods, which in those days meant protecting the Forest Service. When my father found him in retirement, he had become too feeble of mind to explain himself; he has since died.

Sallee was angry about the tampering with his account, but he agreed with the factual conclusion that Dodge's escape fire had not contributed to the deaths of the smoke jumpers. Furthermore, Sallee said that the 1951 statement is pretty accurate about the location of the escape fire and the crevice. If Cramer had wanted to lie outright, Sallee said, he would have placed the escape fire farther down the gulch, where it would have been less likely to impede the retreating smoke jumpers.

"I personally do not believe Wag's fire caused them to die," Sallee said. "The main fire caught up with them before they got to a point where they could have gone to the ridge."

Over lunch, we settled a couple of matters. Sallee had not caved in to pressure to alter his story; it had been altered for him. But the facts in the 1951 statement seemed accurate enough. This left unsettled the dispute between Sallee and the account in *Young Men and Fire* over the locations of the escape fire and the crevice. Another trip to Mann Gulch might help clear up those matters, but why follow such a well-worn trail? The lessons of

Mann Gulch had been taken to heart and kept those fatal circumstances from being repeated.

It took a rerun of the horrors of Mann Gulch to draw Sallee and me back to that lonely piece of real estate. The unwanted echo came with the 1994 South Canyon Fire, which killed three smoke jumpers among its fourteen victims, the first smoke jumpers to die from flames since the Mann Gulch Fire. The two fires were near twins, and there was a direct link to Sallee. In one of the more unusual coping exercises after the South Canyon Fire, Bill Baker, a Spokane native and surviving member of the ill-fated Prineville Hot-shots, nine of whom died in the fire, telephoned Sallee. Baker had been turned off by efforts at grief counseling following the disaster. "Everyone was doing the funeral tour, but I don't like funerals," he said. He had to find some-one to talk to, and who better than Sallee? "I figured he would understand the *magnitude* of a blowup," Baker said. "He would know how to handle it."

The interview turned topsy-turvy.

"Sallee sat me down and said, 'Okay, so tell me, what was it like for *you?*'" Baker said. "'People have been asking me that question about Mann Gulch for forty-five years, and I just wanted to be able to ask somebody else the same thing.'"

As they talked Sallee passed on the spare philosophy that has guided him. "Basically, you'll never be able to understand why you lived and other people died," Sallee remembers telling Baker. "You can't understand that. You can't put Christianity in it, you can't say I prayed and God spared me.

"If you spend a lot of time worrying about why you didn't die, you get messed up. You have to say, That's the way it is, and get on with your life."

The past, though, has a way of asserting itself, like it or not. After the South Canyon Fire, I bowed to destiny, for want of a better word, quit the *Chicago Tribune* after thirty years as a newspaper reporter, editor, and writer, and jumped in my Jeep Cherokee, heading west to write what became *Fire on the Mountain: The True Story of the South Canyon Fire.*

I, too, sought out Sallee to help me understand how catastrophe could strike a second time. If Sallee would return to Mann Gulch with me, he could explain the fatal convergence and perhaps offer wisdom for the future. In the process, we would have an opportunity to check his memory one more time for the locations of the escape fire and the sheltering crevice.

Sallee agreed without hesitation.

We found ourselves at the mouth of the gulch on the bank of the Missouri River one cool, cloudy September day. As we looked into the yawning gulch, Sallee remarked on a continuing mystery of the fire, how it had managed to get below the smoke jumpers without them seeing it.

"The Forest Service found a snag up there, and that's where they think the fire started," Sallee said, pointing to the top of the ridge dividing Mann Gulch from Meriwether Gulch. "They think the embers were picked up by some strange weather phenomenon and dropped into the canyon below.

"It may have started up there, but the fact is when we jumped in, the fire was up on the far ridge, which you can see up there." He indicated a spot more than a mile up the gulch.

"Immediately after the fire when Wag and I got down here, there was a half dozen boats here. And we hollered and some people picked us up and took us down to Meriwether Gulch. And it's entirely possible somebody dropped a cigarette at the bottom of the gulch here. I don't think they'll ever really know for sure how the fire got down below us.

"But we did not jump in the head of the canyon with a fire burning down by the river. The fire was right above us and we had a good escape route down Mann Gulch to the river. It should have been perfectly safe."

We began the hike up the gulch, which was thick with brush. The sides of the gulch rise steeply and are close together at the mouth, and the trail in the narrow bottom was unmistakable.

"One of our water cans broke," Sallee said. "The parachute didn't open. The radio broke, we lost the radio, although there wasn't any radio communication anyhow, so that wasn't any great loss."

"Did you see the radio go down?" I ventured.

"No, as far as I know, we didn't even know that we didn't have a radio. Only Wag Dodge had that knowledge. When Wag started for the fire, he started straight up from where we had accumulated our cargo."

As we continued up the gulch, the vegetation began to change.

"We crossed the line right there, right back there," Sallee said, pointing to the bases of the trees we were passing. "That's where the big fire was. See the difference between that vegetation and this?"

I wasn't sure what he meant, but he quickly explained. The older trees, toward the mouth of the gulch, were untouched by fire. Farther along, we could see scorch marks rising up the trunks of trees.

"As we go along you'll see fewer and fewer of these living trees," Sallee said. "But even up in the gulch itself there are pockets of living trees."

"Storm King Mountain is like that, too," I said, referring to the site of the South Canyon Fire. "It's real eerie. You'll get a strip of juniper or whatever where it hasn't been burned out, and right next to it will be something that is completely obliterated."

"See all the logs laying on the ground?" Sallee said. "By the time the fire got here, it was really doing things."

We walked until we came to the first crosses, the ones farthest down the gulch and closest to the river, marking the spots where the fire caught the first of its victims.

The cross commemorating Joe Sylvia, who was found burned but alive, stands next to a large rock. But Sallee says it may not be the right one: Sylvia's rock was not located until the day after the fire, after Sylvia had been moved.

"They used Sylvia's rock as a starting point," Sallee said, describing how my father and his research partner, Laird Robinson, had fixed their location for the escape fire. If it was the wrong rock, it would have skewed the Maclean-Robinson calculations, which could account for the conflict between their placement of the escape fire and Sallee's.

"You know, there is a marker for Dodge's escape fire up there someplace, but it's quite a ways from where in my opinion it actually was," Sallee said. The wooden marker has been repeatedly knocked down, then put back up wherever it was found.

We walked on until we had a commanding view of the upper gulch and the crosses strung out in a long line.

"See that one standing snag?" Sallee said. "See the grass where the cloud's going over? It looks different, doesn't it?"

"Yes," I said, "it's much greener."

"That's where Dodge's fire was," Sallee said. Dodge's fire was not as intense as the main one, which sterilized the soil. "I was leaning against that tree when he lit his fire. It was right there."

"How do you know it was that tree?" I asked.

Mann Gulch in 1995, looking from the head of the gulch down the slope where Wag Dodge lit his escape fire. Photograph by Dick Mangan, courtesy U.S. Forest Service

"I went up to the cleft, which I have kept a vision of in my mind all these years, and I looked down and there was the tree. Maybe it wasn't the exact tree, but it was a tree right there. Actually there were two of them there. There should be a snag or a tree on the ground right there someplace."

That could be checked. Sallee marched ahead along the same route he had followed to safety many years before, more interested in retracing the route than checking for the fallen snag. He was in his middle sixties at this time, but he kept a swift, steady pace to the top of the ridge. I was glad of a detour to the standing snag, where indeed another snag lay nearby on the ground. Mann Gulch is littered with burned snags, standing and fallen; the evidence, though, did not contradict Sallee.

I joined Sallee at the rimrock above the gulch. There are several openings in the rimrock big enough for a man to squeeze through, but at the time of the fire smoke had blanketed the ridge. Sallee and Rumsey had been lucky to see one opening.

Sallee pointed to a large crevice.

"I think it's that one right there, with the old tree in it," he said. "That's where we came through.

Bob Sallee, the last survivor, retraces his path to escape up the side of Mann Gulch.
Photograph by Dick Mangan, courtesy U.S. Forest Service

The crevice in the rimrock identified by Sallee as the place he and Walt Rumsey made their escape. Photograph by Dick Mangan, courtesy U.S. Forest Service

"And then we just peeled off down through there, on the other side of the ridge. The fire was already burning on that side. We were going to head for the river, and then we saw fire. We hit a rock slide and figured that was as good as we were going to do. We laid down—actually, I poured water from a canteen into my hat, a felt hat. I put that over my face. The fire came on one side of the rocks and we moved down a little bit. It came up the other side and we moved up a little bit.

"I got a couple of sparks in my hair, but other than that it was not hot, not bad in there."

We lingered for a while on the ridge top and then walked out of the gulch.

When Sallee spoke at the fiftieth anniversary of Mann Gulch a few years later, there were no questions about locations for the crevice in the rimrock or Dodge's escape fire. Pinpoint accuracy is a rare thing in accounts of tragic happenings. The facts have to be coaxed out of a variety of sources before they can be turned into useful lessons and, hopefully, keep history from repeating.

"As we move into the next millennium it's time to rededicate ourselves to these fine young men and the lessons their deaths taught us," Sallee told the anniversary assembly. "Wildfires are and always will be dangerous, and we must respect their potential to put a firefighter in harm's way. And life is precious; and for some very short."

He would have been just as happy, Sallee once said, to have been left out of the limelight. By telling and retelling his story, though, he brought the consolation of explanation to a host of others left behind.

4

A Short History of Wildland Fire

THE WORST FIRES in the history of Colorado, Arizona, and Oregon scorched more than a million acres of forest altogether, during the 2002 fire season. Firefighters and home owners near wildlands find themselves increasingly at risk from wildfire. Whole communities are threatened and occasionally overrun by flames.

Environmental groups blame the Forest Service for helping create the situation by decades of fire suppression and support for destructive logging practices. The Forest Service blames the groups for using scare tactics and legal obstacles to block efforts to implement solutions. Scientists say there are no easy solutions and no body of research showing a clear path to follow. Environmentalists say this means that we should proceed slowly. The Forest Service says that action—thinning, prescribed fire, logging—is necessary now.

Following the fire season of 2000, which burned a record 8.4 million acres, the federal government formulated a National Fire Plan. The plan increased funding and committed federal agencies to treat, by burning and thinning, 40 million acres of brush and dense forest during the first decade of the new century. Wildfire would take care of half that acreage, it was assumed, while the remaining 20 million acres would require expensive mechanical thinning, prescribed burning, or both.

Two years later, in 2002, as huge, destructive fires burned in Colorado, Arizona, and Oregon, the Bush administration seized the moment to present a measure to cut red tape in treating forests. The proposed plan would make it easier to log, among other things, which set off alarm bells in the environmental community. Environmental groups had supported thinning activities near housing, but not in the deep woods.

The logging industry can play a positive role in restoring forest health, but even many supporters of the industry say it will have to prove itself. The industry came under intense national criticism during the 1970s over its clear-cutting practices, particularly in the Bitterroot National Forest in Montana and the Monongahela National Forest in West Virginia; it also got a lot of negative press for "below-cost timber sales," the practice of spending more federal money on roads and other logging measures than the sales earned for the government. Those scandals and other past practices have created a powerful negative image for the industry to overcome.

Wildfire has become the nation's business, but it did not achieve that distinction overnight.

The Yellowstone Fires of 1988 were the first act of the modern fire drama to pull a national audience. Americans watched, riveted, as the jewel in the crown of the national park system appeared to go up in smoke. The Yellowstone Fires were the first major public test of a "let burn" policy by the National Park Service, which allows fires started by lightning to burn unchecked. No wildfires in history received more attention, but the swings in public opinion as events unfolded were extreme, an indicator of a lack of familiarity with the role of wildfire.

Initial doomsday reports—the park was "destroyed," according to Senator Alan Simpson of Wyoming, an opinion echoed by many others—gave way within a year to a wave of resurrection stories. "Yellowstone Lives!" *U.S. News & World Report* announced in one typical headline.

Flames touched less than half (38 percent) of the park's 2.2 million acres, it was later determined, and spared additional acres within scorched areas. The fires—there were thirteen major fires, several of which burned into each other—also scorched approximately 400,000 acres outside the park, where the policy was to fight most fires. By the time flames had reached the boundary lines of the national forest, however, they had built up in size and intensity and were not easily contained.

The Yellowstone Fires eventually were fought, at a cost of $112 million, but it was snow in September, not firefighters, that brought the battle to an end.

The Yellowstone Fires sparked a spirited environmental debate. Was "let burn" a good policy? Did the National Park Service have the right to allow fires to become so massive that they could not be stopped when they left park boundaries? The Yellowstone Fires remain controversial to this day, but the policy of allowing fires started by lightning to burn within national parks has survived. The Yellowstone Fires scorched an enormous swath of ground even by historical standards, but they were part of a recurring cycle necessary to bring new stands of timber and grasslands to life. The park's fossil record is clear: Yellowstone, a high bowl with a chill, wet climate, burns every two hundred years or so, when a rare hot summer dries the forest and when enough dead timber has accumulated to sustain wildfire. Scorched forests and grasslands are unlovely to the eye, but they are nature's way.

Spectacular fires have become the norm. In New Mexico, the Cerro Grande Fire of 2000, deliberately set by federal firefighters to clear brush, escaped control and overran Los Alamos, where decades ago employees of that same government had developed the atom bomb. Satellite photos, an arresting novelty, showed smoke from the fire stretching across the Southwest and beyond. If the federal government cannot be trusted to control a fire it had started itself, the watching nation wondered, how much faith should be placed in the government's ability to control the bomb it had invented? Faced with a crisis of confidence, the federal government snatched up the $1 billion tab for property damage, and its program of prescribed fire survived.

No event in the history of wildland fire, however, has equaled the impact of the Big Blowup of 1910, the time the woods roared. Nothing before or since has done as much to influence the way wildfire is fought in America; its effects can be seen today not only in the same-age stands of lodgepole pine growing where the fire burned, but nationwide where fire has been kept in check since then.

A bad fire season was limping to a close in late August of that year when unexpected winds of near-hurricane velocity struck the panhandle of Idaho and northwestern Montana. The Big Blowup raced thirty, forty, and fifty miles in a burst. The smoke reached Boston. Flames scorched more than 3 million acres in two days, destroying a third of the town of Wallace, Idaho. No fewer than eighty-five people were killed, most of them incinerated beyond recognition. Of the seventy-eight firefighters confirmed dead, only twenty-nine could be positively identified. Snow eventually extinguished the flames, but embers were found in snags as late as the following February.

A race with fire is a horrible experience, but most often it is mercifully short. Not so with the Big Blowup. Towering flames and smoke could be seen for hours before they arrived. The sight drove men insane. One firefighter shot himself to death; two others on a crew in the Selway National Forest became unhinged. One of them was held down in a creek by comrades; a ranger later recounted that the other "danced around singing a lullaby." Both men survived, but the "lullaby boy" spent the rest of his days in a lunatic asylum.

The Big Blowup also settled for most of the twentieth century a national debate, the terms of which are familiar today, about how to deal with wildland fire. At that time, the practice of deliberately clearing land with small fires was known as "light burning." It had champions among settlers, loggers, foresters, and others who saw the limited burning as a way to reduce fuel, increase water flow, regenerate pasture, and prevent catastrophic fire—arguments similar to those heard today in support of prescribed fire and thinning. Early advocates of light burning took their cue from regular burning by Indians, a practice denigrated by opponents as "Paiute forestry." The opponents saw the method as primitive and wasteful, not in step with the European model of applying human management to every acre of forest.

During the nineteenth century, as settlers headed west, catastrophic fires burned virtually unchecked. "There were so many trees that no one worried much about waste," Robert W. Wells wrote in *Fire at Peshtigo,* an account of the worst wildfire disaster in U.S. history, the Peshtigo Fire of 1871. That blaze cost the lives of more than fifteen hundred people and scorched more than twenty-four hundred square miles in the vicinity of Green Bay, Wisconsin. There was no organized federal firefighting force to stand against the Peshtigo and other great fires of that era.

Even by the time of the Big Blowup, the national firefighting system lacked the labor force, money, and rationale to put up much of a fight. In 1905, the forest reserves, the national forests of today, had been transferred from the Department of Interior to the Department of Agriculture—an act with symbolic meaning, namely that the forests were to be used for economic as well as recreational purposes—and placed under a tiny new agency, the Forest Service. When the Big Blowup struck five years later, the Forest Service spent $30,000 to fight it, a trifling amount when compared, say, to the $138,000 spent that same year by the State of New York to suppress fire in the Adirondacks Preserve. A large fire today can cost $1 million a day to fight, a considerable increase from 1910, even allowing for inflation.

In 1905, the Forest Service had only about four hundred rangers on fire patrol. When fires struck, the agency often turned a local saloon into an employment office. Early-day rangers considered themselves lucky if their men were merely hungover by the time they reached fire camp.

"In the earlier days of the service we had to gather together such men as we could get from the streets, saloons, and off freight trains," noted Elers Koch, a Ranger hero of the Big Blowup, who later entertained deep doubts about suppressing fires. "As a result, there was almost as much misery connected with handling the men as with fighting the forest fire. Such transients were almost like children, unreasonable, irresponsible, and acting purely on impulse."

Except for a few female lookouts, firefighting in those days was an exclusively male occupation. Firefighters wore cotton shirts and pants and floppy hats. Only the regulars spent a month's wages on thick-soled White's boots, which remain the standard today. The crews worked with two-man saws, communicated by yelling, and (unless of a religious disposition) expected no help from higher up the line.

The Big Blowup's toll of death and destruction turned firefighting into war. Fire was the demon destroyer known by hate terms such as "fire fiend" and "fire devil." The National Forest Plan of 2000, designed to deal with decades of fire suppression spawned by the Big Blowup, describes the effect of the 1910 conflagration: "The ferocity of the Big Blowup, which came on the heels of other devastating fires on both private and government land, triggered a call for a systemic policy change. Less than a year later, the national Forest Service firefighting program was born. *A war on all wildfires was declared* [emphasis added]."

The war had its own guru, William James, the writer and philosopher, who lay dying in New Hampshire as the Big Blowup raged in the West. James had just returned from western Europe and was deeply alarmed by the growing militarism there. That very month, August 1910, *McClure's* magazine carried James's seminal essay, "The Moral Equivalent of War," urging an alternative to military arms "to enflame the civil temper as past history has inflamed the military temper."

James died on August 26, but his idea lived on in the war on fire; James's influence helped turn firefighting from stoop labor into heroic action. "If war was the romance of history, was not firefighting the romance of forestry?" argues wildfire historian Stephen Pyne. "Fire protection would not militarize outright, but it would acquire, in Jamesian fashion, martial values."

Decades later, the foreman of the Prineville Hotshots, Bryan Scholz, who lost nine crew members on the South Canyon Fire, put the analogy succinctly: "Firefighting is like combat—except you're not supposed to die."

Those who fought the Big Blowup united in the desire to never let anything like that happen again. There was no room in the Forest Service for dissent—even from within. Koch, the Ranger hero of 1910, tried to argue afterward that fighting fires in the backcountry often served no purpose. "I firmly believe that if the Forest Service had never expended a dollar in this country since 1900 there would have been no appreciable difference in the area burned over," wrote Koch, who became chief of timber management of Region One, in the northern Rockies, where the Big Blowup had burned. Koch's views were so controversial that for years he withheld publication of his essay "The Passing of the Lolo Trail."

Since fires were to be battled with the utmost zeal, a clear fire policy was needed to guide those who fought them. "Not being sure of their objective, a fatal hesitancy, a lowering of alertness would be bound to result," argued Earl Loveridge, a Forest Service official who advocated the famous Ten A.M. Policy, which required every fire to be put out by midmorning the day after it was reported.

The Big Blowup affected decades of policy making. In 1911, Congress passed the Weeks Act, which allows the Forest Service to cooperate with states in fire protection. Research into fire control began in 1921, when the Forest Service dedicated the Priest River Forest Experiment Station, headquartered in Missoula, Montana; today, research into the nature of fire continues at fire laboratories in Missoula; Macon, Georgia; and Riverside, California. By the time the Ten A.M. Policy was formally adopted in 1935, the nation had arrived at a consensus for dealing with wildland fire: go get 'em, every one.

Reaction to devastation such as this from the Big Blowup of 1910 resulted in a policy of blanket suppression of wildfire, which helped create today's ferocious blazes.
Courtesy U.S. Forest Service

The Nicholson mine shaft, where Pulaski led forty-four men and two horses when the Big Blowup overtook them. When men tried to bolt, he faced them down with a revolver. Courtesy U.S. Forest Service

The Big Blowup also gave firefighting an enduring icon: a stalwart firefighter standing firm as flames approached. The icon had a name, Ranger Ed Pulaski. He had pulled a revolver to hold a crew in a mine shaft, where he had led them to escape the flames. Pulaski's men, at least in legend, staggered from the mine shaft the next morning and stumbled over Big Ed's body.

"The boss is dead!" one called out.

"Like hell he is," Big Ed growled from his prone position.

Pulaski came to have a literal presence on every fire line: the ax-hoe implement called a Pulaski, which he developed, is as common today for fighting fires as a shovel.

The war against fire proved a success, if measured in acres burned. The amount of forest and grassland consumed by fire dropped dramatically, from an average of about 30 million acres a year at the turn of the century, and from highs of 40 to 50 million acres a year in the drought years of the 1930s, to an average of about 5 million acres a year in the 1970s.

Fighting every fire on sight, though, made the Forest Service unpopular in some quarters. Ranchers, hunters, farmers, and others came to detest unbroken stands of brush and forests dense with spindly trees. Burning by humans had formerly kept at least some of this land open. A nineteenth-century shepherd considered brush burning part of his job description. "We burned everything that would burn," remarked P. Y. Lewis when coming out of the Sierra Nevadas with his band of sheep in 1877. (John Muir, the great naturalist, fired a shot from another quarter, calling sheep "hoofed locusts.") Burning had become so widespread by the 1880s, it was said, that California farmers could smoke hams by hanging them out the window.

Arson, or "incendiarism," became a perennial problem after 1910. Major outbreaks during the 1930s and '40s caused the Forest Service to make a special study of California, with its vast brushlands, which disclosed broad citizen support for burning. A fire-prevention officer donned civilian clothes and traveled Mendocino County in northern California, seeking candid opinions. "Every person to whom I talked was quite elated over the fact that the fires of 1944 would improve deer hunting and help the cattlemen," the officer reported.

The climactic 1953 Rattlesnake Fire arson, started by the son of a Forest Service engineer and described in chapter 1, had grotesque echoes during the 2002 fire season, when seasonal federal employees started two of the biggest fires on record. Terry Lynn Barton, a seasonal Forest Service worker, ignited the Hayman Fire, the biggest fire in Colorado's history, at more than 137,000 acres, and an out-of-work firefighter for the Bureau of Indian Affairs, Leonard Gregg, was charged with setting the Rodeo Fire, which merged with another fire and became the Rodeo-Chediski Fire, the largest blaze in the history of Arizona, at nearly 469,000 acres. Together, the fires destroyed more than five hundred homes. Barton pleaded guilty to starting the Hayman Fire, but said it happened by mistake. Gregg was charged with setting the Rodeo Fire deliberately to make work for himself.

Late the same 2002 season, Jonathan Patrick Klausen, a firefighter with the California Conservation Corps, was arrested for allegedly starting five fires that destroyed two homes and prompted evacuations in San Diego County.

The notion that firefighters are more prone than others to set fires is a myth, researchers say. Informal statistics—the only kind available—show that firefighters are no more likely to start fires than anyone else, though when it happens it makes shocking news. Firefighters are drawn to flames, but that does not make them criminals.

Dick Mangan, a retired head of the Forest Service's Missoula Technology and Development Center, estimates that no more than ten to twenty wildfires are deliberately set each year, out of an average of about 116,000 wildfire starts, and rarely is one a year set by firefighters, the 2002 season to the contrary. The nation has about 1.1 million firefighters, urban as well as wildland, but only about 20 percent are full-time professionals. The bulk are part-timers, like Gregg, or volunteers, and it is from these ranks that most problems are said to come. National crime surveys show that if any one group predominates in setting fires it is juveniles, who accounted for 54 percent of arson arrests in 1999, according to FBI statistics.

The impulse to start fires has a variety of causes. Fire was a weapon used by all sides in America's early history: Indians burned out white settlers, and white settlers and the military returned the favor. Cattlemen burned out sheepherders, and so it went.

During the Great Depression, arson became a common way to create employment. In the early 1930s, as many as 30 percent of wildland fires in the Pacific Northwest were started by those needing work, according to Mangan. That number dropped significantly with the creation of the Civilian Conservation Corps, which put men to work fighting fires, among other jobs.

Psychologists say that pyromania, an unhealthy obsession with fire gratified by setting fires, is relatively rare. Arsonists often have disturbed personalities, but their problems are most often unrelated to flames. Stress and personal unhappiness create pressure, which finds an expression in lighting fires. The Forest Service's Barton claimed she was burning an upsetting letter from her estranged husband when the flames grew beyond her control.

"You could tell the progress of the fire by the screams."

By the middle of the twentieth century, the Forest Service policy of blanket fire suppression had rung up an alarming toll in firefighter lives. Fatalities on the fire line had become commonplace—there were seven "tragedy fires" between 1910 and 1957 where the death toll in each case exceeded ten. The

Forest Service convened a special task force in 1957 to study those fires and devise guidelines for safety.

- The Griffith Park Fire of 1933 killed no fewer than twenty-five firefighters when brush exploded into flames in a narrow canyon on the outskirts of Los Angeles, the greatest loss of life among wildland firefighters from 1910 to the present day. "You could tell the progress of the fire by the screams," one witness recounted in the official fire report. "The flames would catch a man and his screams would reach an awful pitch. Then there would be an awful silence. Then you would hear somebody scream and then it would be silent again. It was all over inside of seven minutes."
- The Blackwater Fire of 1937 killed fifteen firefighters in the Shoshone National Forest in Wyoming after a fifty-man crew was delayed in reaching the blaze while it was still small. The circumstances inspired one of the fire's investigators, David Godwin of the Forest Service, to help develop the smoke-jumper program, designed to put firefighters onto blazes swiftly. The first training jump was made two years later, in 1939. Ironically, Godwin, known as the father of smoke jumping, died in an airplane crash in West Virginia in 1947.
- The Hauser Creek Fire of 1943 killed eleven U.S. marines and injured seventy-two other marines in the Cleveland National Forest in southern California; the fire was started by USMC gunnery practice. The men, placed in harm's way by an inexperienced supervisor, were overrun by flames. The fire report cited the supervisor and the fire boss for negligence, but recommended that no action be taken against them. Fatalities on the fire line were unfortunate but inevitable, the report said.
- The Mann Gulch Fire of 1949, described in chapter 3, killed twelve smoke jumpers and a wilderness guard, an ex-jumper himself, when flames unexpectedly blew up in rough Montana backcountry. The famous "escape fire" lighted by the crew foreman, Wag Dodge, is memorialized in today's admonition to firefighters to keep "one foot in the black," meaning stay close enough to a

burned area to step into it for safety. Dodge became an ambiguous icon for fire safety. He saved his own life with his escape fire but not the lives of his crew, and he reproached himself forever after. "Wag died that day," said his widow, Patsy.

- The Rattlesnake Fire of 1953, the California blaze described in chapter 1, killed a Forest Service ranger and fourteen missionaries serving on a fire crew. The fire was nearing control after dark when a wind of near-gale force blew *downhill,* contrary to common sense, and trapped the men.

- The Inaja Fire of 1956 killed eleven firefighters in the Cleveland National Forest in southern California in a blaze set by an arsonist, an Indian who said he got a "mad, crazy idea" to throw a match in the grass to see if it would burn. The area had been without rain for four years. The men killed—three Forest Service firefighters, a corrections officer, and seven inmates of a convict fire crew—were caught by flames when the fire blew up in a canyon bottom after dark, stoked by an unexpected wind shift.

A foreman who survived, Kenneth "Joe" Joseph, described for investigators the nightmare race with fire:

> The fire started making a run up the canyon on the right of the men below me and I could see they were moving along and before I knew it the fire was in front of me on the bluff. . . . I saw Denny Street standing on the other side of the flames yelling, "Joe, get out of there." So I went dashing through in front of the flames. . . . I don't remember how long it was before I saw some men come running out on top of the ridge ahead of the fire. I thought they had all gotten out, but then saw that there were only five or six of them. They said the men behind were trapped and couldn't get out.

The 1957 Task Force produced a lasting contribution to wildland fire safety, the Ten Standard Fire Orders, which are modeled on the general orders of the Marine Corps. Bud Moore, a legendary Forest Service ranger and marine veteran of South Pacific combat, was one of the board members. Moore, unable to remember the marine general orders exactly, left the task force meeting, which was held in Washington, D.C., grabbed the first marine he came across on the street, and made him repeat the general orders.

Just as Moore found the USMC general orders difficult to remember, fire-fighters sometimes have problems remembering—and thus applying—the Ten Standard Fire Orders. This situation is made no easier by the addition of 18 Situations That Shout Watch Out, urging caution. Paul Gleason, a hotshot superintendent, came up with a shorthand list called LCES, for lookouts, communications, escape routes, and safety zones. In 2002, however, the Forest Service reaffirmed strict adherence to the Ten Standard Fire Orders.

The new guidelines coupled with technical advances stemming from World War II reduced the number of multiple deaths; from 1957 until the end of the century, only two fires caused more than ten fatalities each. One, the 1966 Loop Fire in the Angeles National Forest, just north of Los Angeles, killed twelve firefighters when a downslope Santa Ana wind unexpectedly turned uphill and trapped a crew in a narrow defile. The other was the 1994 South Canyon Fire on Storm King Mountain in Colorado that cost fourteen lives.

World War II had a double effect on the fire world, bringing advances in outlook as well as technology. The war's emphasis on discipline and teamwork in pursuit of victory found application in the fire world just as it did in sports, where it sparked the phenomenal popularity of professional football—a sports equivalent for war that William James might have appreciated, at least as metaphor.

Fresh icons for fire emerged from the war years: Walt Disney's epic film *Bambi,* released in 1942, portrayed a crown fire started by a careless hunter turning a wilderness into a ruin, as an adorable fawn and his mother fled in terror. The film's message, that fire is evil, was hokum. Flames do wildfire more good than harm, scientists now believe, creating breaks in forest cover where animals can hide and spurring the growth of succulent feed. "Wild animals deal with fire remarkably well," says a modern National Park Service pamphlet, "Wildfire in National Parks." "Birds fly out of the area, large animals leave immediate danger, some animals escape to ponds or streams." After the Yellowstone Fires, park rangers located the carcasses of 243 elk, 4 deer, 2 moose, and 5 bison within the fire perimeters, a minimal number considering that thousands of elk die in a harsh winter in the park. (The elk population dipped the next year because of poor reproduction, a consequence of the fires, but rebounded as new growth became abundant.) But the *Bambi* image of menacing fire has proved to be one of history's most enduring cultural icons.

The war also produced the lovable Smokey Bear, who first appeared in 1944 as fire's poster boy, designed to shore up antifire attitudes after Japan's generally unsuccessful but disturbing efforts to ignite forest fires on the West Coast with incendiary balloons. A Washington, D.C., disc jockey created Smokey's familiar, throaty voice by speaking into an empty wastebasket.

Consideration was given to shelving the venerable bruin on his fiftieth anniversary, in 1994, the same year as the South Canyon Fire. But the Forest Service was loath to retire the popular symbol—Smokey Bear is the second most recognized figure in America, behind Santa Claus. Smokey's warning— "Only YOU Can Prevent Forest Fires"—refers to human-caused fires and thus remains relevant, it was decided. Smokey lives on.

Tons of surplus military equipment were passed on to federal and other fire authorities after the war—$200 million worth of stuff that ranged from vehicles and radios to C rations and K rations. The most lasting physical effect of the war, though, remains visible above every major wildfire today: the air fleet, including the smoke jumpers.

The jumper program, begun before the war, in 1939, contributed to the development of airborne combat troops, then profited in turn as experienced jumpers returned from the war looking for work. The jumpers embody the Ten A.M. spirit, attacking early to keep small fires from becoming big problems. Continuance of the program is often questioned: jumpers are expensive to train and elitist in attitude. But they are few in number (under four hundred) and very cost-effective when properly employed. And like Smokey Bear, they have a well-cultivated "poster boy" image.

Not long after World War II, in June 1949, when the jumper program was little known, four jumpers were dispatched to put on an aerial show in Washington, D.C. The four movie-star-handsome military veterans took the capital by storm, making a well-publicized jump onto the Ellipse between the White House and the Washington Monument. Thrills from the sky have a price. Among the four were Bill Hellman, killed two months later in the Mann Gulch Fire, and Homer "Skip" Stratton, who led the body-recovery detail into the gulch.

By 1956, the Forest Service had a fleet of air tankers at its disposal. The tankers, operated by private companies on contract with the agency, are surplus military craft such as C-130 transports, refitted and equipped with tanks capable of dumping thousands of gallons of water or retardant, a red mud (made up largely of fertilizer) that slows the spread of flames. The air fleet, supplemented by the versatile helicopter, has become an indispensable arm of firefighting. Helicopters can drop water from buckets, ferry firefighters and gear into inaccessible fires, provide aerial reconnaissance and infrared mapping, or deposit rappellers—the quick-attack firefighters who slide down ropes to reach areas where landing a helicopter is risky or impossible.

Surplus World War II aircraft are still in use in the twenty-first century, though the Forest Service has been warned over and over, including by its own officials, about deterioration of the vintage fleet. The situation reached a crisis point in 2002 when amateur photographers captured shocking images of two air tankers disintegrating in fiery explosions, with no apparent cause, in separate incidents. Five crewmen were killed. A blue-ribbon panel convened to investigate the disasters grounded a quarter of the air-tanker fleet— aging C-130As and PB4-Ys—as well as nineteen lead planes and four smoke-jumper transport planes. Jerry Williams, chief of fire and aviation for the Forest Service, estimated it would take three to five years to bring the fleet back to strength, and fire fighting would lose effectiveness in the meantime.

The first big, organized fire crews emerged during the Great Depression when the Civilian Conservation Corps was enlisted to fight wildfire. Firefighters of that era would be astonished by the look of a modern fire scene— crews in uniforms, aircraft buzzing overhead, bulldozers gouging out fire lines. Firefighters today must wear hard hats, fire-resistant clothing (the ubiquitous yellow shirts and green pants), leather gloves, heavy boots, and face shrouds. Each combatant carries a fire shelter, an aluminized, pup-tent-like device that creates a personal safety zone, in conscious imitation of Dodge's escape fire in Mann Gulch. Two-way radios are so common that the biggest fire-communications problem is too many voices on too few channels. Incident-management teams with high training standards can be dispatched within hours or minutes to any place in the nation; the incident-command system evolved from firefighting and by 1985 was in use by all federal and many state agencies to handle multijurisdictional disasters—everything from an earthquake, flood, hurricane, or volcano eruption, to a terrorist attack.

Line-building crews—the "ground pounders" who cut, dig, and scrape containment lines around a fire and "mop it up" until it's cold to the touch—usually come in standardized units of twenty. Women have been regular members of fire crews since the 1970s; it is common to find around five women on a twenty-person hotshot crew, the most highly trained of the ground army. Deanne Shulman became the first woman smoke jumper in 1981; women today account for about 5 percent of all smoke jumpers.

The social upheaval of the 1970s introduced a different culture to the fire line. "New hires were generally a far different breed than those hired in the sixties," remembers John Chambers, a retired assistant director of fire and aviation for the Forest Service. "Urban and suburban raised with different values and lifestyles, they often preferred not to endure the hardships associated with wildfire suppression and had little appreciation for commodity uses." Old fire dogs were retired in numbers in the 1980s and '90s, often replaced by "ologists," a derisive term for biologists and others with little wildland fire experience.

The work of clearing a fire line, however, has changed little over the years. Hand tools—shovels, Pulaskis, and root rippers—accomplish most of the labor, with the notable exception of the chain saw. One man with a chain saw can do in an hour what it used to take two men with a handsaw a day to accomplish.

The policy of full suppression of fires began to erode during the 1960s and '70s. The 1963 Leopold Report, a study of wildlife management in the national parks, proposed that Yellowstone Park restore a "vignette of primitive America," which included a "let burn" attitude toward fire. Forest Service policy was modified in 1971 to allow lightning fires to burn in wilderness areas. The use of prescribed and natural fires made other inroads, and in 1978 the Ten A.M. Policy was formally abandoned.

Despite a more lenient attitude toward wildfire, about 95 percent of ignitions continue to be suppressed. Forest managers, it is remarked only half-jokingly, spend nine months a year talking about allowing more fires to burn, and three months a year trying to put out every one in sight.

Fighting fires remains an inherently dangerous business. The 1994 South Canyon Fire came at the height of a fire season that took thirty-four lives, which left an abiding, sad imprint on firefighters, survivors, and families, and horrified the public. The fire became a monument to lessons ignored, bad management, and the limits of technology.

On the South Canyon Fire, unlike its near twin the Mann Gulch Fire, supervisors fumbled one opportunity after another to put out the blaze. The South Canyon Fire was not fought for the first three days, though it burned in sight of an interstate highway and threatened the town of Glenwood Springs, Colorado, and other housing. The Grand Junction District of the BLM ignored its own policies, which directed that fires such as this one be put out immediately—the fire burned in a drought year, when all fires were supposed to be extinguished on sight. The South Canyon Fire started on July 2, was first reported the morning of July 3, but was not fought until July 5, and turned fatal on July 6.

When the South Canyon Fire Investigation report blamed the firefighters' can-do spirit for the fourteen deaths, however, the fire community erupted in outrage. Blaming victims for their own deaths was bad enough. The can-do spirit, though, was the heart and soul of firefighting, the slogan made famous by the Seabees, the navy engineers of World War II. For decades, the can-do spirit had saved lives, protected property, and stamped out fires. What alternative, what new icon of the age, existed to replace it?

After the South Canyon Fire, fire crews spontaneously began to question risky assignments as never before. And quickly, so did their supervisors, who, like veterans of the Big Blowup, never wanted anything like the South Canyon Fire to happen again.

The South Canyon Fire became the moment when the old fire world vanished, the time past when firefighters won applause for battling every blaze with everything they had. It ushered in a more uncertain world where fire crews, by common consent, are pulled off fires when winds blow too hard and flames grow too hot. By 2002, the "just say no" lesson had worked its way into official policy in what's known as the yellow book, the federal handbook of firefighting, in a page titled "How to Properly Refuse Risk."

The unusually damaging blazes of the past few years, however, have brought another swing of the pendulum. Aggressive attack in the first hours might have prevented many of these fires from achieving the status of catastrophe. Smoke jumpers and others are now urging faster, more decisive actions on small blazes destined to be fought.

In 2002, the Coal Seam Fire brought flames once again to Colorado's Storm King Mountain. This time, the fire was attacked mostly by helicopters and air tankers; ground crews made no heroic stand against the flames though more acres burned—over 12,000, compared with 2,115 for the South Canyon Fire. Veterans of both fires said the attitude of the townspeople was seasoned by tragedy: most willingly evacuated in 2002. The Coal Seam Fire destroyed twenty-nine homes and fourteen other structures, but no one was seriously injured.

"Having sat through many briefings in the last five weeks," said Stuart Cerise, assistant chief of the Burning Mountain Fire District, "I heard and saw the lessons of South Canyon being taught and implemented. No chances were taken. Ground by the hundreds and sometimes thousands of acres was sacrificed for firefighter safety."

Another marker was set when Tom Shepard, superintendent of the Prineville Hotshot crew on Storm King Mountain, nearly lost another crew on the Sadler Fire in northern Nevada five years later, as described in chapter 2. The disbanding of the Sadler Fire's incident-command team and the recommended demotion in fire grade of Shepard and others broke new ground for accountability for supervisors, an issue raised under fatal conditions a few years later.

The millennium year of 2000 was a costly fire season—the more than 8 million acres scorched was twice the national average for the previous decade. But the safety record was extraordinary: no federal firefighter was lost to flames. Incident commanders, mindful of South Canyon's lesson of "just say no," regularly pulled their crews back.

The federal government's response to the 2000 fire season, the National Fire Plan, pledges years of increased efforts and spending to fight fire and reduce fire risk. "Reversing the effects of a century of aggressive fire suppression will be an evolutionary process, not one that can be completed in a few short years," the report says.

After its own independent inquiry, Congress's investigative arm, the General Accounting Office, agreed with that assessment. "Federal acreage is susceptible to catastrophic wildfires, particularly where the natural vegetation has been altered by past uses of the land and a century of fire suppression," the GAO concluded.

Under the National Fire Plan, the federal fire budget rose from about $1 billion a year to $1.8 billion in 2000, $2.9 billion in 2001, and $2.3 billion in 2002. The initial surge in spending included purchase of capital goods such as vehicles; the budget numbers slowly taper off after 2002. Much of the fresh money goes to hire firefighters, conduct prescribed burns, restore wildlands, and educate home owners about ways to reduce fire risk. The program calls for prescribed burning to rise from about half a million acres a year to 2.6 million acres a year. Already, some good effects can be seen: high-intensity fires drop to the ground when they run into timber that has been thinned and burned, making them less destructive and easier to control. This happened on the huge Hayman Fire in Colorado, though the amount of pretreated forest was so small that it made little difference to the course of the fire.

Besides the usual political and commercial pressures on land-management decisions, the opportunity for public and pressure-group input in managing public lands increased dramatically in the final decades of the twentieth century. The Wilderness Act of 1964 was followed by the National Environmental Policy Act of 1969, the Clean Water Act of 1972, the Endangered Species Act of 1973, the Renewable Resources Planning Act of 1974, and the National Forests Management Act of 1976.

The situation today has become a lawyers' playground. During the Rodeo-Chediski Fire of 2002, an inquiry by the *Arizona Republic* concluded that an environmental group, the Center for Biological Diversity, had blocked plans to thin trees and thus reduce fire danger in the forest where the fire was burning. Arizona's Republican governor, Jane Dee Hull, charged the "greenies" with complicity in the fire, which forced the evacuation of tens of thousands of people and destroyed over three hundred homes, as well as scorching nearly half a million acres.

A spokesman for the environmental group accused Hull of scapegoating environmentalists "to advance her own political agenda." Both sides had studies to back them up. Environmental groups offered what looked like a solid defense: a General Accounting Office study that reported that of 1,671 Forest Service projects to reduce hazardous fuels in 2001, outside groups had challenged a mere twenty, less than 1 percent.

A few days later, the Forest Service issued its own report on legal challenges to fuel-reduction projects, which claimed a dramatically higher rate of intervention. Of 326 cases since 2001 where the Forest Service planned to cut down excess small trees, 155, or nearly half, were delayed by appeals, the study said.

Different methodologies and a rush to put out numbers explain some of the gap between the reports, and the argument about the actual number of challenges continues. But there are so many laws, so many ways to intervene, so many groups pulling in radically different directions that it is not inappropriate to draw a metaphorical comparison between the legal state of affairs in managing forests and the buildup of fuels in those same wildlands—a little thinning would help both situations.

The Bush administration, after failing to streamline the process through legislation, issued rule changes to take effect in 2003 to speed up environmental reviews in ten areas in the West, including the Mendocino National Forest where the Rattlesnake Fire burned. The response was mostly predictable: Democrats and environmental groups assailed it, Republicans and logging interests embraced it. A more bipartisan comment came from Jack Ward Thomas, who served under President Clinton as chief of the Forest Service, who remarked: "I for one am willing to give them a chance. The Forest Service isn't nuts, and I don't think the adminstration is. If they were to do terrible and awful things, the wrath of God will come down on them because everyone is looking."

The new century brought an early reminder that the best plans and most telling lessons cannot prevent every fatality on the fire line. The Thirtymile Fire in the Cascade Mountains in Washington State blew up on July 10, 2001, and killed four firefighters huddling in rock scree. Again, an unbroken string of mistakes and misjudgments led to tragedy on the fire line. From inept management to fatigue to firefighter indifference to underestimating the fire to communications errors, a series of little mistakes led to a rapidly deteriorating situation.

The first investigation report for the Thirtymile Fire had so many errors it had to be revised. Then a multiagency review team, which did not act until the next spring, recommended that eleven Forest Service employees be disciplined, from firing to a letter of reprimand, but the team refused to name the eleven, frustrating victims' families and others. All eleven cases are now on appeal. In the wake of the Thirtymile Fire, a senator and congressman from the state of Washington made some initial legislative efforts to require independent investigations of fatal fires, a long-overdue reform.

Living with fire is a learned experience. It requires knowledge, which often comes at a high price. It takes an attitude of acceptance, for wildfire is an enduring part of the landscape. It demands a heavy commitment of time and money.

Fire is part of a timeless cycle of sustenance and danger, death and resurrection, punishment and glory. It can warm the body, comfort the soul, cook food, and give light. It can be monumentally destructive and steal lives and fortunes, or it can be a tonic to forests, grasslands, and wildlife. Fire remains humankind's unpredictable partner.

A Glossary of Formal and Informal Fire Terms

Air tanker: A fixed-wing aircraft equipped to drop fire retardants and suppressants.

Anchor point: An advantageous location, usually a barrier to fire spread, from which to start building a fire line. An anchor point is used to reduce the chance of firefighters being flanked by a fire.

Another pair of shoes for baby: A new fire assignment.

Baby hose: A half-inch collapsible fire hose.

Backfire: A fire set along the inner edge of a fire line to consume the fuel in the path of a wildfire or drive the fire in a new direction.

Bambi bucket: A collapsible bucket used to dip water for fire suppression and slung below a helicopter.

"Be safe": Parting reminder to those heading out to fight fire.

Bench Warmers (or Home Team): Fire-agency personnel who stay in the office and cover for firefighters.

Big Ernie: The "being" in the sky responsible for lightning, wind, and other natural and supernatural events.

Big Green Machine: Forest Service fire management.

Black mountain–green wallet: A profitable fire assignment.

Bladder bag: A collapsible backpack pump fitted with a sprayer.

BLM: Bureau of Land Management. The acronym is also freely translated as Bureau of Logging and Mining, Bureau of Lotsa Money, Bureau of Lonely Men, and Bureau of Livestock and Mining.

Blowup: A sudden increase in a wildfire's intensity or rate of spread strong enough to prevent control of it.

Blue room or blue hut: A Porta-John in fire camp.

Boot scruff: A fire line constructed by dragging boots.

Bowling for hotshots: Rock and debris rolling down hills.

Brush fire: A fire burning in shrubs and brush.

Bucket: Hard hat.

Bug juice: A fruity drink, such as lemonade.

Bump up: A crew or individual firefighter passing another.

Burn out: Setting fire inside a control line to widen it or to consume fuel between the edge of the fire and the control line.

Burning period: The part of each twenty-four-hour period when fires spread most rapidly, typically from ten A.M. to sundown.

Caffeine transfer device: Coffee cup.

Camp Fifi: A woman in fire camp who wears full makeup and clean fire gear and ties her shirt at the waist.

Candle or candling: A single tree or clump of trees burning from the bottom up.

CDF: California Department of Forestry and Fire Protection; also freely translated as Coffee, Doughnuts, and Fun, Can't Dig Fireline, and the three grades you don't want to get in school.

Cold trailing: Feeling with a bare hand for heat and embers.

Contain a fire: To complete a fuel break around a fire; may be stated in percentages, such as "50 percent contained."

Control a fire: The complete extinguishment of a fire.

Coot and carp: State or federal fish and wildlife agencies, which are also known as fish and feathers or fish cops.

Coyote tactics: Crews resting and sleeping at or near the fire.

Crew: A group of firefighters operating as a unit.

Crew boss: Person in charge of a crew, which is usually about twenty firefighters.

Crown fire: The movement of fire through the crowns of trees.

Cumulus overtimus: Thunderheads, or "money clouds," which carry lightning and thus start fires.

Dead fuels: Fuels with no living tissue.

DIC: Deputy incident commander. Must be said aloud to get the full effect.

Dopes on ropes: Firefighters who drop on ropes from helicopters to attack flames.

Dozer: Any tracked vehicle with a front-mounted blade used for exposing mineral soil.

Drip torch: Handheld device for igniting fires by dripping flaming liquid fuel on the materials to be burned.

Driving for dollars: Driving to and from fires while being paid overtime.

Earthpig or groundpig: Hotshot.

Egg ball: Breakfast served from an ice-cream scoop.

Engine slugs: Engine crews.

Entrapment: A situation where firefighters are unexpectedly caught in a fire-related life-threatening position where planned escape routes and safety zones are absent or inadequate. Can result in near misses, injury, or death.

Escape route: A preplanned route to a safety zone or other low-risk area.

Fingers of a fire: The long narrow extensions of a fire projecting from the main body.

Firebreak: A barrier, natural or constructed, used as a control line from which to work.

Fire front: The part of a fire within which continuous flaming combustion is taking place.

Fire line: A fire barrier that is scraped or dug into mineral soil.

Fire rectangle: Add overhead personnel to the formal definition of the fire triangle; remove one of the four, it is said, and the fire goes out.

Fire shelter: An aluminized tent offering some protection against radiant heat, but intended for use only in life-threatening situations, as a last resort.

Fire triangle: The formal definition is oxygen, heat, and fuel, the necessary conditions for fire; the slang definition is travel-time pay, overtime pay, and hazard pay.

Fire virgin: New firefighter or firefighter who has never experienced life-threatening conditions.

Flash or flashy fuels: Fuels such as grass, leaves, pine needles, and slash that readily ignite. Also called fine fuels.

Fusee: A colored flare designed as a warning device that is used to ignite fire.

Green army: Forest Service fire forces.

Ground pounder: Firefighter on a hand crew.

Hand line: A fire line built with hand tools.

Head of a fire: The side of a fire having the fastest rate of spread.

Head shed: Supervisory office.

Heavy fuels: Fuels of large diameter, such as logs, snags, and large limbs, which burn more slowly than flash fuels.

Helitack crew: Firefighters trained to use helicopters for fire suppression. Slang terms: dopes on ropes, rotor heads, rotor toads, propeller heads.

Hoods in the woods: A prison-inmate crew.

Hooters: Forest Service firefighters paid to look for spotted owls, an endangered species.

Hose jockey or hose wienie: An engine crew.

Hotshot crew: A highly trained fire crew used mainly to build fire lines by hand.

Hunker: To take it easy on the fire line.

Incident: A human-caused or natural occurrence, such as a wildland fire, that requires emergency action by trained personnel.

Incident-action plan (IAP): A summary of objectives, overall strategy, and tactics for an incident.

Incident-command post (ICP): Command location for an incident.

Incident-command system (ICS): The combination of resources and organizational structure used to deal with an incident.

Incident commander (IC): The person responsible for incident operations.

Incident-management team (IMT): The staff assigned to manage an incident.

Juice slugs: Fire-camp workers.

Lawn darts: Smoke jumpers; also called dirt darts.

Lookie loos: Members of the public who gawk at fires and firefighters.

Major rager: Large fire.

Mop shots: Ground pounders who wish they were hotshots; or hotshots who complain about a mop-up assignment.

Mud droppers: Air tankers.

Mud flap on a stick: A tool to swat fires that is widely used in the South.

On the board: A firefighter, crew, or other resource listed as ready for assignment.

Pack test: The physical test used to determine the aerobic capacity and strength of firefighters. The test consists of walking a specific distance with or without a pack in a predetermined period of time (most commonly, three miles in forty-five minutes or less with a forty-five-pound pack).

Parent company: The Forest Service.

Parkies: National Park Service personnel.

Pavement queen: A fire engine that must remain on pavement.

Pencil hose: Fire hose five-eighths of an inch in diameter.

Pole patch: An area of downed and crisscrossed trees, usually lodgepole pines.

Prescribed fire: Any fire ignited by purposeful management actions.

Pulaski: A combination chopping and trenching tool.

Punkin' pine: A large ponderosa pine.

PWAC: Person without a clue.

Red army: The CDF, which uses red trucks and engines.

Red-flag warning: A formal alert for critical fire-weather conditions.

Red zone: *See* Wildland-urban interface.

Run (of a fire): The rapid advance of the head of a fire.

Safety zone: An area cleared for flammable materials used for escape in the event of trouble.

Scratch line: An unfinished preliminary fire line.

Shake and bake: A fire shelter.

Slimed: Hit with a load of retardant.

Slopover: A fire edge that crosses a control line or natural barrier.

Smoke jumper (often spelled *smokejumper*): A highly trained firefighter who travels to fires by aircraft and parachute.

Squeak or friction trees: Trees crossing each other that squeak when the wind blows. Rookie firefighters are told to locate these "dangerous" trees, fill out a friction-tree form, and apply for a reward for each one found.

Squirrel channel: A radio frequency used for intercrew communications.

Tanker kitten: Cute girl who works on an engine.

Tie in: To connect, as when constructing a hand line to tie in with a dozer line.

Touron: A cross between a tourist and a moron.

Twig pig: National Park Service law-enforcement ranger.

Vollies: Volunteer firefighters.

White bite: The pinch on the top of the feet caused by new White's boots.

Wildland fire or Wildfire: Any nonstructure fire that occurs in wild or open lands.

Wildland-urban interface: The line, area, or zone where structures and other human development intermingle with wildlands; also called the red zone.

Acknowledgments

THE SPARK FOR this book came from reaction to a short opinion piece written for the wire service of *High Country News,* a western newspaper, about the 1999 Sadler Fire, in which six firefighters were trapped and nearly killed. According to the official Sadler Fire report, more experienced crews had refused an order from Division Supervisor Tom Shepard that put the six in harm's way.

After the piece appeared in several newspapers, Shepard got in touch with me. "John, it didn't happen that way," he said. According to Shepard, nobody had refused an assignment from him. In fact, the six firefighters had been trapped largely as a result of precipitous actions by others.

Shepard and I talked many times, beginning with a taped interview in Boise, Idaho; I spent two years looking into the events of the fire. My account is an attempt to sort out the complex circumstances that nearly cost six lives. I could not have written the story without Shepard's sustained cooperation.

Members of the National Park Service crew known as Golden Gate 3 were helpful in reconstructing events, but none more so than Alex Naar, crew-boss trainee. He helped arrange a stay for me at Marin Headlands and put me in touch with supervisors and many other crew members, notably Angela Hawk.

I interviewed all six members of the burn squad: Naar, Tim Horton, Keren Christensen, David "Ty" Deaton, Peter Giampaoli, and Derek Hyde. I've profited from continuing talks with Christensen and Hyde. I also want to thank Dan Bowmen, a squad leader on Golden Gate 3; I reached him late in the writing process, but his input was substantial.

Talking with the burn squad was a rare opportunity to find out what goes on in people's heads in the final moments of a close encounter with death from fire. It took courage for them to reveal their thoughts and feelings, and I hope the result gives other firefighters a sense of the serious, occasionally terminal nature of their job, and the reading public a better idea of the risks involved in protecting lives and property.

None of the dialogue in this book is made up. The words are what the people involved remember saying or hearing. No liberties have been taken, but not all memories are equal in accuracy; I have tried to make clear in the text the source and reliability of direct quotations.

I thank Bob Lee, who led the fire investigation, for talking with me in Boise, Idaho. My criticism of the practice of naming serving fire supervisors to fill the ranks of fire-investigation teams, and not appointing law-enforcement or other independent members, should not be taken as a criticism of Lee or the other members of the Sadler Fire investigation team. I believe they struggled hard with a tough assignment. I also thank Tom Boatner, another member of the investigation team, for introducing himself a few weeks after the fire, at a book-signing event in Billings, Montana, and especially for making the remarks about the fire that are quoted in the text.

Ed Storey and Dan Huter from the incident-command team also talked with me. They are proud, accomplished men and it could not have been an easy or pleasant experience for them; I thank them.

The Rattlesnake Fire of 1953 was suggested as a subject by Dick Mangan, a retired head of the Forest Service's Missoula Technology and Development Center. The fire, Mangan said, is a significant marker in wildlife history but not well known outside northern California. Mangan pointed me toward J. W. Allendorf of the Forest Service, who became an amateur historian of the fire while a ranger in the Mendocino National Forest. Allendorf was instrumental in collecting the fire documents now kept for serious inquirers at the Forest Service headquarters in Willows. It was Allendorf who interviewed Paul Turner, the missionary who doubted. Allendorf's research and openness in sharing information were much appreciated. Now based at the Helena National Forest in Helena, Montana, Allendorf can look out his office window and see the mountains that form Mann Gulch, the site of the legendary 1949 Mann Gulch Fire, which is the subject of the book's final story.

I was assisted at Mendocino National Forest headquarters by Phebe Brown, the public affairs officer, who asked Greg Greenway, a forest archaeologist, to work with me. They made available all the documents and photographs of the Rattlesnake Fire at the headquarters, including the envelope with Raymond Sherman's watch, which came to play a pivotal role in my research.

The Glenn County courthouse in Willows has the transcript of the grand jury proceedings in the Pattan arson case. The murder charge, which was not sustained by the grand jury, resulted in extensive testimony, which is the source of a number of the firsthand accounts used in the text.

Survivors of the Rattlesnake Fire interviewed included: Stanford Pattan, the arsonist; David Pesonen, then a young firefighter and later the director of the CDF; Robert Werner of the Forest Service; and New Tribes missionaries Duane Stous and Don Schlatter. I also talked with relatives and friends of the firefighters involved; their names appear in the text. Kenneth Johnston of New Tribes Mission was interviewed two weeks before his death at age eighty-eight, on September 23, 2001. I am grateful to everyone who agreed to relive those terrible times.

I thank Daret Barclay, a relative of Ranger Robert Powers, for his open-handed generosity in giving me his only copy of the September 1953 issue of *Official Detective Stories,* with the story about the Rattlesnake Fire. The staff of the Meriam Library, in Chico, were most helpful. Mike Nobles, a bookman as well as a private investigator, was a source of inspiration and advice. Darren Dalrymple of the Mendocino Hotshots also gave valued help.

Many members of the California Department of Forestry and Fire Protection, the CDF, provided me with continuing assistance, from Battalion Chief Mike Brown's expert help in identifying types of vegetation to the effort required to reconstruct the race with fire, which was organized by John R. Hawkins, assistant chief for Butte County. Hawkins helped at every stage of research. At one point, he introduced me to Battalion Chief Mike Shorrock, a Rattlesnake Fire buff, who passed along a sheaf of documents on the fire used at the CDF fire academy.

Those who participated in the January 2002 reconstruction of the Rattlesnake Fire included Don Karvonen of the California Department of Corrections and the following CDF firefighters: from the Valley View Camp, Fire Captains Skip Barber, Ron Bravo, and Chris Ruggle and Assistant Chief Case Butterman; from Butte County, Fire Chief Jim Broshears, Assistant Chiefs John Hawkins and Bill Holmes, Battalion Chief Rob Cone, Fire Captains Mike Carr, Kyra Ireland, Greg McFadden, Fred Middleton (ret.), Sean Norman, Todd Price, Lloyd Romine, and Bruce Yuhasz, Battalion Chiefs Jim Bishop (ret.), Mike Brown, Mark Nelson, Bill Orthel, Mike Shorrock, Wayne Wilson, and Fire Apparatus Engineers James Derington, Todd Garber, and Sims Hawkins.

Chapter 3, "The Last Survivor," is based on documents that I compiled and that were collected by my father, Norman Maclean, and his research partner, Laird Robinson, and on interviews I conducted as noted in the text. Robinson has made himself available on many occasions as a source of information and expert comment. My father conducted his research while he was in his seventies and eighties, and as I pursue my inquiries, I marvel at how he kept it up.

The descriptions of historic fires in chapter 4, "A Short History of Wildland fire," come almost entirely from official fire reports—the remark by Patsy Dodge (now Patsy Wilson) about the effect of the Mann Gulch Fire on Wag Dodge was made in conversation with me; I thank Patsy, too, for passing on Wag Dodge's poem "The Lookout." Steve Dunksy, audiovisual manager for the Pacific Southwest Region of the Forest Service, did much to help dig up the fire reports, other documents, and photographs. I also thank Patricia Pepin, librarian for the Forest Service's Pacific Southwest Region at Mare Island on San Pablo Bay, California, keeper of Firebase, the invaluable archive of historic fire documents, who made my visit there most worthwhile.

This book had many helpers. I especially thank Jack Macrae, my able editor at Henry Holt and Company, who among other things gave unifying vision to the book. My agent, Jennifer Lyons, has been there from the first as friend and supporter. I also thank those who read portions of the book along the way: they include Chris Cuoco, John Hawkins, and Kelly Andersson. Nick Lyons's early editing advice was most helpful, as well as generous. Doctors John E. Campbell and Michael Lumpkin of Gerogetown University Medical Center have been generous in sharing their medical knowledge.

I extend to many in the fire community my gratitude for their support, criticisms, questions, and companionship during a long journey.

Lastly, I once again offer my thanks to my wife, Frances, who tolerates a great deal with style and grace.

Index

About the Author

John N. Maclean was a writer, reporter, and editor for the *Chicago Tribune* for thirty years. His first book, *Fire on the Mountain,* was the Mountains and Plains Booksellers Association best nonfiction title of 1999.